The Ones We Remember

Scholars Reflect on Teachers
Who Made a Difference

A volume in
Adolescence and Education
Tim Urdan and Frank Pajares, *Series Editors*

The Ones We Remember

Scholars Reflect on Teachers
Who Made a Difference

Edited by

Frank Pajares
Emory University

Tim Urdan
Santa Clara University

INFORMATION AGE PUBLISHING, INC.
Charlotte, NC • www.infoagepub.com

Library of Congress Cataloging-in-Publication Data

The ones we remember : scholars reflect on teachers who made a difference /
edited by Frank Pajares and Tim Urdan.
    p. cm. – (Adolescence and education)
  Includes bibliographical references.
  ISBN 978-1-59311-943-0 (pbk.) – ISBN 978-1-59311-944-7 (hardcover)
  1. Teachers–Anecdotes. 2. Teaching–Anecdotes. I. Pajares, Frank. II.
Urdan, Timothy C.
  LB1775.O54 2008
  371.10092–dc22

                                                              2008022728

Printed in the United States of America

For Saucy.
My best and most patient teacher.

—*Frank Pajares*

For all of the inspirational and memorable teachers I have had
the opportunity to work with and learn from, especially C.M.,
M.M., P.P., and Mr. Smith.

—*Tim Urdan*

CONTENTS

FOREWORD

The primary aim of our book series, *Adolescence and Education*, has been to highlight the insights of prominent scholars from a wide range of disciplines united by a common interest in adolescence. Our first volume, *General Issues in the Education of Adolescents*, published in 2001, provided an overview of some of the central issues regarding the education of adolescent students. Volume 2 focused on the *Academic Motivation of Adolescents*, and Volume 3 provided much needed *International Perspectives on Adolescence*. In our fourth volume, we identified a number of *Strategies and Challenges of Educating Adolescents*. Last year, we published Volume 5, which provided an overview of *Self-Efficacy and Adolescence*. In all, prominent national and international voices on adolescence and adolescent development have contributed to our series.

For our current volume, we decided to attempt something quite novel and, we hope you will agree, valuable. Paulo Freire wrote that "sometimes a simple, almost insignificant gesture on the part of a teacher can have a profound formative effect on the life of a student." Sometimes, of course, this formative effect is not the result of a simple, isolated gesture but rather of a proactive and sustained series of gestures on the part of a teacher. Many of us have been deeply influenced by one or more teachers who have exercised a formative effect in our development as students and individuals. We remember these teachers with fondness, tell their stories to our own children, think of them with affection, respect, gratitude, even reverence. Sometimes, we recognized this influence as it was happening, and we grew close to these remarkable individuals, keeping them in our lives even after we graduated from their classes. Often, however, they themselves were unaware of the influence they exercised over us, for it was not until years passed that we realized their effect. If time and distance did not prevent it,

The Ones We Remember: Scholars Reflect on Teachers Who Made a Difference, pages ix–xi
Copyright © 2008 by Information Age Publishing

perhaps we found our way back to these educators and shared with them our appreciation and gratitude.

With this in mind, we asked some of the finest scholars in the fields of education, educational psychology, adolescence, and adolescent development to provide us with a short story or vignette describing their most memorable teacher. Our instructions gave authors a great deal of leeway. They could provide the story on its own, or they could follow it with a brief analysis drawn from theory and research in education, psychology, and human development to identify key concepts and principles that would seem to apply in explaining why the selected teacher was so effective and memorable. They could also choose to write a story about one specific teacher, or they could instead choose to write about the qualities that they believed contribute to teaching excellence, including anecdotes from various teachers and experiences to support the qualities they identified. We left it to our authors to decide how to tell the story and how to, or even whether to, conceptualize the analysis. What we emphasized, however, was that we asked our authors to write their stories with an eye toward being accessible to a wide audience of readers. One need not be an academic, or an expert in education or psychology, to understand and find meaning in these stories.

We conceived of "adolescence" as broadly as possible, from middle elementary to the undergraduate years. Some of our authors, however, experienced the sort of teacher we had in mind during their graduate study, and they asked to be able to write about these experiences. We happily approved.

In essence, we were looking for stories and analyses that capture just what it is that makes a particular teacher, as our title describes, unforgettable. Who are these teachers that we remember? And why? But we wanted to hear these stories from scholars who had themselves become experts in education, who were well versed in the literature on teaching effectiveness, and who understood the process of teaching both personally and, for lack of a better term, theoretically. Indeed, in addition to being international authorities in their own academic fields, the scholars we selected are themselves master teachers about whom a future generation of scholars will write about.

Through the stories our scholars tell, we hoped to create a volume that describes and vividly illustrates the critical qualities that make teachers of adolescents both effective and memorable. Culminating the volume is a wonderful and insightful chapter by Professor Marshall Gregory, a scholar of the first rank and a leading authority on teaching who has published widely on the subject. In his delightful treatise, Professor Gregory puts his finger on the very essence that is required of teachers who aspire to becoming effective educators of youth. He asks, also, the humorous and thought provoking question, "Must a teacher be charismatic and sexy in order to be the one who makes a difference?"

It is our hope that these stories, anecdotes, and analyses will prove especially valuable to preservice and classroom teachers who are engaged in the important process of educating our youth. In a sense, we hope it provides a series of templates that help identify the attitudes and behaviors of those teachers who make a difference in the lives of their students. Of course, we believe that these stories about exceptional classroom teachers and professors of adolescents will also further the mission of our series.

Over 100 years ago, William James made the observation that "the teachers of this country…have its future in their hands." Indeed. But it is the exceptional, unforgettable teachers who best chart that future.

We thank our contributors for their excellent work and dedication in this volume.

—**Frank Pajares** and
Tim Urdan

CHAPTER 1

LEARNING NOT TO BE A CHILD

Lessons From a Master Teacher

Tim Urdan
Santa Clara University

MEETING MR. SMITH

I sat on the oversized window sill outside of classroom 25 with my friend Chris, anxiously awaiting the first glimpse of our new teacher. We were excited because, in addition to being the first day of 5th grade, we had been assigned to Mrs. Taylor's room, and she had the best reputation of all the 5th grade teachers at our school. When a black man in his early 30's turned the corner and strode toward us with a big grin on his face, Chris leaned over to me and whispered, "Here comes Mrs. Taylor!" Just as the words left his mouth, the man bellowed at us: "Good morning, beautiful children!" He stopped in front of the door to room 25, took out a set of keys, unlocked the door, and propped it open, motioning for us to enter the room with grand sweeps of his right hand. "Welcome to 5th grade!"

When all of the students were seated in our classroom, Mr. Smith explained that Mrs. Taylor was pregnant, so he would be our teacher for the

The Ones We Remember: Scholars Reflect on Teachers Who Made a Difference, pages 1–9

year. I think all of the students were disappointed. We had felt fortunate to have landed in Mrs. Taylor's room, but instead of the challenging yet supportive teacher we were promised we were faced with a man that nobody knew. He was about five feet nine inches tall with wavy, longish hair and badly stained teeth. He always took tremendously long strides when he walked, even in relatively small spaces like the classroom. When he talked, he was usually animated, and had odd pronunciations of certain words, such as "Warshington, D.C." And when people spoke to him, be they students or adults, he always listened intently, his right hand stroking his beard. Although I did not know what the coming academic year would be like, I knew it would be different from my previous years in school: All of my teachers before Mr. Smith were middle-aged white women. I was anxious to see what a class with a relatively young black man would be like.

LEARNING THE LESSONS OF ADOLESCENCE

Whatever our initial anxieties were about Mr. Smith, they were quickly replaced by a devotion that most students rarely, if ever, experience. By the end of 5th grade, we had become so enamored of Mr. Smith that we begged our parents to lobby the principal to let Mr. Smith teach our entire class, intact, in 6th grade the following year. Our parents were successful in their efforts, and Mr. Smith became a 6th grade teacher, allowing almost my entire class to stay with Mr. Smith for two academic years.

Although I am confident that Mr. Smith competently taught us what we needed to know in the core academic areas, I remember almost none of the specifics of what we learned. I can recall that we learned long division and often played a multiplication game in class, but the lessons that have stayed with me from Mr. Smith's class had much more to do with getting along in the world than with academics. Mr. Smith taught us about race, about social class, about commitment and values, about expanding one's view to see opportunities for learning that are not always readily apparent, and about breaking rules while being willing to pay the consequences for breaking the rules. And, at the end of our 6th grade year, he taught us about human frailty.

In the 1970s, as today, Berkeley, California, was a segregated city with integrated schools. Relatively wealthy families lived in the hills of Berkeley whereas less affluent families lived in the flatlands. Most of the hills residents were white or Asian American and, the majority of flatlands residents were African American and Latino. At the time, public elementary schools were divided into K–3 and 4–6 configurations. The K–3 schools were all in the hills, so young black and Latino children rode school buses up into the hills to attend school for their first four years of schooling. The upper elementary schools were in the flatlands, so the white and Asian kids were bused to these schools for grades four, five, and six. The injustice of asking very young black and Latino students to ride the bus to school while allowing White and Asian American students to delay their bus riding until 4th grade was lost on me and my friends, but Mr. Smith thought it was important for us to recognize it. One day, while standing outside of our portable classroom on the edge of the playground and talking with Mr. Smith just after the end of the school day, he asked me to take a look at the crowd of students heading for the buses parked on the street across the playground. "Notice anything?" he asked?

"Not really," I said, unsure of what he wanted me to notice.

"You ever wonder why the schools for little kids are all up in the hills but the schools for older kids are all down here?"

I never had, but once he said it I wondered why I never had. Mr. Smith did not lecture me about race relations and everyday injustices, although I'm sure he could have. His style of teaching was usually marked by asking the right questions of his students and then letting them think it through for themselves. Once he pointed out the disparity, I could not help but notice it, and think about it. More importantly, he offered me an approach to considering similar issues. I began to look for other examples of racial injustice in Berkeley, a town that has always congratulated itself much more than it deserved for its racial progressivism.

Mr. Smith offered frequent lessons on race, social class, and navigating the social world with some savvy. As emerging adolescents in a largely segregated society attending an integrated school, Mr. Smith seemed to feel obligated to teach us about each other. He rarely developed lesson plans for these topics (although he did assign a fair number of Richard Wright books and Langston Hughes poems for us to read). Rather, he waited for, and created, teachable moments and then took advantage of them. Sometimes, these moments emerged spontaneously. For example, one day while working with a small group of classmates, my pencil broke and I got up to sharpen it. When I came back to my seat, I found it occupied by Jason. Jason was the most feared student in my 5th grade class. He was much taller and heavier than the rest of us, had an observable mustache, and seemed to be somewhere around 15 years old. One day, Jason got into a physical altercation with Mr. Smith, and Jason got the better of the exchange. He simply was not a kid to mess with. But I had a big mouth and little impulse control. So when I saw Jason in my seat I did not mince words.

"Get out of my seat," I told him.

"You ain't sittin' here now," he replied. "Go find another seat."

"If you're such a baby that you need to steal my seat to be happy, go ahead and keep it," I shot back.

"What did you say?" Jason asked, offering me a chance to back off without getting hurt. I didn't take it.

"I said, 'If you're such a baby that you need to steal my seat to be happy, go ahead and keep it.'"

Upon receiving confirmation of my lack of concern for my personal safety, Jason took his pencil, jammed it into my left thigh, and then snapped the pencil in two, leaving the sharp end embedded in my leg. I immediately stumbled over to Mr. Smith's desk to show him the evidence of Jason's criminal behavior, and I had little doubt that Mr. Smith would take swift action against Jason. Instead, Mr. Smith asked me what happened. I told him that Jason had stabbed me in the leg with his pencil. "What did you say to him to make him stab you?" Mr. Smith asked. When I told him what I'd said, Mr. Smith looked me in the eye and said "If you are dumb enough to say that to Jason, you deserve to get stabbed with a pencil." With those few words, Mr. Smith offered me an important lesson: Being "right" is not always the smart option. True, Jason should not have taken my seat nor stabbed me with his pencil. But Jason was a very large, volatile kid, and baiting him with wisecracks was not a smart move. To avoid trouble and pain, one must know who one is dealing with, and how to best handle difficult situations. It was a lesson I have not forgotten.

In addition to the spontaneous teachable moments that arose in our class, Mr. Smith was also very good at creating teachable moments. One way he did this was to bring a variety of adults into our classroom. These visitors had no connection to the school other than their friendship with Mr. Smith. One of these visitors was a Spanish-speaking woman who taught us several songs in Spanish and offered us basic Spanish lessons. Our school offered no second-language instruction, a gap that Mr. Smith filled as best he could through his own personal contacts. Another frequent visitor was a sort of grungy man that was a friend of Mr. Smith's. None of the students knew what this man did or why he visited our classroom, but we were used to Mr. Smith's friends sitting in on our class so we did not think much of it. Several of us made fun of this visitor (privately) because of his appearance and body odor, and we assumed he was simply a homeless man that Mr. Smith had befriended. One day, Mr. Smith gathered up the students in the class and marched us all outside, off the school property, and around the corner. There we saw a large, bright yellow boat-truck with Mr. Smith's friend perched atop it. This man that had underwhelmed us all explained that the truck was amphibious, that he had built it himself, and then invited us all on board and took us for a ride. Mr. Smith looked at all of his students and beamed, knowing that he did not need to say anything. He had taught us all, again, not to judge people too quickly or to rely too heavily on superficial evidence.

THE UNRAVELING

One of my favorite things about Mr. Smith was his willingness to violate school rules if he felt that doing so would benefit his students. Like most elementary schools in California, our school had a tiny library with few books and a part-time librarian. About a half mile away from our school was the public library, well stocked with books and librarians. So when Mr. Smith wanted us to do something in the library, he would march us up to the public library, always stopping, either on the way there or the way back, at a seafood restaurant and talking the manager into "donating" several loaves of sourdough bread for us to eat while we walked. Of course, any trips off of school property were supposed to be planned well in advance and involve gaining signed permission from parents ahead of time. But Mr. Smith felt that such rules were the enemy of spontaneity, so he rarely followed them, at least for these short trips near the school. Every time we returned from such trips, a note from the principal would be waiting on Mr. Smith's desk. Mr. Smith would read the notes and then instruct us to work on something independently while he went to talk to the principal. He usually returned in about 15 minutes, smiling broadly.

During the spring semester of 6th grade, Mr. Smith's demeanor began to change. We had substitute teachers more often as Mr. Smith began arriving late to school or skipping the day completely. Mr. Smith had always been playful with his students. My friends and I would often punch Mr. Smith in the leg as we were leaving for the day, then sprint across the playground to the bus with the hope of a clean escape. But Mr. Smith always chased us down and punched us in our legs or shoulders, never trying to hurt us. He was physical with us in a rough-housing way, but never when he was angry. In the spring of sixth grade, however, this began to change as well. He began grabbing students by the shoulders when he was angry with them. As the semester continued toward summer break, Mr. Smith became more sour, more disheveled, and more angry.

One day, about two weeks before the end of the school year, Mr. Smith again led us on an outing to the public library. At the library, some of the students were talking loudly and running around, being rowdy. The behavior was not appropriate, but it was nothing extraordinary. Mr. Smith felt otherwise. He grabbed one of the misbehaving students by the arm, pulled him into a side room off the main room, flung him face-down over his knee, pulled his pants down, and beat his naked rear with his belt. The beating lasted for a minute or two in full view of the rest of the class. When it was over, the beaten student pulled up his pants and we all marched back to school, walking quickly and silently. The student who received the beating walked a few paces ahead of the rest of us, crying quietly, his unbuttoned pants sagging the entire way. Instead of coming back to the class with us when we arrived back at the school, this student veered off onto another street and walked home.

Back in the classroom, we all sat at our desks in silence for a few minutes. Then, one of our classmates dared to speak: "Why did you have to beat him, Mr. Smith?" she asked.

"Shut up, girl!" he snapped at her. "You don't even know what was going on."

A friend of mine, a white boy, then said to the girl who had asked the question, "Just don't say anything right now. Mr. Smith is too angry." As the last word left his mouth, Mr. Smith was rushing toward my friend. Mr. Smith grabbed him under the armpits and carried him to the back of the room, where he slammed him up against the blackboard. Their noses were almost touching as Mr. Smith yelled in his face. "Who do you think you are? You have no right to tell people they can't talk!" When Mr. Smith released my friend, he walked out of the room. Those of us remaining in the room were too scared to talk.

Mr. Smith then gave us a speech about race and class. He explained that he had asked the parents of each child in the class how he should discipline us. All of the parents of the black children had given Mr. Smith permission to use corporal punishment, he told us, whereas none of the white parents had. He told us that respect for parental authority (or teacher authority) was more highly valued by parents in rougher neighborhoods whereas independence and questioning of authority was more highly valued by wealthy parents living in safer neighborhoods. He informed us that the white students in the class were ignorant about our own privilege, and about the lives and values of students in our own classroom that were less privileged. The lecture concluded with Mr. Smith telling us that the parents of the student who had been beaten had expressly given Mr. Smith permission to punish their son that way in just such situations.

When the class broke for lunch, another friend and I met up with my friend who had left the classroom earlier. The three of us went to the principal's office to report on the events of the morning. Our parents were called to pick us up so we would not have to return to the classroom that afternoon. The next day, when we returned to school, we had a substitute teacher. Mr. Smith never returned to the school.

FORGIVENESS

Although I felt justified in the actions that I took, resulting in Mr. Smith's dismissal, I never felt good about it. Before his meltdown, Mr. Smith had been the best teacher I, or any of my classmates, had ever had. His dedication to teaching, and to his students, was best exemplified at the beginning of our sixth grade year. The year began with a teachers' strike, and the school was shut down. Mr. Smith made some arrangement with a church in the same neighborhood as our school to allow our class to use space in the church during the day. Every day (Monday through Friday) for the full duration of the strike, my entire class met with Mr. Smith at the church, and he taught us, without pay. When he could have been out earning money to make up for his lost income during the strike, Mr. Smith decided to teach our class instead. And Mr. Smith was not a wealthy man, so this was a tremendous personal sacrifice.

For several years I felt badly about my role in Mr. Smith's dismissal from teaching. Throughout the rest of my years in Berkeley schools, I never saw Mr. Smith again. I went off to Michigan for college, and during the winter holiday break of my first year I returned home to Berkeley. One day, I went back to my old high school to visit some of my favorite teachers and friends that still attended the school. As I left the high school, I stepped to the curb and looked at the car coming to a stop on my left, allowing me to cross the street. I glanced inside the car and the driver was looking at me, a hint of recognition on his face. When he broke into a broad smile, I recognized it as Mr. Smith's smile. He pulled his car over and jumped out, then wrapped me up in a warm hug. "Well, well, well," he said. "The boy has become a man." I was suddenly presented with the opportunity that I thought I would never have; to thank Mr. Smith and to ask for his forgiveness.

I began by telling Mr. Smith how sorry I was for my role in getting him fired. I went on to tell him what a fantastic teacher he had been, and how grateful I was for all that he had taught me. He listened intently, scratching his beard, as he always had in his classroom. When I finished what I had to say, he looked at me and said, "I had no business being around children at that time in my life. You did the right thing." He went on to explain some of the difficulties he was experiencing in his personal life during the spring of sixth grade (divorce, substance abuse) and told me that his break from teaching had led to a new career as a writer. He had published some books of poetry and was content in his new career.

Mr. Smith's absolution gave me immediate and lasting relief of the guilt I had felt since that awful day in the spring of sixth grade. During the last two weeks of that school year, after Mr. Smith's dismissal, a couple of his old friends who had been regular visitors to the classroom continued to visit, and they asked me why I had ratted on Mr. Smith after all he had done for me and my classmates. I told them that Mr. Smith had become scary, and told them they might have done the same thing if they had seen him on the day he lost control. And although I knew what I was saying was true, I also felt that his friends had been right in their condemning questions of me. Perhaps I had overreacted. Mr. Smith was the only person who could have possibly convinced me that I had done the right thing. And when I finally ran into him as a young adult, Mr. Smith had the grace to do just that.

LESSONS LEARNED

The years leading up to fifth grade had been pure childhood. All of my teachers had been motherly, and all of my interests and concerns had been childish. I was not a particularly sheltered child, but my school years to that point had been easy and relatively carefree. But, in 5th and, particularly, 6th grade, I began a transition into adolescence that most kids encounter around that time. I was fortunate to have a teacher that was willing to teach me lessons, beyond the regular school curriculum, that would help me in this transition. He understood that many of his students had limited interactions with adults beyond their teachers, parents, and parents' friends, so he introduced us to an eclectic mix of adults, each with talents, abilities, and interests that were not immediately apparent but revealed themselves over time. This taught us not to judge, or fear coming into contact with, people outside of our familiar groups. He taught us that rules, while important, could be trumped by personal beliefs and convictions, so long as one was willing to accept the consequences of violating the rules. After a childhood spent learning the importance of rules, it was important, on the brink of adolescence, to learn that rules could be violated.

Most importantly, for me at least, was the lesson that one must navigate the social world with awareness and intelligence. When I stepped outside of my middle-class, mostly white world as a child, it was mostly as a tourist. My family would take brief visits to the flatlands of Berkeley, or to Chinatown in San Francisco, or Oakland, and then return home without learning much. My fourth grade year, spent in the same elementary school as my fifth and sixth grade years, involved no discussions of race, class, or privilege, despite the diversity in the classroom. But Mr. Smith made sure that diversity was a prominent component of our instruction, partly by virtue of the fact that he was a black man himself. The norms of classroom discourse and climate often tilt toward the norms found in white, middle-class culture simply because most teachers are white and middle class. But Mr. Smith had no inclination to favor such norms. His language use in the classroom was a model of code-switching, between ebonics and the Queen's English, as the situation dictated. And he explained to all of his students why it was important to know how to communicate in a manner that was appropriate for the situation without favoring one style over another. Mr. Smith taught me that I could no longer count on adults to protect me from larger, more violent students, so I better exercise good judgment in my interactions with them. I had spent my childhood making biting and insulting comments to bigger kids and then hiding behind parents and teachers for protection. Mr. Smith offered no such protection, and he let me take my lumps.

Given the changes in public schools since I was in fifth grade—no touching between students and teachers, the threat of lawsuits for every transgression of rules—it is difficult to imagine that there are many Mr. Smiths out there. Even then, there were few Mr. Smiths—teachers willing to follow their own beliefs and principles, even if it violated school rules, in order to offer students valuable learning experiences. Indeed, it was his exceptionality that makes Mr. Smith one of the few teachers that I can vividly remember from my K–12 education. Eventually, through trial-and-error, I probably would have learned on my own many of the lessons about life and getting along that Mr. Smith taught me. But I got lucky. Mr. Smith came into my life exactly when I needed him to, and the wisdom he shared has stayed with me to this day.

CHAPTER 2

PASSING THE TORCH

The Legacy of Inspirational Teachers

Jeffrey Jensen Arnett
Clark University

When I think back to the teachers of my youth, one of the things that strikes me is how vivid they remain to me. I turned fifty this year, and I still remember the teachers I had 35, 40, even 45 years ago, along with specific events I experienced in relation to them. This illustrates, I think, how deep the impressions are that teachers leave on us. They are iconic figures of our childhood, larger than life. For better and worse, they play a large role in shaping the kinds of adults we wish to be, and the kinds of adults we become.

I am a developmental psychologist, which means that I do research on how people develop and change with age. Developmental psychologists describe how each stage of life has distinctive characteristics that set it apart from other stages. In this chapter, I will recall the most memorable teachers I had from first grade through college, and how my experiences with them fit—or, in one case, jarringly didn't fit—the developmental stage I was in at the time.

The Ones We Remember: Scholars Reflect on Teachers Who Made a Difference, pages 11–18
Copyright © 2008 by Information Age Publishing

FIRST GRADE: A SUBSTITUTE MOM

The earliest teacher I remember was my first grade teacher, Mrs. Sterlitz. Memory that far back is indistinct, but I remember that she was young and lively and had bright red hair. I was very fond of her and deeply wanted to impress her, so I was a good kid in her class and worked diligently.

Developmental psychologists talk about the importance of the *attachment relationship* in childhood, meaning that children need to have one special person, usually the mom, who loves them, protects them, and provides for their needs. If children are secure in their love from this "primary attachment figure" it gives them the confidence to explore the world around them and gradually become more independent, because they realize that if a crisis arises—they become hungry, or hurt, or frightened—they can always retreat to the "secure base" provided by this attachment figure. Gradually children form additional attachments to persons within and outside the family.

I was well-loved by my mom, and I think I found that same kind of love in Mrs. Sterlitz. In those days most American kids had full-time moms and didn't have much experience with day care or preschool before they entered kindergarten, so the transition to starting school was a much sharper break from life at home with mom than it is today. I'm sure I missed my mom when I started school, but Mrs. Sterlitz became an important secondary attachment figure for me. My mom always made me feel like she thought I was just wonderful, and so did Mrs. Sterlitz.

At the end of the school year, she gave me a little school picture of herself and wrote on the back (I still have it):

$$\begin{array}{r} \text{You are} \\ \text{2 good} \\ + \text{2 be} \\ \hline \text{4 gotten} \end{array}$$

So was she, and I have not forgotten her.

THIRD GRADE: HUMILIATION AS A TEACHING TECHNIQUE

Most of my experiences with teachers were good, so the one especially bad one really stands out. It provides a textbook example of how *not* to teach children.

Middle childhood is a time of beginning to gain the skills necessary for performing the work required in your culture. In many cultures, including the American middle-class I grew up in, that means learning reading, writing, and arithmetic. It's also a time when, according to the developmental psychologist Erik Erikson, the primary challenge is *industry vs. inferiority*. If a child is encouraged and supported in learning cultural skills, a sense of industry develops that includes enthusiasm for learning and confidence in mastering the skills required. However, a child who is neglected or humiliated in the learning process is likely to experience a sense of inferiority.

My third grade teacher—I can't remember her name, and in any case it would probably be best not to name her—came up with an idea that seems like it was designed to promote inferiority rather than industry. We were told to bring a favorite story from home, which we would then read to the class. I chose *The Curious Cow,* about a cow whose curiosity led to all sorts of mayhem and disorder. I really loved that story, and I looked forward to reading it to my classmates.

However, a strange thing happened when I stood up before the class and began to read. No sooner had I started reading when *the whole class started laughing*. I stopped and looked at them, puzzled and hurt. Why were they laughing? I had not reached any of the funny parts yet, I had just begun the story. I tried again, and the same thing happened. They all laughed, and worse yet, I realized that they were not laughing at anything in the story, they were laughing at me! I tried yet again, and they again interrupted me with howls of laughter after I had spoken only a few words. Humiliated, bewildered, and tearful, I slunk off and retreated to my seat.

As I sat burning with shame and pain the teacher stood up and explained that she had told the class to laugh when I began reading, as a way of showing—what? I can't remember what educational goal this exercise was supposed to achieve, I only remember my humiliation, and my horrified astonishment when she announced that she had instigated it.

More than 40 years later, it makes no more sense to me than it did then. What on earth was she thinking? Did she really think that I would benefit from being humiliated, or that the other students would be edified from humiliating me? How, exactly, would that be instructive for anyone involved? I remain horrified and astonished.

Teachers are iconic figures, and that can be good when they are loving, encouraging, and inspiring. But their iconic status also gives them vast power to hurt. We remember our whole lives the ones who especially loved, encouraged, and inspired us, but we remember, too, the ones who used their power over us to cause us pain.

SIXTH GRADE: LOVE PRACTICE

Physically, socially, mentally, and in pretty much every other way, adolescence is an earthquake that changes everything. In the course of a few years, our bodies change in ways that amaze us, sometimes delight us, and sometimes appall us. Perhaps most importantly, we reach sexual maturity, and sexuality, to which we had been merrily oblivious in middle childhood, now bestirs us and presents us with daunting puzzles and mysteries. For most boys, the girls we had as friends through childhood now become— well, something else, but it takes us a long time to figure out exactly what.

I remember early adolescence as the most difficult time of my life, and I'm not alone. For most people—boys and girls alike—self-esteem takes a sharp drop in early adolescence, not fully recovering until late high school. Moods fluctuate more, and dark moods are more frequent. In a study by Reed Larson and Maryse Richards, in which 5th to 8th graders wore wristwatch "beepers" and reported their moods and activities when beeped randomly in the course of a day, the authors described the changes of early adolescence as an emotional "fall from grace." Times beeped when feeling "very happy" declined by 50% from 5th to 8th grade, and similar declines took place in reports of feeling "great," "proud," and "in control." According to Larson and Richards, a key source of early adolescents' negative moods is their fumbled attempts to figure out how to interact with the other sex.

This definitely fits how I remember my early adolescence. I had always played happily with girls as well as boys, but suddenly girls terrified me. One little girl in particular, with long blonde hair and a sunny smile, inspired my deepest adoration and fear, in equal parts. I heard through the peer grapevine that she "liked" me, too, but that only deepened my terror. I never actually spoke a single word to her. Suffice it to say that, anywhere near her, I never felt "great," "proud," or "in control."

However, that same year, sixth grade, we had a student teacher, Miss Davis. She, too, had long blonde hair and a sunny smile, but I felt no fear in her presence, only adoration. She was young enough to be a target of my youthful infatuation, but old enough to be safe. In retrospect, I see my relationship with her as a way of practicing normal flirting without the remotest prospect of actual sex intruding.

I was smitten enough with her that, after she left her student teaching internship to return to college, I sent her two dollars from my allowance, along with a letter encouraging her to buy something nice for herself. Thinking of this now, I can imagine the laughs this gesture provided to her and her friends, but she handled it with kindness and grace. She sent the money back to me along with a letter thanking me for thinking her, and a little pennant from her college. I still have that pennant, and I still have my warm memory of her as the first girl/woman outside my family that felt safe for me to love.

FIFTH TO SEVENTH GRADE: HOW TO BE A MAN

One of the most influential teachers of my childhood was someone outside of school, my Boy Scout leader Ken Bourgon. I loved Boy Scouts. I was involved in it from about age 10 to 13, from fifth to seventh grade. I loved camping out and hiking, and I loved learning about the natural world. But perhaps even more importantly, at an age when relationships with girls were new and daunting it was wonderful to have an all-male social haven.

I think the Boy Scouts is a great organization, but having Ken Bourgon—"Mr. B" as we all called him—as Scoutmaster was the key to my enjoyment of it. I know this because I briefly had two other Scoutmasters before Mr. B, and although I enjoyed Scouts with them it was not nearly as important in my life as it became once I met Mr. B.

Part of early adolescent development is figuring out how to be a woman in your culture, if you are a girl, or a man in your culture, if you are a boy. All cultures have gender distinctions, that is, different roles and ideals for men and for women, and all children are urged to conform to the roles and ideals specific to their gender. Some cultures teach gender roles and ideals explicitly, as part of puberty rituals. Others, like ours, teach them implicitly, through the models that parents, teachers, and others provide, and through the ideals presented in the media.

My father was a remote, cantankerous figure who taught me little about being a man, either explicitly or implicitly. He had five children, and he regarded it as his fatherly duty to keep them all fed, clothed, and housed, but he didn't see fatherhood as involving much beyond this. In old age he has mellowed out, and he is a much better grandfather than he was a father, but when I was young he was not someone I looked to as a model for how to be a man.

Mr. B came as a revelation. Where my father was remote, Mr. B was open and accessible. Where my father was grumpy and easily irritated, Mr. B was jovial and serene. Where my father was humorless, Mr. B was full of laughs and gentle ribbing. He seemed to know everything about the skills of Scouting, and he taught them with patience and good humor. I wished Mr. B were my father, but since that was not possible, at least I wished to be like Mr. B. He was my model for how to be a man.

Once at a Boy Scout summer camp I got into some trouble, accidentally breaking a window, and I came to him full of tears, expecting to be admonished. I should have known better. He trusted me when I said it was an accident, and he consoled me and dried my tears with his handkerchief. He let me keep that handkerchief, and I still have it, with his monogram in the corner, JKB, for John Kenneth Bourgon. Recently I bought handkerchiefs of my own, and had them made with my own monogram in the corner, JJA. Forty years later, I still aspire to be like Mr. B.

ELEVENTH AND TWELFTH GRADE: A REBEL TAMED

I was a "good kid" throughout most of my childhood, well-behaved and eager to please my parents and teachers, but this changed once I reached high school. I decided there was more fun in being a rebel, rule-breaker, and risk-taker than a good student. I often exasperated my teachers with disruptive behavior in class, being more interested in a good laugh than in learning anything they had to offer.

However, my classroom antics varied depending on the teacher. I suspect this is true of most classroom rebels: we calibrate our behavior to the teacher, pushing just as far as we think we can get away with but not so far as to get into any real trouble. Perhaps because I was generally a good student, most of my teachers tolerated a lot from me—perhaps, as I see it now, more than they should have.

The teacher who ran the tightest classroom ship during my high school years was Jerry Smith, the choir director. In many schools being in choir lowers rather than raises a student's social status, but Dr. Smith made choir cool. The choir was a perennial winner of the highest state music awards, and performed at many school functions. Every year selected members of the choir took a "Spring Tour" for a week to some fun place—such as Washington, DC, my senior year—funded by the money raised at choir concerts and other fund-raisers.

You might think that, as a devoted hell-raiser, I chafed under Dr. Smith's discipline, but the opposite was true. I thrived under it, and I loved him for it. Adolescence is a time when unruly impulses surge. Developmentally, adolescents may need independence, but they need to learn self-restraint, too. They grow rapidly bigger and stronger, they become suddenly sexual, and for boys especially, the hormones that incite aggression rise sharply. I had perhaps more intense impulses of all kinds than most of my peers, so I was especially in need of training in self-restraint, and I wasn't getting that training at home or from most of my teachers. But Dr. Smith required it, and I eagerly complied.

I admired him tremendously. Like Mr. B, he provided me with a model, an ideal, of what a man can be. He was a dynamic choir leader and he drew the best possible performances out of us. He was always in complete control on the stage, and we sang our adolescent hearts out for him.

My senior year of high school I sent him a Christmas card expressing my admiration and devotion. At the choir Christmas dinner he stood up and told us he wanted to read aloud some of the cards he had received from us. I still remember vividly the moment when he began reading mine: "To the richest man I know..." I don't remember anything he read after that because I was weeping like a baby, unashamed despite the presence of my peers, my heart overflowing with love and gratitude.

Alas, this is a story that does not have a happy ending. Although I behaved well for Dr. Smith, outside of his presence I remained a wild child, and eventually my behavior within and outside choir came into collision. At the end of the year we made a record album, as the choir did every year. On the day we were to record the album, I went to the beach with my friends before the recording session and drank many beers. I wasn't drunk when I came to the session, but I wasn't exactly in top form either.

Dr. Smith knew it immediately. I could tell he was eyeing me as we warmed up our voices, and I tried to be inconspicuous, but to no avail. I still remember the dreadful moment when he stopped the warm-up, called my name, and asked me to leave. My voice does not appear on the album we recorded, and I have never been able to bring myself to listen to it. But that awful experience taught me a permanent lesson about the costs of selfishness and indiscipline.

COLLEGE: THE INSPIRATION OF IDEAS

I had many good teachers in college, as an undergraduate at Michigan State University and as a graduate student as the University of Virginia. However, none of them evoked the emotional intensity of the teachers I have described so far in this chapter. They were not lesser teachers than the ones I have described so far, but I was at a different developmental stage by then. Childhood and adolescence are stages when our selves and our views of the world are first being formed, so during those stages we look to teachers and other adults as models and ideals for the kinds of persons we might become. We focus a great deal of emotional intensity on the teachers we love best, partly because childhood and adolescence are times of high emotion, partly because we transfer some of the emotional intensity in our relations with parents to other adults we love, including teachers.

College and graduate school years, from the late teens through the twenties, are a much different stage of life. This is the age period that has been the focus of my research and writing as a developmental psychologist, and I call it "emerging adulthood." It is distinct from adolescence, because emerging adults are no longer going through puberty, are no longer in secondary school, and many of them no longer live with their parents. It is not really "young adulthood" either, because emerging adults have not yet entered the roles we associate with adulthood: marriage (or other stable partnership), parenthood, and stable full-time work. Emerging adulthood is an age in between adolescence and young adulthood, an age of exploring different possible futures in love and work. It is an age of freedom, instability, and high hopes.

Emerging adults are often optimistic and idealistic, and they can be inspired by their college teachers to see life differently than before, an inspiration that often carried a strong emotional charge. Relations between students and college teachers are sometimes emotionally close, as I know well from my own experience in two decades of college teaching. However, in my experience as a student, perhaps because I went to a large state university rather than a small college, the inspiration provided by college teachers was less about the personal relations and more about the ideas. I remember especially the power of the intellectual revelations of my first year of college. I took an excellent short story class my first semester, and one of the stories we read was "The Dead" by James Joyce. In the course of the story a man comes to realize that his beloved wife has an emotional life and a past to which he has been excluded. We can never really know each other, I concluded. The next semester I took my first course on psychology, and read Freud's "Introductory Lectures on Psychoanalysis," with its descriptions of the workings of the unconscious mind. We can never really even know ourselves, I concluded.

These are not happy revelations, yet discovering them was somehow exhilarating. Although my view of life has changed in many ways in the 30 years since (and now includes a healthy skepticism of everything Freudian), the exhilaration of new ideas has remained with me throughout my life as an academic.

MY OWN LIFE AS A TEACHER

I have been a college teacher for about 20 years, and I have taught a wide range of courses, ranging in size from five students to 300, at a wide range of institutions, from a small liberal arts college to large state universities. As a teacher I try to bring the same inspiration of ideas into the classroom I felt as an emerging adult years ago. Because I still feel the thrill of ideas in my life as an academic, it is natural for me to communicate that excitement to my students.

When I receive praise from students in their end-of-semester evaluations, I know they will remember me and my course always, as I remember the best teachers of my own youth. That is one of the great rewards of being a teacher, that you leave an enduring legacy in the lives of your students, hopefully a good one. Erik Erikson writes about development in midlife as, at its best, a time of *generativity,* meaning a time of doing what you can to nurture, support, and encourage the next generation. In my teaching I see myself as taking the torch of inspiration from my best teachers, from Mrs. Sterlitz and Miss Davis to Mr. B and Dr. Smith, and passing it on to my students to carry forward.

CHAPTER 3

TEARS OF A TEACHER

Mimi Bong
Korea University

EPISODE 1

I was a transfer student.

During the summer of 1977, my parents decided to move in with my grandfather, who had expressed a strong desire to spend the last several years of his life under the same roof with his eldest son and grandchildren. He had even built a new house for this purpose in one of the booming towns near the outskirts of Seoul. I was a fifth grader with a year and a half left till graduation from an elementary school.

I clearly remember the first day that I met my teacher, Miss *Kim Myung-Sun*. My mom and I were in the backseat of a car that was taking us to my new school. Even before I started attending this new school, my mom had managed to intimidate me with all these horror stories about what would soon become my new school.

"*Mimi*," she was starting it again in the car. "You should remember that kids in this school are really, really smart, much smarter than the kids you used to hang around with in your old school." She kept on going, closely studying the apprehensions on my face that were only getting deeper every minute of the way. "I heard most of them get average scores above 90 points on most of the exams. I know you've been a very good student in your old

The Ones We Remember: Scholars Reflect on Teachers Who Made a Difference, pages 19–29
Copyright © 2008 by Information Age Publishing

school...quite honestly though, things might become somewhat different in this new school...I mean, there could be so many kids who are at least as strong as you are academically in this new school."

To this date, I honestly do not know who or what her sources were for these exorbitant anecdotes. My best guess is that she largely made up the stories on the basis of what little she knew about the school in this new town we were moving to. As any mom, or should I say any "Korean" mom, I bet her motive was pure and simple—to prevent her daughter from letting the guard down and her achievement scores slide. She was successfully turning one transfer student into a scary little rat.

What I also did not know at the time was that this new town was quickly earning a reputation for establishing schools that produced students with excellent academic performance, which was far superior to the average performance of students in other districts in Seoul. The whole town was being developed as part of a strategic expansion plan by the government in response to the saturation problem in downtown Seoul. Families were encouraged to move to this new area and schools with superb academic records worked as powerful baits for Korean parents to consider moving for the sake of their children's education. I am not sure whether the government provided any reward for so doing but principals of these new schools were working very hard to make sure that their schools made part of this honorable reputation. In fact, the superior achievement level of schools is the primary cause of ever-increasing housing prices in this and neighboring areas even today.

My new teacher had freckles on her face. She looked very young. I do not remember what she said to me or my mom when we first met her. All I remember was that I thought she was really pretty with this long black hair and a shy, yet beautiful, smile. The classmates in my new school did not seem much different from the classmates in my old school, either. A couple of days had passed and I was cruising, despite my mom's continued warning. "Just wait until you get your first test scores back."

In the morning of my fourth or fifth day in this new school, the teacher made what to me was a surprising announcement. "We'll have a math quiz today as I announced to you last week. Please clear up your desks." No one told me about this math quiz, so I got caught completely off guard. I was relieved when all five problems she put up on the board were what I already learned well in my old school. After we turned in our answer sheets, she made another dreadful announcement. "As I also warned you last week, you'll be slapped on the palm by the number of problems you missed on this quiz." What? Oh, my God. I was almost losing my mind.

Surely she won't slap a transfer student...I'm sure I'll be spared...I mean, I didn't even know we were going to have this quiz...I wasn't here when they made this stupid agreement.... What if I missed any of the problems? What if I missed two?

There were two students who got all five problems right and I was one of them. The teacher, without even a slightest trace of smile remaining on her face, began slapping students on their palms with a plastic ruler, starting from the very first row on the left corner of the classroom. "*Kyung-Mi*, you missed two problems, so two slaps." "*Hyun-Jung*, one problem missed, one slap." There were more than fifty of us in the classroom and the slapping seemed to last eternity. I remember seeing a vice principal's face outside the classroom window. I did not know how long he had been standing there. He was looking into our classroom from the hall. I don't recall if he had entered our classroom or said anything to us.

When our teacher was finished slapping the last student, she collapsed on her chair. Then she began talking to us, "Class, you know we are falling so much behind on our math achievement compared to other classes..." She didn't finish. She was just sitting there, covering her face with her both hands. There was dead silence in the classroom. Several minutes had passed and we realized our teacher was crying. Some girls started sobbing after her. We were only fifth graders but we understood why she cried. Well, sort of.

That was the first and the last time that I saw my teacher slapping anyone for whatever reason. In fact, she seemed to have fully recovered from the frustration and vulnerability she revealed to us by the very next day. She was back to the gentle, cheerful, and diligent teacher that we knew and stayed that way for the remainder of the school year.

And I continued enjoying my new school. Neither my new teacher nor my new classmates treated me like an outsider. They were all very warm and instantly accepting of the transfer student. I did not clearly realize it then but it had a lot to do with how the teacher treated and positioned the new student in her classroom. My new teacher called upon two girls, whose homes were close to mine and whose names and faces I still remember, to help me adjust to the new surroundings as quickly as possible. I started coming back home with them after school, chatting with them and asking questions about the new school, teachers, and friends. They showed me around the neighborhood as we walked along together.

My teacher regularly checked how I was doing and always tried to find ways to make my transition to the new environment easier and less anxious. I remember seeing her talking to another female teacher in the hallway one day. When I made a bow to her (as any Korean student is expected to do when they see a teacher), she stopped talking to her friend teacher and turned to me again with this big smile that became her trademark in my mind. "Good morning, *Mimi*. Oh, Ms. so and so, this is *Bong Mimi*. She is a new student in my class. *Mimi* is such a terrific writer." She started telling her friend teacher about the poem and the paper flower that I gave her on her birthday. She told her friend teacher that the poem was so good and touching that she could not believe it was written by only a fifth grader. I was totally embarrassed because I did not expect that the teacher would introduce me to her friend, who was an adult and, on top of it, another "teacher." It must have been very pleasant embarrassment, nonetheless, because this "terrific" poem writer was standing there feeling proud.

I soon felt as if I had been attending that school for a long time. I did not miss my old school or my old friends any more. I liked my new teacher a lot and she liked me back. I did not think she liked me any more than she did my friends but I knew she liked me a lot and that was all that mattered. All the kids in my class liked her and she liked every kid in her class. She had a way of making us feel that we were very special. She did not try to bombard us with absent-minded compliments. Rather, she showed us deep and sincere appreciation for the small things we did.

I became liking her so much as did my mom, who even tried to arrange a blind date for her, which was more like a marriage meeting, with my uncle. She gracefully declined, citing she was waiting for her fiancée to finish the three-year military service mandatory for all Korean men. She got married to him the next year and all my friends, my mom, and I attended her wedding. None of the weddings that I have attended in my life so far had so many children guests.

EPISODE 2

I was a transfer student again.

It was the summer of 1981. That spring, my dad ran for a seat in the National Assembly and won it. My brothers and I had to transfer to schools that were located in one of his electoral constituencies. We moved to an apartment that was only two minutes away from the school that I was going to attend, the *Yongsan Girls' Middle School*. Our house was on the seventh floor and I could see the school yard from the window of my room.

I clearly remember the first day that I met my teacher, Mrs....? Funny, I vividly remember her face but can't remember her name. It wasn't one of those common last names like *Kim, Lee, Choi,* or *Park*...or was it? Anyhow, it was a couple of days before the school resumed from its summer break and my mom told me we needed to go see my new teacher. Because it was hot and the school was so close from where we lived, my mom and I didn't feel like we needed to dress up. We took a short stroll down the street to my new school in one summer afternoon.

It was around 4 o'clock in the afternoon and the main administrative office was busy with teachers getting ready to leave after the day's work. No one really paid any attention to us, so my mom told one female teacher that

I was a transfer student to the 3rd Year (equivalent to U.S. 9th grade). She said, "3rd Year? Oh, then you belong to Homeroom Class 4. The teacher is in the classroom now for an end-of-day assembly but will be here shortly." My new teacher did come down to the office shortly and was told that we had been waiting for her. She approached us with what I thought was a very tiring and annoyed look on her face.

"So you are the transfer student?" She turned her head away from me and began talking to my mom. "Well, you know, the class is already full with (how many) students. I really can't accommodate any more students but one of the students in my class recently transferred to another school, so they assigned the new student to my class..." She paused and glanced at us up and down for several seconds. She continued, "I hope she won't be causing any trouble.... How is she in terms of school achievement? The student who transferred out of my class had good grades.... Oh well, that's alright as long as she doesn't cause any trouble." Trouble? I was sure that she had not even looked at my school records. She showed us where the classroom was and that was it. We didn't get to say much. The teacher didn't ask us whether we had any question before she said good-bye.

I remember feeling humiliated and insulted at the same time. I checked on my mom. She did not say a word but I bet she felt the same way. We didn't talk about my new school or my new teacher on our way back home. Actually, I don't think we talked at all. After all, it was only a two-minute walk.

Weirdest things began to happen one after another, starting the very next day. My new teacher called me to the teachers' lounge first thing in the morning. She had an awkward smile on her face. "*Mimi,*" she called my name. "I am afraid I was not courteous enough to your mom yesterday...I mean, how humble your mom was!" She laughed a little from time to time as she spoke. "I must say that I truly respect her modesty...I bet you must be very proud to have such unassuming parents!" I was confused by the sudden change in the tone of her voice because nothing really changed since we met yesterday, approximately eighteen hours ago.

Several days had passed, and I became friends with three girls who were sitting in front and back of me. One day, one of the girls suddenly asked me a strangest question none of my friends had ever asked me before. "*Mimi,* so tell me. Where do you live, *Dongbu Echon-dong* or *Seobu Echon-dong*?" What? What was *Dongbu Echon-dong* and what was *Seobu Echon-dong*? I was clueless. My address said I lived in *Echon 1-dong*. It didn't say anything about *Dongbu* (Eastern) or *Seobu* (Western). "OK, then just tell us where you live exactly." "Me? I live right there—that apartment you see right there." A sneer flitted across her face. "So you are a rich kid. Why have you played with us? Were you trying to pull our legs?" They stopped playing with me that instant and never played with me again. In fact, they stopped talking to me altogether.

One girl wanted to remain friends with me but the other girls wouldn't let her. It was an extremely difficult situation for me because I had not made other friends yet and we were still sitting in front and back of each other.

It was weird. Several more days had passed and students from other homeroom classes started visiting ours during the break. They pointed a finger at me from the door. "That is the girl. That is the daughter of *Bong Du-Wan*." *Bong Du-Wan* was the name of my father. During each break, a different bunch would come swarming about at our classroom door. I felt like a monkey in a zoo. Then a group of students approached me. "*Mimi*, we would like to have you in our group. Will you join us?" There were about six of them in that group. One of them lived in the same apartment as I did. I was glad to have friends again.

My new homeroom teacher taught music classes. Music was one my strong subjects, along with English. In one of the first music classes since I transferred, the teacher posed several questions about scales and notes. I raised my hand to answer them and got them right, not knowing that would mark the very beginning of a completely new schooling experience for me.

Suddenly rumors started to spread. The stories were about how my homeroom teacher showed favoritism toward me and how I chose who to make friends with on the basis of family wealth and school grades. "Did you know the first thing she said after she came to our school was, 'Who is the top performer in this class? I only make friends with best students.' How obnoxious!" "She boasted she always gets perfect scores on English exams." Those were just two rumors that a girl in my class told me she had heard. I was speechless. I even heard some of the students in my class confronted the teacher, accusing her of preferential treatment. Through these rumors and gossips, I learned that the six students in the group, with who I had newly made friends, were those who other students believed the teacher strongly favored. Apparently, my name was now on top of that list. Other students resented that all the girls in this cliquish group, including this transfer student who happened to be the daughter of an influential figure, were from well-to-do families, achieving well academically, and favored by most teachers in their school.

My homeroom teacher called me again to the teacher's lounge. I was so glad and relieved. She must have heard what was going on. I wanted to tell her how difficult it had been for me for the past couple of days and how pent-up I was feeling with all these baseless accusations. My teacher asked me. "Do you know there is this rumor among the students that I favor you, giving you all the special treatments?" She didn't call me by my name. She continued. "You know, I didn't have this problem before you came to my class. Unless you are spreading these rumors yourself, I cannot understand why all these rumors are suddenly rampant. The whole thing really puts me in an awkward position. Why did you want to create an impression that I favored you? Give me one good reason why I should favor you."

I didn't want to go to school. The school started at 8:30 am and I wouldn't start heading for school before 8:20 am. I cried every morning. In Korean middle and high schools, it is the teachers who go to different classrooms in each class period, while the students stay in the same classroom. Tears started to pour right after I sat in my classroom and would not stop until the second or third class period. I sobbed helplessly in my seat. All the subject matter teachers who taught our class in the morning saw this transfer student sobbing helplessly in her seat. None of them said anything to me. They all pretended that they didn't see me. I guess they felt there was nothing much they could to. Besides, I wasn't one of their homeroom students. The crying lasted a little over a month. Meanwhile, my school performance hit rock bottom. My homeroom teacher didn't try to help me. I think if anything, she tried to distance herself from me.

I graduated from that middle school after one semester and went on to high school. It was the only graduation ceremony in my family history that none of us, including the graduating student, attended.

CARING, COMMITMENT, AND COLLECTIVE EFFICACY

If someone asks me to name just one thing that most clearly distinguishes the two teachers in my mind, I can say without hesitation it is "caring." Caring for students was what Miss Kim Myung-Sun had and showed to her students. She might not have been the best teacher in terms of teaching skills or classroom management but she cared for students. It was not merely one or two special events that made me feel that she cared. Rather, it was how instantly I felt safe after the transfer, how quickly I developed a sense of belonging to my new school, and how happy I continued to be in this new learning environment. Miss Kim Myung-Sun took me in under her wings as she did all the children in her class and this made other children to be more accepting of me.

The two major transitions I experienced during my school days, one in elementary school and the other in middle school, initially put me in a similar psychological state. I was feeling nervous, anxious, and somewhat excited at the same time. However, I was a completely different student several weeks after the transition, a happy and confident child in one setting and a miserable and helpless one in the other. Here are a few quotes Bandura (1997) offers:

> Socioeducational transitions involving new teachers, regrouping of classmates, and different school structures confront students with adaptational pressures

that inevitably shake their sense of efficacy. These adaptational problems are likely exacerbated if the teachers to whom the students are entrusted doubt they can achieve much success with them. (p. 242)

It is funny how I should recollect the slapping incident, which happened only once, over all the pleasant memories I had when I was asked to share a story about my most memorable teacher, Miss *Kim Myung-Sun*. It is even funnier how that incident is ingrained in my memory as undeniable evidence of her caring and compassion and not her neglect or abusiveness. I am not saying that I believe Miss *Kim Myung-Sun* resorted to slapping purely out of love. It was more likely out of frustration that her class was lagging behind in math achievement and she did not know what to do to make her students study harder for it. Perhaps she took a wrong advice from more experienced colleagues around her or simply emulated what was then part of common practice in Korean classrooms. Although it is my personal belief that no circumstance could justify teachers for exercising corporal punishment to children, my friends and I were able to feel our otherwise caring teacher's agony in her tears.

Teachers who genuinely care about their students do not show favoritism. Every student is as dear to them as every other student in her or his own special way. Students in the classrooms of caring teachers are protected from the harms of an outside world by forming a caring community of their own. I find it intriguing that it is not the corporal punishment per se that leaves a scar in children's minds. It is the simplest utterance without heart, fleeting sneer, or cold facial expression of a teacher that could leave everlasting scars in students' minds.

I had often wondered why the teachers in the *Yongsan Girls' Middle School* did not try to help me. I could not comprehend that teachers would do nothing to help a transfer student who was sobbing for hours every morning in class. Wouldn't they have wanted at least to find out what was going on? After having moved back from South Carolina to Seoul in 2003, I called one of my high school teachers to say hello and let her know that I was back in Seoul. She happened to tell me that she was now teaching at this relatively new coed middle school, whose predecessor was none but the *Yongsan Girls' Middle School*. So I had to tell her, "Did you know that I'm a graduate of the old *Yongsan Girls' Middle School*? Boy, I had such a difficult time while attending that school.... The school had a terrible culture with students forming factions on the basis of achievement scores or family backgrounds and teachers doing absolutely nothing about the situation...but that was twenty-some years ago. It must be different now, being a new school, coed and all."

Her answer really surprised me. "So it was already like that then, when you were attending this school? How amazing. What you just described is exactly the way it is now in this school. I guess nothing changed."

Like most K–12 schools in Korea, the *Yongsan Girls' Middle School* was then and still is a public school, which means students are designated to the school from nearby areas. The problem is, a majority of the feeder areas for this particular school are relatively underprivileged, whereas few of them are known to be highly affluent. Two of the neighborhoods with the same block name, *Echon-dong*, are divided by a main road with its well-to-do East and its far less prosperous West. The economic difference has narrowed significantly in recent years due to major development efforts but it has been creating tension among the residents and a source of friction even among the students in this school. What is worse, public school teachers rotate schools within their provincial system every five years and many teachers simply opt to wait out the five-year term, turning a blind eye to problems they see in their "temporary" workplace.

"The teachers here have absolutely no commitment. They don't care about the students or the school. They don't try to fix anything. Most of them just wait until their "five-years" is over. *Mimi,* this school has the worst culture that I have seen so far."

Teachers in this school tend to see clear differences in students' achievement scores by the districts the students live in. Because only a small fraction of the students come from affluent neighborhoods, the superior achievement levels of some of these students are more easily discernible. Probably for this reason, some teachers show unmistakable favoritism for so-called "rich" kids. When students perform poorly, the same teachers are too quick to blame the students' unsupportive family background. Not only these teachers lack caring for students and commitment to teaching, they also appear to suffer from lack of collective efficacy. Below are some more quotes from Bandura (1997):

> Teachers who view intelligence as an acquirable attribute and believe they can attain academic successes despite students' disadvantaged backgrounds promote a collective sense of efficacy, whereas teachers who believe that intelligence is an inherent aptitude and there is little they can do to overcome the negative influence of adverse social conditions are likely to undermine one another's sense of efficacy. (p. 248)

Clearly, what the teachers at the *Yongsan Girls' Middle School* exhibited was, and according to my former high school teacher still is, a defeatist attitude. The way they showed favoritism toward certain groups of students resulted from their belief that students' family background and other innate factors that often come with it largely determine how and how well students would perform in school, academically or otherwise. It partly explains the cold and indifferent initial reactions of my new teacher toward me and my mom when we first met her. She must have performed an instant assessment of my background, solely on the basis of how my mom and I were dressed that hot and humid summer afternoon, and decided that I could not possibly belong to the category of the select few who she favored. Here is Bandura (1997) again:

> Staff's collective sense of efficacy that they can promote high levels of academic progress contributes significantly to their schools' level of academic achievement. Indeed, perceived collective efficacy contributes independently to differences in school achievement levels after controlling for the effects of the characteristics of student bodies, teachers' characteristics, and prior school level achievement. With staff who firmly believe that, by their determined efforts, students are motivatable and teachable whatever their background, schools heavily populated with poor and minority students achieve at the highest percentile ranks based on national norms of language and mathematical competencies. (pp. 250–251)

Students can successfully overcome any adaptational or achievement pressure and perform well when their teachers let them know that they care about them, trust that they can achieve success, and will help them achieve and adapt well in the new learning environment. I sometimes hear from Korean teachers that no matter how hard they try, it is the family background that ultimately makes the needed difference in the end. Teachers often underestimate the power they can exert on their students and nowhere else is this more evident than this type of comments.

It is an interesting coincidence that both of my transfers occurred near my graduation from the particular school level. Korea maintains a 6–3–3 school system with six years in elementary and three years each in middle and high school levels, respectively. I spent the last one and a half years of my elementary school years and the very last semester of my middle school years in a new learning environment. Teachers and parents alike tend to believe that students' achievement levels fluctuate less as they move to higher grades within the given school level. Whereas this is true in many cases, it is also true that a single, dedicated teacher still brings about remarkable changes in schools, classes, and individual students with achievement records and cultures that seemed to have become bolted. Just like how my school performance soared right after I transferred to Miss *Kim Myung-Sun*'s class and how it plummeted so dramatically within such a short period of time after I joined the *Yongsan Girls' Middle School*.

Teachers who act as agents of positive changes share several notable characteristics. They genuinely care about their students' overall wellbeing. They are committed not only to help their students achieve better but also to make them feel safe and happy when they are in and outside school.

They are firm believers in their capabilities as an individual teacher and as a member of their team to bring about desired changes in their students. These caring and committed teachers with strong personal and collective convictions do make undeniable and constructive marks in their students' lives that often last a lifetime.

Several weeks after Miss *Kim Myung-Sun* slapped us on the palm by the number of problems we missed on the math quiz, the school administered its regular end-of-month examinations. I do not recall exactly how well our class performed on this school-wide exam. I do remember, however, that our teacher was quite pleased with our overall achievement and we, as a class, felt very proud of ourselves. We were proud that we performed well academically but we were more proud that we made our teacher happy. Because, you know, the last thing we wanted to do was to make our teacher cry again.

REFERENCE

Bandura, A. (1997). *Self-efficacy: The exercise of control.* New York: Freeman.

CHAPTER 4

THE MEMORABLE SISTER CANDIDA AND HER PASSION FOR POETRY

Revathy Kumar
University of Toledo

Each year I teach educational psychology to pre-service teachers, grounding students in the concepts and theories of psychology and encouraging them to examine their instructional practices from these theoretical perspectives. On the first day of class, I ask students to draft an essay identifying a favorite teacher and reflecting on qualities that set this teacher apart from other, less well-liked teachers. As the semester progresses and we discuss topics such as motivation in the classroom or instructional strategies that promote learning, students regularly revisit this essay and analyze the behaviors, beliefs, and attitudes of their favorite, and sometimes their least-liked, teacher. Thus the request to reflect on my favorite middle-school teacher was a pleasant surprise.

Decades have elapsed since I was in middle school. Yet, when I received the invitation to write about my favorite teacher, the image that sprang immediately and effortlessly to mind was that of Sister Candida, my seventh grade English teacher. I am surprised at how vivid my memory of Sister

The Ones We Remember: Scholars Reflect on Teachers Who Made a Difference, pages 31–42

Candida is. Before I talk more about Sister Candida and what it was that made her so special, I would like to describe briefly the sociocultural and historical backdrop of my middle school years.

Most of my formal education took place in India. I was in middle school in the late 1960s, about twenty years after the overthrow of British rule in India, at a time when two centuries of British domination over India retained a strong hold on the collective Indian psyche. Among the educated populace, for example, a strong command of the English language was admired and considered essential. What indeed was education if one could not navigate the intricacies of grammar (from the Wren and Martin grammar textbook published in Cambridge, England); quote Shakespeare at the drop of a hat; or recite William Wordsworth's "Daffodils" when called upon by doting parents to perform for guests. Belief in the absolute necessity of a mastery of English was certainly true of my family—particularly my father, a medical doctor with a passion for English and Tamil literature, who comes from a long line of very highly educated South Indian Brahmins. In the hope that I would receive the best education possible and an earnest desire that I, too, would develop a love for English literature, he enrolled me in a missionary school run by Carmelite sisters. It was in Carmel Convent, New Delhi that I spent my elementary and middle school years and there that I encountered Sister Candida.

FROM UNMOTIVATED TO MOTIVATED STUDENT: THE DIFFERENCE A TEACHER CAN MAKE

I have a confession to make. To the despair of my parents and the exasperation of a long line of teachers, I was a classic example of the unmotivated and disengaged student, doing just enough work to get by. I cared little about school and less about English literature—that is, until Sister Candida came into my life at the beginning of seventh grade.

She was unlike any teacher I had ever had. The austere nun's habit could not hide the spring in her step or the sparkle in her eyes; her vivacity was infectious. Sister Candida was universally loved by her students, not only for the energy and enthusiasm she infused in her classes, but for her ability to reach out to every student in the class. What drew *me* to her, surprisingly enough, was her passion for poetry. Emotions embedded in poems came alive when she read them. In contrast to the apathy I displayed for other classes, I looked forward to sister Candida's English class, particularly if it was "poetry" day.

We never learned poetry within the confines of the classroom. These sessions were often held either under a large shady tree in the school yard or on the steps leading up to the school terrace. On these occasions, she would have all the students sit on the staircase while she stood at the bottom, observing every student's facial expression and ensuring that each of us pronounced and enunciated every word in the poem correctly.

We learned several poems that year. As was traditional in most convent schools rooted in Western traditions, we memorized classic poems written by renowned English poets such as Tennyson and Wordsworth. Sister Candida thrilled us with eloquent renderings of famous Shakespearean speeches. There we were, a class of seventh grade Indian students reciting Mark Anthony's speech from *Julius Caesar*—"Friends, Romans, and Countrymen"!—with great gusto. I am amazed that after all these years I remember most of these poems and speeches verbatim.

However, Sister Candida went beyond teaching the usual list of poems taught in Indian schools, and more particularly in convent schools, at that time. Together we explored the poems and writings of great Indian philosophers, thinkers, and poets. She transported us to the time when India was in the throes of the national struggle for freedom. It was with a great sense of pride that we read poems written by Sarojini Naidu, named the "Nightingale of India" by Mahatma Gandhi. She was a distinguished poet, a champion for womens' rights, freedom fighter, and a great orator. Many of Sarojini Naidu's poems reflected on Indian themes—the social milieu, the grandeur and beauty of the mountains, oceans, and rivers of India. I still recall how entranced I was by the lyrical beauty of "The Palanquin Bearers" and "Coromandel Fishers." At the end of the year we were required to select and memorize a poem that we first recited in front of Sister Candida, and then in front of a panel of teachers. I must confess it was thrilling to see the surprised and incredulous expression on the faces of many of the teachers who did not expect me to do quite as well as I did when I recited Sarojini Naidu's "The Lonely Child." The highlight of the year came when our class was selected to represent our school and present a rendition of Rabindranath Tagore's "Where the Mind is Without Fear" at then-Prime Minister Jawaharlal Nehru's residence in celebration his birthday. Tagore, a Nobel Laureate in literature, wrote this poem, which he titled "The Prayer," first in Bengali and only later in English (see Appendix). This exquisite poem calls readers to break away from the bondage of parochialism and narrow-mindedness.

Sister Candida's class was most memorable for me for both the pure enjoyment of poetry the class evoked and for the personal interest that she took in me. Such personal attention was a novel experience. Never until then had I felt that my teachers genuinely cared for me. For example, towards the end of the year, Sister Candida encouraged me to participate in the yearly inter-school poetry competition, helping me select and prepare Walt Whitman's "O' Captain, My Captain," a eulogy written for Abraham Lincoln. I do not recall how long I practiced, but I do remember staying after school to learn the poem and to pay careful heed to Sister Candida's critique of my elocution. I do not recall ever feeling that I was not competent enough when she critiqued me; I understood that she was merely helping me improve my diction and presentation.

The competition was held on Children's Day, celebrated across India on Jawaharlal Nehru's birthday. My parents were in the audience. Strangely, I was oblivious to the audience when I recited the poem, but I experienced all the emotions of a soldier mourning the death of his Captain. I received the first prize at the competition.

My parents and I moved to another state in India shortly after I completed seventh grade, and I enrolled in another school. But my experiences with Sister Candida and her "poetry classes" have always remained with me. At the expense of sounding trite, she taught me to believe in myself. During that year I learned not only poetry, I learned that I can achieve anything I want—if I want it badly enough. Her passion for poetry kindled a real spark of interest in English literature in me and in many of my classmates, and her vitality and enthusiasm taught us what it means to enjoy learning.

None of my high school English teachers held a light to the dedicated Sister Candida, and my enthusiasm for poetry was somewhat dampened. However, her lessons were far-reaching. I threw myself into algebra and geometry with the same enthusiasm with which I memorized and recited poems. I relished the aesthetic beauty of a simple solution to many of the geometry problems I solved. The transformation that occurred during the seventh grade drove me to do my very best in most of my school subjects thereafter. I think my parents were more than a little relieved and extremely happy as I transitioned from an unmotivated and disengaged student in middle school to a highly motivated student in high school.

A Retrospective Analysis of Sister Candida's Poetry Class

My perspective is filtered, because I am attempting to analyze a learning experience situated in a different cultural context and a different era using current learning and motivational theories developed within a Western cultural framework. Likewise, my perceptions of a classroom that existed in a different time and place are necessarily filtered through my life experiences and, more importantly, through my immersion in the motivational and educational literature produced in the United States over the past decade or so. Despite this, I believe that an analysis of this nature lends itself to identifying features of optimal learning environments that transcend time and cross cultural boundaries. Specifically, I hope to explore what was it about Sister Candida's class that made her universally loved by all her students and how my experiences in her class affected me.

Sister Candida the Universally Loved Teacher

To get at "what it was about Sister Candida's class that made her universally loved by all her students," I examine features of her classroom context from the perspective of a social cognitive theory of motivation known as achievement goal theory. Relative to other social cognitive theories of motivation, achievement goal theory has focused on creating learning environments that encourage the development of cognitive skills by promoting adaptive motivations.

Critical Analysis of Sister Candida's Poetry Class from an Achievement Goal Theory Perspective

Early research in achievement goal theory identified two classes of goals that students pursue in a learning context: mastery and performance (Ames, 1992; Maehr & Midgley, 1991; 1996). While the former focuses on self-improvement, progress, and intellectual development, the latter focuses on demonstrating superior ability or avoiding the appearance of being incompetent. The two goals reflect vastly different conceptions of school success and vastly different reasons that students engage in academic activities. More recently, some have suggested that the valences, approach and avoid, associated with performance goals are also significant. For example, the desire to look smarter than one's classmates has been labeled as a performance-approach goal, while concern about appearing unable has been labeled as a performance-avoid goal (Elliot & McGregor, 2001; Pintrich, 2000). Achievement goal theory is grounded in the Western cultural belief that individuals are driven to engage in behaviors that have direct consequences for the self, whether adaptive or maladaptive, for example self-improvement, self-enhancement, or self-protection (Kumar & Maehr, 2006).

Achievement goal theory also emphasizes how perceptions of the goals emphasized in the learning environment influence students' personal achievement goals. Ames (1992) and Maehr & Midgley (1996) have detailed the critical facets of classrooms and schools that determine whether they are more mastery-focused or more performance-focused. Ames suggested that students would be better-served if teachers engaged in instructional practices that are meaningful and challenging to the students; actively solicit students' participation in classroom decisions; minimize social comparisons among students; recognize students' effort, progress, and accomplishments; and adopt criterion-referenced rather than norm-referenced evaluation techniques.

When examining Sister Candida's classroom in light of these important aspects of the classroom, it is important to understand the school climate and culture within which it was situated. Carmel convent was an all-girls' school, and teachers maintained strict discipline in the classroom. We were required to sit in a quiet and ladylike manner when the classes were in session. At the same time it was also a very competitive environment. Beginning in first grade, report cards were issued at the end of every quarter that ranked students' exact position within the class. Needless to say, with my "don't care" attitude toward learning (probably a self-protecting strategy!), my name was never anywhere near the top of the list. The control exercised over students, the power differential between teachers and students, and the clear distinction between winners and losers was not designed to create a community of learners. In the language of achievement goal theory, Carmel convent was a highly performance-focused school. Against this backdrop Sister Candida's poetry class featured several characteristics associated with mastery-focused classrooms. What set her class apart was *how* she taught, *what* she expected of her students, and the *kind of relationship* she forged with her students.

There was a clearly articulated demand for mastery in understanding the poems, perfection in presentations, and expectations for high effort in Sister Candida's poetry class. At the same time, she provided the necessary scaffolding and support for each one of us to do our best. In recalling the support she offered, I am reminded of the words of a seventh grader from a Midwestern school whom I interviewed some years ago. This student talked at length about his reasons for feeling disengaged from school and reflected on the general lack of teacher support. However, he said that he was fond of his science teacher because she provided, in his words, "good criticism" instead of "bad criticism." When asked to explain what he meant, he replied, "She does not embarrass me in front of the class and takes time to explain things I don't understand. She knows what I am about." Sister Candida provided her students with "good criticism."

In this class we experienced a relatively greater sense of autonomy than we did in most of our other classes. The very act of leaving the confines of the classroom and moving us outdoors for the poetry class created a sense of freedom. Along with this sense of freedom was also a sense of shared identity, a positive interdependence as we worked to make clear the meaning of the poems and recited them together. I recall that this feeling of togetherness, of having a shared goal, was particularly strong towards the end of the year as we learned the Rabindranath Tagore poem recited at the prime minister's residence. We were encouraged to work with each other to improve our performance, and there was a feeling of collective efficacy as we regulated our own and our peers' presentations in progressing towards a common goal of being selected to represent our school.

Ample social cognitive motivational research (Ames, 1992; Bandura, 2001; Deci, Vallerand, Pelletier, & Ryan, 1991; Iyengar & Lepper, 1991; Ryan & Deci, 2000) suggests that providing choice is central to providing a sense of autonomy. Based on this definition, which emerges primarily from research with Western student populations, Sister Candida's class did not provide the level of autonomy considered optimal. She did not involve us in the selection of poems she taught or the books that we were required to read for her class. While I recognize and believe that autonomy is essential for student motivation, at that time I do not recall feeling controlled or that my autonomy was curtailed because our choices for poem selection were not solicited. But then, the standards of autonomy and its effect on psychological well-being are culturally defined and determined (Kumar & Maehr, 2006), and the phenomenological experience of autonomy is relative. We certainly had more autonomy in this class than in the other classes, and Sister Candida's evaluation of students' performance was based both on our efforts through the course and on the presentation of a poem of our choice at the end of the year.

Creating a Culturally Responsive Classroom

I would argue that Sister Candida engaged in culturally responsive teaching, an approach that requires teachers to incorporate culturally valued curriculum and create culturally appropriate situations for learning (Ladson-Billings, 1995). Her selection of poems written by famous Indian poets who worked alongside freedom fighters like Gandhi and Nehru to liberate India was designed to promote social consciousness and feelings of empowerment by instilling in us pride for our national heritage. It was uplifting, for example, to read Rabindranath Tagore's vision for a democratic India in "Where the Mind is Without Fear." I do not recall exactly how she taught this poem, but I do know that every line in this poem came alive as we read and interpreted it together and that it remains by far one of the most meaningful and beautiful poems I have ever read. Again, it was the cultural relevance of Sarojini Naidu's description of the shade of a coconut glade or scent of a mango grove in the "Coromandel Fishers" suggestive of the coastline of South India that made it meaningful to the students. While Wordsworth's "Daffodil," which we also learned, is a beautiful poem, full of visual imagery, it could evoke neither the emotion nor the visceral reaction that the poems by Rabindranath Tagore and Sarojini Naidu evoked in young, post-independence Indian students. I am certain Sister Candida was aware of this as she selected poems that carried a historical significance for Indians and described people, places, and events that her students could identify with.

I do not know if it was by accident or by design, but her practice of teaching poems that emphasized a more encompassing national identity helped bridge the tremendous variability in language and religion that was manifest in Carmel Convent's student body, as well as that evident among students and teachers. The language and religious diversity in our school reflected the cosmopolitan nature of New Delhi which, as the capital of India, drew people from across the nation. The only language common to all students was English. My perception (and I may be wrong) was that even though many of the teachers were Christians and most of the students were Hindus who spoke different languages at home, these were not the salient issues that one might expect them to be. Regardless, I believe that creating a strong sense of national identity, a shared destiny, and a sense of national pride can have a powerful impact on middle grade students when issues of personal and group identity take on added importance. Through the poems she taught, Sister Candida emphasized the commonalities that existed among us, her students, while simultaneously acknowledging our cultural differences to promote positive intergroup relationships within the classroom.

THE WELL SPRING OF MY MOTIVATION
IN SISTER CANDIDA'S CLASS

Motivation is that factor which energizes and directs behavior. The emphasis in this definition is usually on the terms "energizes and directs behavior." I believe the key word in the definition is "that." It is the wellspring of any motivated behavior. In an effort to understand my own motivations in Sister Candida's class, I will attempt to identify the "that" in the definition of motivation. Upon reflection, there were two inter-related sources for my motivation in that class. The first was Sister Candida's own passion for poetry. It was simply infectious. It was not as if I had not been exposed to poetry before; it had never touched me in quite the way it did in her class. In Sister Candida's poetry class, the beauty and emotions embedded in the poems came alive. It was a powerful experience. I invested so much effort in that class, but it seemed effortless. This was the "flow" experience that Csikszentmihalyi (1990) wrote so eloquently about. This was the "interest and excitement" that, Deci and Ryan (1985) explained, accompanies intrinsic motivation.

The second wellspring, closely related to the first, was the quest for aesthetic experience that spurred me to read and reread these poems. Indeed, it was the very act of reciting the poems that was motivating. How and where do concepts like "aesthetic experience" and "inspiration" fit in within the current literature that explores motivation? While the act of reading could be described as agentic, it was not the need for agency or control that motivated me in the context of Sister Candida's poetry class.

The notion of agency is central in all current social cognitive theories of motivation. For example, Deci and Ryan (Deci & Ryan, 1985; Ryan & Deci, 2000) explain that agency and control are necessary antecedents for intrinsic motivation. Thus motivation is closely tied to individuals' ability to choose to engage in a course of action and not be controlled by external environmental constraints. Achievement goal theory, too, emphasizes the intentional nature of goals in which we make a rational and conscious choice to engage in specific behaviors to achieve specific goals in a learning context. How, then, can we describe motivation and understand the learning that occurs as a consequence of engaging in an aesthetic activity, such as the one that I was engaged in without any conscious thought of control or any attempt at making a considered and rational choice?

Not surprisingly, social cognitive theories emphasize the cognitive underpinnings such as choice, decision-making, self-regulation, and metacognition for understanding motivated behavior. However, emotional underpinnings of motivated behavior that can also lead to learning and behaviors, such as deep processing of information, are not as clearly articulated or widely discussed. Wong (2007, p. 216) suggests that "deeply moving experiences are more likely to emerge when students are less cautious, self-aware, skeptical, objective, and intellectual and more venturesome, un-self conscious, trusting, subjective, and emotional." This statement exemplifies my experiences in Sister Candida's class. I am deeply grateful to her for creating the non-threatening environment that made this kind of learning experience possible.

THE LONG-TERM EFFECTS OF MY PERSONAL EXPERIENCES WITH SISTER CANDIDA

I grew to love and respect Sister Candida, as I am sure many of my classmates did. It was the first time I felt that a teacher took personal interest in my learning and education. Never did I ever feel that she expected any less of me than of the other students in the class. As the year progressed, she realized the impact the class was having on me, and I think this created a closer bond between the two of us. Sister Candida's expectations for me and the task-oriented and non-judgmental feedback she provided for improving my performance spurred me to do my best.

Research documenting the lasting effect that teacher expectations can have on students (Smith, et al., 1999) certainly proves true in my case. As I mentioned earlier, I moved to a new school in a different state at the beginning of eighth grade. While several factors, including transferring to a new school and developing friendships with peers who were oriented toward doing well in school, also acted in my favor, it was Sister Candida who first sowed the seed of wanting to learn and do my best in school. For this I am grateful.

A FINAL REFLECTION

As I reconstruct my memories of events that occurred so many years ago, it is very likely that my current beliefs and expectations may taint this reconstruction. There may have been occasions when I was not as involved in or committed to learning in Sister Candida's class. But I have no recollection of these occasions. I think the very fact that I can recall not only the names of many of the poems I learned, but the poems in their entirety attests to the impact this class had on me. Again, the fact that I cannot recall the names of most of my other teachers while her name is etched in my memory also attests to her impact on my life.

Several years ago I interviewed 54 seventh-grade students who indicated on a survey in the sixth grade that they experienced dissonance between their home and school cultures. Almost all the students interviewed talked about their feelings of disconnection from school. While some of the reasons they articulated were closely tied to ethnicity, they also discussed reasons for disengagement that cut across ethnic lines. Among other factors, they voiced their unhappiness about the lack of teacher support for learning, the unfair treatment they received from some of their teachers, and the intense competition they experienced in the classroom. They also talked about the occasional caring teacher who made a significant difference in their lives. I find that many of my descriptions of my favorite teacher and my middle school experiences in 1960s India resonate with many of the responses made by the seventh grade students I interviewed in the late—1990s United States. Qualities that make a teacher eternal are timeless and transcend cultural and national boundaries.

REFERENCES

Ames, C. (1992). Classrooms: Goals, structures, and student motivation. *Journal of Educational Psychology, 84*, 261–271.

Bandura, A. (2001). Social cognitive theory: An agentic perspective. In S. T. Fiske, D. L. Schacter, & C. Zahn-Waxler (Eds.), *Annual Review of Psychology*, (Vol. 52, pp. 1–26). Palo Alto, CA: Annual Reviews.

Csikszentmihalyi, M. (1990). *Flow: The psychology of optimal experience.* New York: Harper-Perrennial.

Deci, E. L., & Ryan, R. M. (1985). *Intrinsic motivation and self determination in human behavior.* New York: Plenum.

Deci, E. L., Vallerand, R. J., Pelletier, L. G., & Ryan, R. M. (1991). Motivation and educations: The self-determination perspective. *Educational Psychologist, 26,* 325–346.

Elliot, A. J., & McGregor, H. A. (2001). A 2 x 2 achievement goal framework. *Journal of Personality and Social Psychology, 80,* 501–519.

Iyengar, S. S., & Lepper, M. R. (1991). Rethinking the value of choice: A cultural perspective on intrinsic motivation. *Journal of Personality and Social Psychology, 76,* 349–366.

Kumar, R., & Maehr, M. L. (2007). Cultural interpretations of achievement motivation: A situated perspective. In F. Salili (Ed.), *Culture, Motivation and Learning: A Multicultural Perspective* (pp. 43–66). Charlotte, NC: Information Age Publishing.

Ladson-Billings, G. (1995). But that's just good teaching! The case for culturally relevant pedagogy. *Theory into Practice, 34,* 159–165.

Maehr, M. L., & Midgley, C. (1991). Enhancing student motivation: A school-wide approach. *Educational Psychologist, 26,* 399–427.

Maehr, M. L., & Midgley, C. (1996). *Transforming school cultures.* Boulder, CO: Westview, Harper Collins.

Pintrich, R. R. (2000). Multiple goals, multiple pathways: The role of goal orientation in learning and achievement. *Journal of Educational Psychology, 92,* 544–555.

Ryan, R. M., & Deci, E. L. (2000). Self-determination theory and facilitation of intrinsic motivation, social development, and well-being. *American Psychologist, 55,* 68–78.

Smith, A. E., Jussim, L., Eccles, J., VanNoy, M., Madon, S., & Palumbo, P. (1998). Self-fulfilling prophecies, perceptual biases, and accuracy at the individual and group levels. *Journal of Experimental Social Psychology, 3,* 530–561.

Wong, D. (2007). Beyond Control and Rationality: Dewey, Aesthetics, Motivation, and Educative Experiences. *Teachers College Record, 109,* 192–220.

APPENDIX

Rabindranath Tagore's Vision

Where the mind is without fear and the head is held high.
Where knowledge is free.
Where the world has not been broken up into fragments
By narrow domestic walls.
Where words come out from the depth of truth.
Where tireless striving stretches its arms towards perfection.
Where the clear stream of reason has not lost its way
Into the dreary desert sand of dead habit.
Where the mind is led forward by Thee
Into ever-widening thought and action.
Into that heaven of freedom, my Father, let my country awake.

Rabindranath Tagore

CHAPTER 5

THE ART AND HEART
OF THE SKILLED TEACHER

A Personal Reflection

Julian G. Elliott
Durham University

To be a teenager in London in the summer of 1966 was—if I may amend Kipling's famous line about being born English—to have won the lottery of life. England were newly crowned soccer World champions, the music and fashions of the period were enervating and exciting, and there was a widespread feeling of confidence on our part that this was the time to be young. This feel-good factor was increased by my perceived good fortune in respect of my schooling. In the Fall of 1966 I transferred to one of South London's most academically prestigious selective boys' secondary schools. This was the school that my parents had long dreamed about; an academy that had educated three recipients of the Victoria Cross (the U.K.'s most revered military honour), a Secretary of State, an Oscar winner, a famous comedian, and multiple captains of industry and government.

I was not so naïve as to fail to realize that the school would have its dark side; its reputation was more redolent of Tom Brown's Rugby than Harry

The Ones We Remember: Scholars Reflect on Teachers Who Made a Difference, pages 43–51

43

Potter's Hogwarts. I had heard about the bullying of the new boys (having your head stuffed down a toilet bowl, a favoured initiation ceremony, was not a prospect I relished), and stories of the fierceness of the teaching staff and their predilection for the use of corporal punishment as a means of character formation. However, I was reassured by the knowledge that most of the really tough kids were attending very different institutions—"secondary modern" schools that catered for the 80% of each annual cohort who had failed the selection examination. In addition, the school was run by priests of a greatly revered religious order. My experience of the parish priest, based on regular attendance at church and service as altar boy, was that he was typically an avuncular figure with a strong sense of fun, a twinkle in his eye and a paternal affection for his parishioners. Surely, our teachers would be cast from the same mold? In all honesty, my major concern was that I was required to wear short trousers in the first year—an experience I found shameful and demeaning. Having worn long trousers in my final year of primary school, a sign of having "grown-up," I was mystified by this ruling which, even then, seemed to my young mind to be primarily a mechanism of social control and subjugation.

Dr. Hemmings was quite a teacher. His age was difficult to determine. While clearly younger than many of the crusty old hands—many of the non-cleric teachers, entitled "Major This" or "Colonel That" having seen action in the '39–'45 War—he exuded a certain air of maturity and worldliness that was impressive. Unlike other teachers of a comparatively youthful age, he did not seek to win over his pupils by behaving in ways that might be perceived as "trendy" or fashionable. Nevertheless, he clearly understood the needs, anxieties and, importantly, the humour, of young people and could navigate our world while maintaining clearly signposted generational and professional boundaries.

Dr. Hemmings' classroom authority was rarely directly challenged. His professional confidence and sense of composure, manifested through his posture, gesture, voice, gaze, and facial expression, were such that challenge or resistance rarely entered our heads. Of course more indirect challenges, manifested in the typical format of very bright adolescents—questioning banter—were easily dealt with by his superior oral skills and his ability to regulate and control classroom discourse patterns. He instinctively knew that to maintain control, it was important not to be overly responsive to all student interrogations unless the educational needs of the moment merited this.

Even at the tender age of twelve, the precocious boys at my school could quickly calculate which of our teachers were a) highly intelligent and b) masters of their particular academic specialisms. This process of divination was made easier by the school's tendency to timetable the more academically able teachers with the most gifted academic streams. Of course, intellectual and pedagogical ability were in no way correlated. We could, therefore, take heart from the fact that while many of our teachers were inept pedagogues, at least they "knew their stuff, academically"; while those who were clearly not masters of the academic discipline for which they had been timetabled, tended to have a certain degree of classroom presence or otherwise disappeared.

Interestingly, this highly selective school rigidly streamed its annual intake into four classes such that the lowest stream, endearingly described by teachers and children alike as "The Thickies," consisted of students operating at above the eightieth percentile in terms of national performance. However, despite what appeared at the time to be a massive intellectual void between the streams, I learned about the true range of ability (for example, that difficulty in conjugating Latin verbs was *not* a sign of severe intellectual deficiency) only when I began my teacher training. As Marsh has shown through the "big fish, little pond effect" (Marsh, Chessor, Craven, & Roche, 1995), the practice of placing very bright students in selective groups can result in social comparison processes that lead some high achievers to develop a negative, and potentially damaging, academic self-concept. The relative high wastage of very capable students from such institutions is a phenomenon that has often been overlooked in the debate about the merits of selective schooling.

Dr. Hemmings seemed equally at home teaching any stream. He was able to differentiate by level, pace, and degree of abstraction. His key strategy for making often very complex ideas meaningful to us was to start from our own everyday life experiences and, from these, highlight those issues that could be applied to the particular lesson content. Such an approach helped us to grasp key principles and embedded new learning within our existing frames of understanding.

While his apparent excitement and curiosity about even the most mundane curricular elements was infectious, we were also spurred on by the encouragement he offered. Not that he was given to roseate and voluble exclamations of affirmation—English grammar schools in the 1960s had not yet encountered the practice of ubiquitous and non-contingent affirmation that would sweep across the Atlantic a decade or so later. Nevertheless, Dr. Hemmings' approval, largely signalled by subtle, often non-verbal, forms of communication—a nod, a gaze or a smile, was important to us. By such means, he indicated an approving recognition that we had grappled with an idea, a concept or a task. Of course, even he could not render all aspects of the academic grammar school curriculum, intrinsically motivating. However, the temptation to let our thoughts wander to whatever phenomena typically occupy the minds of teenage boys (it's so long ago, I can no longer recall what these were) or to engage in banter or warfare with classmates, was constrained by Dr. Hemmings' impressive capacity to be wholly aware of everything that was happening in the classroom, all of the time—"The Eye of Sauron" as we ironically joked. Exhibiting an uncanny knack of managing multiple events in the classroom simultaneously, his tendency to call upon a child to answer a question or to undertake a task, just at the moment that his concentration was wavering, or his interest declining, kept the class alert and expectant. Such skills helped to prevent problems from emerging and, therefore, there were few occasions when he was required to respond to significant misbehaviour.

While Dr. Hemmings appeared to understand that his key role was principally that of educator rather than social worker, nurse or probation officer, he was more than merely an exceptional teacher of his chosen discipline. While clearly passionate about his subject specialism, he also demonstrated a strong belief that the broader development of the child was a goal that should be of equal importance for all teachers. In the harsh atavistic environment of a boys' secondary school, he realized that teachers played an important role in creating a school environment characterised by caring, sensitivity and thoughtfulness. While we were never sure of his religious beliefs, his approach to life exemplified the Christian principles of goodness and concern for others that we were explicitly taught each day.

By now, the reader may be wondering whether the portrayal of Dr. Hemmings in this chapter might be a little too eulogistic. Perhaps the picture that is being presented has been distorted by the passage of time—some four decades? In truth, the answer is more complex. Dr. Hemmings never physically existed, yet he is a very real product of my experiences—my memory of those times is vivid and, I am sure, accurate. In composing this chapter, I first tried to follow the prescribed brief of identifying a key influence at my secondary school. Very quickly, it became clear to me that there was no such individual. I decided, instead, to generate positive aspects of a number of my best teachers in order to create a fictional composite figure. Sadly, this also proved impossible—there were just too few elements available to me. Finally, I decided to identify a list of negative teacher aspects—those elements that reduced my enthusiasm to learn, stifled my desire to please, led me to disengage intellectually and emotionally from school and, ultimately, to fail miserably in subsequent public examinations. Having composed such a list, I then produced their antithesis—Mr. Hemmings was the resulting incarnation.

So what were my formative experiences of my teachers during my adolescent years?

AN APPARENT AND PERVASIVE ABSENCE OF INTEREST IN THE EMOTIONAL SECURITY AND WELL-BEING OF THE CHILDREN

Teachers always addressed the boys by their surnames, a format we therefore adopted when addressing our classmates. Discipline was enforced by frequently administered corporal punishment. There was no sense that teachers were ever cognisant of children's fears, insecurities or personal crises. Rather paradoxically for a school run by a religious order, a strongly Darwinian principle of "survival of the fittest" seemed to operate. There seemed to be a sense, perhaps echoing from the Victorian independent school tradition, that the future "officer class" needed to be made of stern stuff and should always maintain self-control under duress. In contrast, I remember my amazement some years later, when I began teaching in an inner-city secondary school, that my streetwise and physically hardened students would so often dissolve into tears, and even run away, when challenged. When I was at school, such displays of emotion were perceived to be indicative of weakness and thus were almost never witnessed.

While I was unsurprised by the behaviour of the lay teachers, I was greatly discomfited by the behavior and orientations of the priests. Unlike those in my local church, these men often appeared to be sadistic, and in a few cases, lascivious. Even to this twelve year old, the notion of housing celibate priests on the top floor of a school catering for pubescent boys was seemingly inadvisable. While appearing to be eager to ensure the salvation of our souls, at the same time, most appeared to be wholly uninterested in our social or emotional security. While preaching love, generosity and tolerance, they usually displayed none of these virtues to their charges.

In this, as in many other schools of the time, physical education teachers threatened the self-esteem of many children (thankfully, things in the U.K. in this respect have greatly improved in this respect nowadays). It seemed as if these athletes' own personal biographies, whereby they had found sporting achievement easy to come by, yet had failed to reach the highest levels, had resulted in a strong antipathy towards those who lacked their abilities or motivations. To be a skilled and committed "player of the game" was to gain their favor, while their disdain for the uncoordinated, the unfit and the reticent was palpable and often communicated very directly. I can speak here from personal experience. Although I was greatly enthusiastic about racquet sports, I lacked any sense of physical coordination and my physical strength had failed to grow in proportion to my height. For this reason, the gymnasium was a nightmare for me, a very public space where I struggled to conceal my inadequacies. However, unlike those who seek to protect themselves against observer perceptions that they lack ability by going out of their way to demonstrate an absence of interest (Covington, 1992),

I was eager to demonstrate that, despite my clumsiness, I had some competence in sports. My coping strategy in the gym, therefore, was to avoid engaging with the more challenging apparatus and conceal myself from the teacher's scrutiny as far as possible. On one occasion, however, I was called upon to demonstrate a handstand to the class. As my muscles and coordination failed and I collapsed on the floor, his sneering, contemptuous public evaluation ("You're just pathetic!") was an intensely humiliating experience that still evokes an emotional reaction whenever I recollect the experience. Labelling theory has shown how the use of a derogatory label by an authority figure in a public setting can often result in the labelled person acting in accordance with the label (Hargreaves, Hestor & Mellor, 1975). This is a lesson that has yet to be learned by many teachers even today.

A LACK OF UNDERSTANDING OR INTEREST AS TO HOW TO CREATE INTRINSICALLY MOTIVATING LEARNING EXPERIENCES

This school was, to all intents and purposes, academically successful. Catering for highly able and largely compliant, students, its diet of rote, mechanical learning and daily repetition resulted in significant success in public examinations and high acceptance rates to the most prestigious universities. The pressure to perform, to be better than everyone else, to be accepted by the elite universities, was sufficient motivation for most of the students. The key to success was to cram an immense amount of factual knowledge into our heads and regurgitate this in our examinations. Unlike some achievement motivation researchers, I am not surprised that a high emphasis upon performance goals predicts examination success as, in my experience, the latter rarely requires deep understanding of the material to be covered. However, the mind-numbing nature of my lessons, a difficulty to defer gratification and an irrational belief that I could come good by revising at the last minute proved, for me personally, to be an unfortunate combination.

While I doubt that pedagogy was a matter of hot debate in the teachers' lounge, if there were an educational philosophy operating in the school, it was seemingly that the boys' flabby minds had to be shaped by means of the traditional academic disciplines. Much material, at this stage in the boys' education, was there merely to be memorised. However, at our school, the classical languages, Greek and Latin, were pre-eminent—the principal means by which rote learning—*Amo, amas, amat, amamus, amatis, amant*—could be supplemented by the inculcation of logical and analytical processes. The procedure typically involved a child translating a sentence or phrase in front of the class leading to a reaction of horror or chagrin on the part of the teacher. The aggressive challenge by the centurion as to the correct way to decline the graffiti "Romans Go Home" in *Monty Python's Life of Brian* perfectly captures the adversarial quality of the standard teacher-pupil exchange in these classes.

In the majority of my lessons, the main pedagogic method consisted largely of recording material with the expectation of subsequent memorization. I recall hour upon hour of writing down dictated notes in my exercise books; the tedium was stifling. To break this, I used to write one line of text sloping to the left, the next to the right, the third upright and the fourth, upside down. On other occasions, I would experiment with colored inks. Much of the time I would transfer the teachers' words to paper without any consideration of their meaning.

Other, forward-thinking, teachers embraced a visual rather than auditory modality! Here, instead of dictating content, the teacher would write his notes onto the blackboard and we would copy this material into our books. It was in such lessons that I learned the important lesson that would serve me well in my later teaching career: Never turn your back on the class for other than very brief periods unless you are very secure in your ability to manage classroom behaviour. In similar vein, throughout my teaching career I always tried to remember that I should never spin around to face the class and ask, "Who threw that?"

In an educational culture of rote learning and memorisation there is unlikely to be a significant emphasis upon children's existing understandings and experiences or any consideration as to how these might impact upon learning. Thus, the material to be learned was imparted as fact with the expectation that this would be absorbed and reproduced as and when necessary.

Most of my teachers singly failed to communicate any sense of excitement or enthusiasm in their academic discipline. Any suggestion that we should take pleasure from our studies only became evident as we moved towards our final years of schooling. I recall the words of my Latin teacher, a priest in his late twenties: "I know that declensions and conjugations are dull. I know that Latin is boring. But we've got to do it so there's no point in moaning. Let's get on with it and stop pulling faces." This appeal to demonstrate the British stiff upper lip in adversity, to buckle down and do the right thing, seemed as inappropriate as a motivational device to me then as it does now. However, his frequent public condemnation of those who struggled to grasp the finer points of Latin as "cretins" would certainly be more frowned upon today than it was then.

A FAILURE ON THE PART OF SOME TEACHERS TO DEMONSTRATE APPROPRIATE CLASSROOM AUTHORITY AND MANAGEMENT

To be fair, many of my teachers did display that powerful sense of awareness in the classroom that I ascribe to Mr. Hemmings. They were aided by the fact that we were expected to work in silence most of the time, and movement around the classroom was largely forbidden. In attributing this skill to my fictional teacher, I draw upon my memories of those poor souls who lacked the necessary classroom awareness and presence and thus failed to signal any sense of professional authority. As in many highly regulated schools, these teachers suffered greatly. Their lessons were the valves that permitted the release of the pent up pressures of our adolescent lives. Each evening on the way home, we would share our stories of the various escapades that had taken place during their anarchic classes. For these teachers, the array of punishments available, which they were usually not averse to drawing upon, seemed to have little or no effect upon the children's behavior. Despite this, some of the teachers who encountered the greatest disciplinary problems were among the more humane and personable members of staff. However, our behavior towards our teachers seemed to be more conditioned by their level of classroom expertise than by their personal qualities or any obvious concern they had for our wellbeing. Being friendly, responsive and caring, while vitally important, are insufficient if there is an absence of professional teacher expertise and authority. This proved to be an immensely important lesson that I have endeavored to pass on to several generations of student teachers.

CONCLUSION

While academic success only came to me in my post-adolescent years, I learned much at my secondary school that I have subsequently drawn upon in a lifetime in education. That this resulted largely from a succession of negative experiences is personally unfortunate yet, paradoxically, may have proven invaluable in making more salient to me what really matters when educating students of all ages.

REFERENCES

Covington, M. (1992). *Making the grade: A self-worth perspective on motivation and school reform.* New York: Cambridge University Press.

Hargreaves, D., Hestor, K., & Mellor, J. (1975). *Deviance in classrooms.* London: Routledge & Kegan Paul.

Marsh, H., Chessor, D., Craven, R., & Roche, L. (1995). The effects of gifted and talented programs on academic self-concept: The big fish strikes again, *American Educational Research Journal, 32,* 285–319.

CHAPTER 6

IN SEARCH
OF MISS STEEPLETON

Vanessa Siddle Walker

The day Miss Steepleton abruptly left our class and our school remains as stark in my memory as the shock that she would be leaving. I tried to explain the imminent departure to my mother. My comments must have seemed liked the incoherent babblings of a pre-adolescent.

"She's leaving, Mom," I said for the second or third time since we drove away from the newly built school for Black children. We were riding in my mother's sporty white Corvair with the red interior and had traveled three miles or more since my first effort to explain. Despite the forward motion of the car, we were still stuck on the same rotation sequence in the conversation.

"Vanessa," Mom patiently explained, "You must mean that she is leaving for the weekend. She's probably going to her home in Kannapolis to visit." Back in those days, a weekend trip home for a Black teacher would have made perfect sense. After all, Black teachers often left spouses and families to reside in other areas where they could locate suitable employment. Since they were routinely expected to maintain some presence in the community, even on the weekends, they might easily be in their adopted residence for two or more consecutive weeks before returning home. My mother's specu-

The Ones We Remember: Scholars Reflect on Teachers Who Made a Difference, pages 53–61

lation that Miss Steepleton was merely going home to visit for the weekend was eminently logical, except that it didn't resonate with the words the revered teacher had spoken to our class earlier that Friday afternoon.

Many of my friends and I had been Miss Steepleton's students for more than a year. Although the wintery days were now upon us for the new school year, the class had settled into the easy familiarity of a comfortable school routine. The previous year we had been together in a Black segregated school where students labored to perform operettas and Christmas plays and enjoyed our Friday afternoon dances. Parents still came in droves to the Parent and Teachers Association Meetings. This year we had a White principal, a White secretary, and a White cafeteria manager—and they called our brand new building an integrated school. Yet, somehow neither the so-called integrated facilities nor the civil rights conversations around us mattered very much. Up and down the halls of our school walked the teachers we knew. And, Miss Steepleton was still the same.

We had had a typical week of school—one so typical as to be completely unmemorable. I know Miss Steepleton taught, and we learned. The particulars of how she taught us escaped my memory. I just know she did. She always did. That pattern was just the way her class operated, and I was sure it operated that way during this particular week. At the end of the afternoon, just minutes before we would be dismissed, had come the shocking announcement. She stood in the front, near the new blackboard. "Class," Miss Steepleton began. "I'll be leaving to go home. I won't be coming back. You will have a new teacher on Monday." We had stared quietly, with not a word uttered that I can remember. I think we were numbed by disbelief. "I want you all to be good boys and girls and do well," she concluded. I think those were her words. I don't remember. All that registered and remained was that she was leaving.

Choking some unnamed emotion deep within me that afternoon, I was trying to make sense of the events that had just transpired. No matter how many times I repeated myself, my mother seemed incapable of understanding. Mom and Miss Steepleton were colleagues. Perhaps my mother thought if the departure were true, she would have known. Now five or more miles down the road, we were making no headway on the issue. She was still maintaining that Miss Steepleton was leaving for the weekend. I, on the other hand, insisted that she didn't understand and that I knew what I had been told.

Why should it matter anyway? Why was I working so hard to explain, to convince my mother that this sense of loss welling inside me was real? Why was I feeling this strange emotion, something akin to abandonment? She was, after all, just a teacher. I had had teachers before, even loving motherly ones. In fact, one had given me a lovely *Little Red Riding Hood and Other Stories* hardback book for Christmas, and had even saved me from getting spanked by my mother one afternoon by just happening to put me in the top reading group that day. As I made my pronouncement of my first-grade success in the car that afternoon, a proud mother had changed her mind about delivering the promised, and well-deserved, spanking I had been informed that morning I would receive in the afternoon. Instead, she expressed her joy in my accomplishment, while pointedly reminding me to stop leaving my new sweaters at school. As I breathed a sigh of relief, I knew I owed that teacher a good deal. But, even with a vague sense of being helped by this teacher, the sense of gratitude soon diminished.

Miss Steepleton was somehow different. Maybe her appearance and carriage shaped my feelings about her. She looked like an elegant Ethiopian queen. Slim and impeccably dressed, she carried herself with a grace and gentleness that commanded my attention and admiration. I can not remember another teacher who so captured the images of the "me" I hoped to become. I admired her voice also. In soft tones, she corralled the attention of an exuberant girl who liked very much to talk. Though I had received a less than satisfactory grade once in conduct, I seemed to be able to keep my talkative nature at bay in her classroom. Her soothing, affirming manner that first year had also been a balm after I had been frightened by a teacher the previous year who talked rather loudly. My mother had had to convince me that the former teacher was a caring person who also just happened to have a loud voice.

Two episodes, one inspiring me academically and one inspiring me personally, stand out as I reflect on the ways Miss Steepleton taught me that were different from my other teachers. The first appears a non-story, unless you were the student who lived it. Typically, I grasped concepts rather quickly. Long division had me stumped, however, and my failure was becoming frustratingly evident to me. Not realizing the problem was my increasing near-sightedness and my concurrent inability to see the board well from my seat near the back, I was just beginning to entertain the sinking sensation that I was dumb. Miss Steepleton did not publicly reprimand me for my repeated mathematical errors, but moved in close to my seat. She leaned over my desk, examined my work in progress, and softly explained my error. I had missed a simple concept—the need to subtract at the end, and that lack of understanding was the reason for all my wrong answers. A simple function, simply explained. I learned the math, and I maintained my self-esteem. I was especially grateful the whole class didn't have to know my difficulties. In a way that expressed caring to me, she taught the concept, but allowed me to keep my head up. That was just how she taught. I don't remember her students being embarrassed.

I also remember the private reprimand that made me a better human being. The new girl in our class was not one of my favorite people. She had become a member of the class several months after the school year began, and she just didn't fit in with the rest of us. I do not remember a thing she ever did to me, but I quickly decided she was an outsider who was not behaving according to the standards of myself and my posy. I rigidly ignored her, abruptly silencing her every effort to fit into the class. I knew my mother and the girl's aunt were friends, but their relationship did not deter my behavior. Convinced I was right, I maintained my unforgiving distance, at least until Miss Steepleton asked me to stay late after class. Not very happy about the summons, I wondered if my mother or the girl's aunt had set me up. I now question that interpretation though. My mom was fairly rigid about refusing to interfere in my education, despite the fact that she was a teacher in the school. Years later, when I began to write about segregated schools, I would discover that this belief that one teacher should not interfere with the classroom of another teacher was a strong unwritten policy. My guess is that the reprimand emanated from the observation of Miss Steepleton, who more than anyone was in a position to see the dismissive behavior I daily exhibited toward the girl in class.

"Vanessa," she calmly began. She was moving in close again, trying to help me solve a different kind of problem. I remember being invited to think about how I would feel if I were new to the school and didn't have any friends. I also remember being introduced to the idea that I was somehow a class leader. In this role, I had certain leadership responsibilities, and I wasn't living up to my possibilities. If I were to be nice, other students would follow, she explained. The talk achieved the effect she intended. I changed my behavior, although I never remember liking the girl.

Memories such as these were too new to have been explained at the time I sat in the car. I only felt the loss growing bigger and bigger in my chest that Friday afternoon. We were nearing a little country store where there was a one-pump gas station. The store was in the middle of a White neighborhood, and I don't remember it as a place my mother routinely stopped. I don't know why she stopped that day. Perhaps it was because she recognized Miss Steepleton's car parked at the gas pump.

That afternoon outside the little store was the last time I saw Miss Steepleton, and the events remain as a blur. Gas. Someone going inside the store. Someone coming outside the store. I glimpsed Miss Steepleton. Somewhere, maybe inside, they talked. Then we were gone. I don't know who bought gas. I don't even remember waving good-bye. I was too choked up by my mother's affirmation of the point I had been trying to make these past miles. "You were right, Van. Miss Steepleton is leaving." Mom only called me Van as a term of endearment. She must have known how much I was hurting.

Only a short time later, I knew for sure Miss Steepleton was gone. We had another teacher, one brand new to the profession and not very inviting. Apparently, she had not been around long enough to be mentored in any forms of teacher caring. We were completing an assignment that involved utilizing words with the "dis" prefix. I asked her about the use of "disconsolate." She told me no such word existed. I knew she couldn't be right because I sang something that sounded a lot like that word on Sundays in the church choir. Returning to my desk, I sought a dictionary and flipped pages until I found it. Then, I proudly carried the dictionary to the new teacher's desk to show her the word. I thought she would be pleased that I knew such a really big word. Miss Steepleton would have been. Standing close to her desk—about the spot that I had come to associate as a safe place with teachers, she glared at me and told me that I should be the teacher if I knew so much. In retrospect, I can see why she thought me a little know-it-all. But, at the time, I just felt dejected by her reproof. Apparently, all teachers were not the same.

What was it about Miss Steepleton that captured my heart and still captures my imagination? Her style of teaching was neither quantifiable nor easily identifiable. Nothing was particularly brilliant about the curriculum or the pedagogical style. Ashamedly, I would admit that I don't even remember many of the topics we studied. Instead, somewhere deep within me was the unalterable conviction that this teacher deeply cared about my success. She was approachable and willing to help solve my personal and academic problems. Some of my other teachers seemed to care about the class as a whole, but Miss Steepleton managed to convince me that she cared about me—even though I don't remember her doing anything different for me than she did for anyone else.

I now believe that I was captured by the type of teacher caring that reportedly dominates the attributes of successful teachers of Black children in segregated schools. Long before scholars began to posit the significance of teacher care in schools, many Black teachers consistently and repeatedly inspired Black children to believe in what they were capable of achieving. Their style of caring was communicated in deeply personal interactions, where the teacher was unafraid to move closely into the life of a student and inspire him or her to craft a new vision of his or her potential. In fact, the professional associations of Black teachers encouraged this behavior, and their principals consistently modeled it in their own interactions with students. Miss Steepleton may have been a gentle and beautiful person by nature, but she was a caring teacher by intent (Siddle Walker, 2001). In this professional world of Black teacher caring, as evidenced in Miss Steepleton's response to my misbehavior toward a classmate, caring was not merely a praise session that dismissed a student's poor behavior. Rather, the caring for the student was demonstrated in the willingness of the teacher to be direct about behaviors that were inappropriate. The caring was real and up-close, not phony or dehumanizing.

I can now see how her type of caring influenced my academic success. "If a teacher teaches, but the student doesn't learn, has the teacher taught?" It was a favorite saying my mother would later use in professional development sessions with her own teachers when she subsequently became a principal. The phrase captured her belief that the teacher had a responsibility for presenting content knowledge *and* for caring whether the student actually learned the material. It exemplified the beliefs of Black teachers who worked with Black children in the segregated schools such as I attended. Teaching for Miss Steepleton would not have been merely standing at the front of the room and providing explanations. Teaching would have been spotting misunderstanding and coming to the aid of a child who never asked for help. Thus, she would not be an effective teacher if I did not learn, and caring was the mediator through which she made sure no barriers inhibited my learning.

Of course, this feeling about teachers as people who cared about you pretty much left with Miss Steepleton. In the years that passed, as desegregation was upon us all, teachers came and went. However, my heart was always drawn to teachers who in any way exhibited some of the caring behaviors I had taken for granted with Miss Steepleton. These teachers, only two that I can remember, looked at me as an individual with potential and also moved in close to my life to make sure I would fulfill the possibilities. One teacher showed concern about my personal well-being during a time when I was just learning how to transition to the young woman who needed to carry a purse to the bathroom; perhaps as a result, when she later wrote in class prophecies that I would become a journalist, I took her seriously and later headed off to the University of North Carolina to the school of journalism. The other teacher, who was my instructor for all three years of high school, also invited me into the space near her desk during that first year to talk with me about college plans. From class, I knew that she took silent pride in my typing skills, especially when I, a Black girl, would be the first to zing the return button on the type-writer, alerting the whole class that I could type the most words per minute in the class. I don't think I raced to be first because I needed to be admired by the class. I didn't even know the people in the class. I think I typed quickly because I loved her smile of satisfaction. (To be completely frank, I probably also enjoyed the look of exasperation from one White girl who sat in front of me and who seemed genuinely annoyed that a Black girl kept beating her.) By calling me up to talk about college and expressing interest in my typing achievement, I began to get the message that I also mattered to this teacher as an individual.

I really knew I mattered to her when she went to bat for me and my rowdy friends during our senior year. The loudest friend and I had been called to the principal's office for writing an editorial in the school newspaper that announced the presence of worms in the school soup. The White cafeteria manager was enraged. Passing the White secretary to be escorted to his office, we were unsurprised to discover that the White principal also did not take very kindly to this kind of publicity. Nor was he impressed with our free speech arguments. The teacher called us in close to her desk when we returned, and we were reprimanded for our behavior (although she never made us believe she thought we were wrong). In the behavior of this teacher and the one previous, I saw a glimpse of Miss Steepleton. But, not until writing this piece did I realize why I may have liked them so much.

In elevating the salience of caring in teacher behaviors I do not seek to dismiss the creativity of teachers who have strong content knowledge and are able to teach in exciting and challenging ways. Some of my other teachers were encouraging and led interesting class discussions. Others were extraordinarily creative. The latter assigned fascinating projects that kept me happily engaged in the wee hours of the morning, and that still inform my understanding of some world and national events. From these teachers, I learned that an engaging curriculum, powerfully executed, could introduce liberating new ideas to a teenage mind. I appreciate all of their efforts. But, while content and creativity may help generate good grades, I am not convinced they prompt the inspiration that makes a child want to succeed in life. On the other hand, convincing a child of his or her academic and personal potential may inspire beliefs about a future life that no lesson plan, however well executed, can replace.

Of course, a fair critique of my memories of a favorite teacher could posit that my elevation of care may be a function of the segregated time period during which she was my teacher. This perspective has merit, as the larger national context and the internal school messages may have been particularly important for children who were devalued in the larger society. During the 1960s, many Black teachers wanted to be sure that their children could become full participants in the desegregating world around them. They inspired children to become their personal and academic best. Many are remembered as creating classrooms that shielded their young charges from negative messages that would diminish their potential and, instead, creating a safe learning environment within the school where Black children could believe we were as good as anyone else. They were preparing us for a world that did not exist. In this cocoon of safety, messages about potential could be reinforced and believed. Miss Steepleton's caring was surely a product of this world.

However, I am also amazed at how little the needs of Black children have changed, despite the external differences in society. I note with interest (and with sadness) that even today Black children report being greatly influenced by what a teacher thinks about them. In recent studies, the influence of teacher expectations is reported to be three times as great for African American students as for White students. Indeed, 81% of Black females and 62% of Black males want to please the teacher more than their parents (Singham, 2003). Their desire for teacher approval contrasts sharply with the negative teacher encounters that discipline them more frequently, even for the same offense as that of a White classmate. One wonders what kind of caring messages these children are receiving. Perhaps in a world of continuing inequalities, Black children still need to be made to believe in what they can become. If so, the overlooked quality of a teacher caring enough to move in close to encourage and to reprimand, both personally and academically, may be lost in the mad scurry of standards and teacher-proofed curriculum that purport to be the best measures of their success.

In all these years, I have only spoken with Miss Steepleton once since the day she left for her home in Kannapolis. The phone number came years later—after undergraduate and graduate school, when I was beginning my first university job at the University of Pennsylvania. I don't remember who gave me the number. I do remember I called her. When she answered the phone, I strove to connect the voice with the remembered portrait. I thanked her for the beautiful letter she had sent me in response to my own good-bye and thank you note, sent so long ago by a hurting little girl. I tried to find words to tell her that I had indeed tried to be smart, just like she had encouraged me to do. I didn't know what else to say. It had been so many, many years. How could one explain that her belief in what I could become, exemplified by her caring, had made an indefinable impact on my life? I don't know that I was particularly successful in explaining all of this, although she made me believe that she was really happy to hear from me. When we ran out of talk, I said good-bye.

I still think of her almost every time I travel through Kannapolis on my many trips to the childhood home I still maintain in North Carolina. I always say I want to stop, to see if I can relocate the phone number, to see if I can find Miss Steepleton. So far, I never have. Maybe I am afraid. I think she married a man named "Brown." (After a name with such a lilt—Steepleton, calling her "Brown" seems dull and uninspiring.) Maybe I am afraid to meet this Mrs. Brown. As teaching has changed in the intervening years, perhaps so too has she. Maybe the style of caring that imbued her teaching wasn't valued or rewarded in a new setting. Perhaps school climates focused on pedagogical excellence did not provide the freedom to continue to move in close to children and to inspire their personal and academic best. Maybe Mrs. Brown won't be the Miss Steepleton I remember. Perhaps I don't want to know, and that's why I haven't tried harder to visit her.

One day, just as my young daughter and I were approaching Kannapolis, riding along happily in my white, family-style car, we saw the breathtaking beauty of the full arc of a brilliant rainbow before us in the sky. I have never seen a rainbow so lovely, either before or since. We were awed by its beauty and majesty, especially since the interstate led us directly under its high peek. To my daughter, the rainbow was an array of colors, a beautiful piece of art searing the darkness of the surrounding clouds. To me, it was a symbol of the mythical pot of gold, especially since Kannapolis was the next city on the other side. I thought again of Miss Steepleton. I wanted her to still be there, living on the other side of that rainbow. I wished she would be there for me and for all the children who need a teacher like her. Every child deserves a Miss Steepleton.

REFERENCES

Siddle Walker, V. S. (2001). African American teachers in segregated schools in the south, 1940–1969. *American Educational Research Journal, 38,* 751–780.
Singham, M. (2003). The achievement gap: Myths and reality. *Phi Delta Kappan, 84,* 586–591.

CHAPTER 7

MRS. MILLER

Frank Pajares
Emory University

I was thirteen years old, insecure, and in the eighth grade. I wasn't attractive, I wasn't athletic, and I wasn't popular. I had an accent, and my hair was far too long for an era that favored crew cuts. The Beatles were just around the corner but, alas, they hadn't yet arrived. I was bony, gaunt, lank, lean, thin, and scrawny, and I refused to go swimming with anyone lest I should have to remove my shirt and expose a body so emaciated and feeble. I did feel "smart," but what few brains I might have had were no advantage to me in such a capricious world. You might think that simply out of a sheer sense of inadequacy I should have developed a bit of humility, or perhaps a quiet and introspective nature. You might infer that I should have been shy. No. I was loud, obnoxious, and arrogant. Always the class clown. Such were the tools with which I began my teenage trek to adulthood.

I'll not bore you with sad anecdotes or melancholy memories of my eighth grade year. Suffice it to say that thirteen has never been my favorite age. In retrospect I should have put my own children to sleep for the duration of their thirteenth year. There must be something to that number. I'm not at all surprised that hotels avoid having a thirteenth floor.

I guess I survived by enduring. I was beaten up at the bus stop for mouthing off to the bus stop bully. I had a crush I still remember with longing—

The Ones We Remember: Scholars Reflect on Teachers Who Made a Difference, pages 63–65

Susan Patrick where are you and why didn't you want to kiss me when we played post office at your birthday party? Ah, well. I was beaten up on the basketball court for mouthing off to the basketball court bully. I fell over while leaning backwards in my desk soon after the teacher told me it would happen, and everyone laughed. I was beaten up after school for mouthing off to the after-school bully. During physical education dance classes the jocks would cut in on me when I was assigned a nice-looking girl as my square-dancing partner. I was beaten up several times while square dancing. There, I've gone and done it. I've bored you with my sad anecdotes and melancholy memories.

But, honestly, was life really all that bad? I don't know. I don't remember most of it. But I think so. Until that day, and recalling this makes recalling all those gloomy memories worthwhile, when I took my yearbook to Mrs. Miller for her signature.

Mrs. Miller was my math teacher, a lovely mad woman given to feverishly sucking pieces of chalk because, she proudly declared, it helped her to give up cigarettes. Everything about Mrs. Miller was alive and in a constant state of motion and emotion. When she looked at you after asking a question she did so with vibrant, dancing eyes that beckoned the answer from you. And if you hesitated, a raspy, nicotine voice would cajole you. "Come on, duckie! I know you know it. You know you know it. Tell the world!!" And you did, because Mrs. Miller never asked you a question you couldn't answer. She also endeavored to call all her students by a name no one else would call them, a name reserved for her use alone.

"Manuel, you dear matador, swagger to the board and do problem seven!" How deliciously embarrassing.

Age is at best a nebulous concept for eighth graders, but I think Mrs. Miller must have been close to retirement. She dressed oddly, everyone said so, she wore too much make-up, sometimes people laughed at it, and she always wore a crazy blonde wig that was never on straight.

When she could tell I was having a particularly difficult day, and she could always tell, she would keep me after class. After our math class, Mrs. Miller had her planning period, and how well I recall those splendid, rambling chats in the blissful solitude of that empty classroom. Only empty cathedrals have since elicited that same mood in me. There, for however long it took her, Mrs. Miller would unruffle my bruised feathers, reorient my perspective, and sit quietly while I cried. She nursed my wounds and dried my tears. Some days I would tell her my great secrets, others my great fears.

"Don't you worry Manolito, it will pass." And so it would.

After observing the proper rites, she would get me to laugh at some silly joke. Soon after, I'd be laughing at myself and my foolish predicament. And then I would find myself babbling on about my hopes and my dreams and my ambitions, and our chatter would transform the empty classroom and fill it with magic fantasies and dazzling possibilities. I know now that our chatter was not at all responsible for that magic transformation. The magic was Mrs. Miller. When we were done, she would carefully write me an all-powerful pass to my next class in order that I suffer no harm for my transgression. I would leave quietly and renewed, a smile confidently in place and eyes moist with gratitude. Mrs. Miller was outrageous, she was eccentric, she was bizarre, and I loved her.

And so, at year's end I took my brand new yearbook to Mrs. Miller to sign.

"Manuel," she gasped, "this is empty! No one has written in it! I have no juicy tidbits to read and entertain me!" She slapped the virgin yearbook on her desk, leaned precariously over me on one hand, and rearranged her wig with the other.

"Bring it to me filled to the brim!" she bellowed. "I want to be the last to write in it." And so I did, even at the embarrassing expense of asking near strangers to write in my book.

"Anything. Just write something."

Triumphantly, I brought my exhausted yearbook to Mrs. Miller. She read it with utter delight and abandon, giggling at the compliments, what few there might have been, chuckling at the inanities, and howling at the cruelties. And when she was done, and after we'd both laughed, she took my book and said, "Let me keep it a while, Manuel. I want what I write to be the great truth about you. I will return it Monday. Now off with you. Find yourself a señorita."

And so Monday morning I raced from the bus to Mrs. Miller's classroom to retrieve my book. She smiled and whispered, "I have found the great truth about you."

I darted from the classroom to discover my great truth alone, and I found solitude under the basketball bleachers of an empty gymnasium. There I opened my yearbook and searched. Under her photograph she had written, "Become a heart specialist, Manolito. You understand them so well."

I became a teacher, Mrs. Miller. I'm pretty sure that's what you meant.

"I cannot but think that to apperceive your pupil as a little sensitive, impulsive, associative, and reactive organism partly fated and partly free, will lead to a better intelligence of all his ways. Understand him, then, as such a subtle little piece of machinery. And if, in addition, you can also see him *sub specie boni*, and love him as well, you will be in the best possible position for becoming perfect teachers."

William James
Talks To Teachers

CHAPTER 8

AN AMOTIVATED ADOLESCENCE

How One Rugby Game and Two Teachers Changed My Self-Beliefs and the Course of My Academic Life

Robert Klassen
University of Alberta

Most academic motivation researchers study positive or functional motivation, and try to understand how self-efficacy, or learning goals, or self-determination positively foster academic achievement. But many adolescents do not display functional academic motivation, and discussions of the flip side of functional motivation—dysfunctional motivation or academic amotivation—may be instructive when exploring the motivation of certain groups of teens. Few researchers focus on academic amotivation, but Canadian researchers Legault, Green-Demers, and Pelletier (2006) have recently discussed how some adolescents feel disconnected from typical academic and social contexts, and are likely to be bored, lack concentration, feel higher levels of stress, and in extreme but all-too-common cases,

The Ones We Remember: Scholars Reflect on Teachers Who Made a Difference, pages 67–75

67

drop out of school. Adolescent amotivation leads to frustration and discontentment, and hampers academic productivity and general well-being. For academically amotivated adolescents, school is drudgery, with few rewards available from a system that rewards academically motivated students, and with teachers that usually spend time and attention on the students who learn quickly, who appear interested, and who display high levels of effort, persistence, and who make sound academic choices.

My story of "teachers who made a difference" is set in the context of adolescent amotivation. The rise and fall of my academic motivation in childhood and adolescence is not atypical, and is described well by findings from Jacquelynne Eccles and colleagues (e.g., Wigfield & Eccles, 2002) who have noted the decline in academic motivation in the transition from elementary to junior high school. The challenge for teachers of adolescents, as we shall see, is in (a) understanding how previously academically engaged children transform into bored and disinterested adolescents, and (b) knowing how to make a difference in the lives of students who lack academic confidence and show little academic motivation. In this account of my childhood and adolescent schooling, I will discuss how although few teachers inspired me during early adolescence, two teachers—one in my last year of junior high school, and one in my last year of senior high school—planted the seeds that grew during late adolescence and eventually resulted in a reawakened belief that I could be a successful learner in an academic environment. I will first describe the family context, and then the social and school contexts that influenced my academic motivation and functioning. Next, I will examine how a sports-field epiphany and contact with two teachers changed my self-beliefs and inspired my learning. To complete the essay, I will provide some analysis of these adolescent happenings, and offer suggestions to teachers who want to make a difference in their students' lives.

FAMILY CONTEXT

Educational psychologists too rarely explore the influence of the family and the family learning environment, yet the educational and social modeling and training provided at home have considerable influence on children's academic and social development. Growing up in the 1970s in a working class Vancouver suburb, there wasn't much talk, at least among my family and social network, about the need to strive in the academic world. My parents were first-generation Canadians, whose parents had fled the communist regime in Russia in the 1920s to rebuild their lives in western Canada. My early childhood was strongly flavored by socializing with other children whose parents or grandparents were immigrants from Russia. Our family's academic roots were shallow, and although my parents loved me and supported me, they did not provide my two brothers and me with any particular academic direction or encouragement. The family support for learning was decidedly neutral, with opportunity for intellectual growth provided by weekly trips to the local library and through exposure to our sets of Childcraft and World Book encyclopedias left over from one of my father's less successful sales ventures. Although our family's indifferent learning milieu seemed to provide an adequate foundation for achievement in elementary school, it proved less effective in my early adolescent transition into junior high school, when the academic and social influence of peers grew stronger, and when academic self-beliefs were uncertain.

TRANSITION: ELEMENTARY SCHOOL
TO JUNIOR HIGH SCHOOL

Elementary school was a positive experience for me with a number of teachers that inspired my learning. In our school district, elementary school ran from kindergarten to Grade 7, junior high schools from Grades 8 to 10, and senior high schools for Grades 11 and 12. My friends in elementary school were generally bookish and academically competitive, and we spent much effort competing to be the top of the class in the weekly reading, spelling, and arithmetic tests. Equally importantly, we worked hard for teachers who grew to know us well, and who were able to point out our academic strengths and weaknesses, and who displayed a concern for us that went beyond our academic performance. I functioned reasonably well academically and socially in elementary school, connected well with my teachers, and was even placed in a pilot program for bright students in Grade seven (in what must have been the world's worst gifted education program, consisting of four students left in charge of their own learning, with virtually no teacher guidance or supervision. Discovery learning might work well when properly implemented, but it was a remarkably ineffective guiding theory for four 13-year olds left to their own devices in Burnaby in 1974…but it was a memorable year).

My transition to junior high came with a change in social network, with friends from elementary school moving into a variety of different schools in the city. The social environment in the working class junior high I attended was dramatically different from elementary school, and relationships with teachers were usually strained and sometimes antagonistic. I played a few sports, but badly, and did not associate much with the more athletic students. I had a few close friends, but was generally clueless when it came to popular culture and the social goings-on of most of my school peers. In junior high school the academic expectations and workload increased, but my interest in learning decreased, and indifferent or challenging relationships with teachers resulted in lowered grades and declining academic confidence. My academic motivation and achievement plummeted in the first two years of junior high school, and I quickly joined the ranks of the disaffected early adolescents who experience little academic success and who find themselves on the social and academic fringes.

Friends and peers have a strong influence on the development of motivation beliefs, and it's no surprise that children and adolescents typically seek out peers who share their level of academic functioning and motivation. My lack of any real connection with teachers morphed into a growing lack of interest in attending classes and completing assignments. I gravitated towards peers who shared a lack of interest in formal learning, were minimally involved in school activities, and skipped class regularly. My closest friends were under-achievers, on the fringes of high school life academically and socially, and who had poor relationships with teachers. Social support for academic achievement was not a factor in my circle of friends, and we neither talked about academics nor had expectations that our schooling could be of any benefit or interest to us.

My memories of junior high school still make me cringe—the school seemed full of bored and sullen adolescents with little interest in learning, but plenty of interest in smoking pot and hanging out in the wooded area beside the school. The school subjects seemed irrelevant and badly taught by teachers who struggled to maintain order in their classrooms. The teachers were quicker to point out academic flaws than academic strengths— I did poorly in English because my handwriting was messy; did poorly in social studies because I colored maps badly; did poorly in math because I missed too many classes to catch what was going on; and did poorly in PE because of poor performance on the dreaded Canada Fitness Tests. I missed many days of school in Grade 8 due to migraines brought on by puberty and anxiety, and was frequently absent in Grade 9 due to hanging out with like-minded disaffected peers. My academic life took a turn for the better in Grade 10 and beyond, when I began to attend more regularly, and when two things happened that changed the direction of my education. First, I came to a new understanding—during a rugby game—of my personal agency, and a realization that I had the capability to influence my environment and my life's direction. Second, I encountered two teachers, one in Grade 10 and one in Grade 12, who made an effort to establish a personal connection with me and who influenced my understanding of my own capabilities.

RUGBY, PERSONAL AGENCY,
AND TWO INFLUENTIAL TEACHERS

Rugby was the big sport in our school, and I played, although usually not very much or very well. But in Grade 10 the rugby field provided me with an epiphany—a sudden intuitive understanding—that influenced my self-beliefs, and laid the foundation for the development of more positive academic and social functioning. I remember the very moment when I realized that I was an agent, and realized that—at least on the rugby field—I had the capacity to act and to impose my actions on the world. It was in the third and final year of my inglorious rugby career, playing at the back of the scrum as the eighth man. My usual mode of playing was to stay on the fringes of the action, with little involvement in or impact on the game, even though I was big for my age and my coaches harbored the hope that one day I'd tackle somebody or pick up the ball and run with it. One beautiful fall day, and I can still remember the smell of the grass and dirt of the playing field, and my green and black striped rugby jersey, I realized, *Hey, I can tackle that ball carrier. I can run over there, and stop that guy. There's nothing preventing me from being the one to be the person that influences what happens in this game.* I understood, in one of those rare moments of adolescent clarity, that I had the capacity to act, and to influence what happened not only during that game, but in a broader sense. (The game result? I can't remember, but it was near the end of the season, and I recall getting more playing time for the remainder of the season.) Albert Bandura states that agency begets self-belief, and that the process begins in early childhood, but for me, a sense of physical and personal agency was grasped in adolescence in a single moment on a rugby field in Burnaby. A realization of human agency is important, because academic and other self-beliefs are born from the understanding that individuals have the capacity to act, and to influence their own and others' lives. My understanding of my agency was tied to another Aha! moment in grade 10, but this one came from interaction with a teacher who made a difference.

Our rugby coach, Mr. Campbell, was also my Grade 10 science teacher. Bruce Campbell was one of the few teachers I can recall in junior high who was respectful of students, and seemed to like his work as a junior high school teacher. His was one of the first classes I can remember that offered clear and relevant instruction from a teacher who was genuinely interested in his subject and in his students, and who actually seemed to enjoy teaching his classes of often-unruly adolescents. As a science teacher, he made regular use of hands-on participation, and he also injected his enthusiasm about the subject into his teaching, and made science relevant to our adolescent interests. Was it the subject matter? Partly, because what adolescent boy doesn't enjoy taking a sample of his own blood for blood-typing, or being challenged to figure out how to distill crude oil from samples of tar sands, or using microscopes to look at cells from anything and everything? But it was more than that—it was his encouragement that we were capable of conducting science, and it was his personal connection with students that make him stand out in my memory. I can hardly remember *any* positive results on assignments in junior high school, but I remember clearly my science assignment on biofuels (maybe my first "A" on an assignment since elementary school) and his comment that I had done *excellent work*. And he was right—for me it was an assignment I had taken seriously, and I had produced the best work I was capable of doing. He recognized and supported my efforts, and encouraged the belief that I was capable of a higher level of achievement than I had shown.

Most importantly for me, Mr. Campbell seemed to care about his students as people, and he regularly talked to me outside of class, sometimes discussing what we had covered in class, and sometimes talking about other happenings of the day. For at least one disaffected, unmotivated adolescent, a small amount of personal attention made a huge difference, and I became an interested learner in that class, and still remember many of the things we were taught. (In contrast, I can't remember even the names of the science teachers in the previous two years.) Maybe more importantly, Mr. Campbell made me see myself as a learner, and as someone who could make an academic contribution, and I gained a positive learning experience that helped me to understand that I had the capability to succeed as a student.

TRANSITION: JUNIOR HIGH SCHOOL
TO SENIOR HIGH SCHOOL

Moving from junior high to senior high after Grade 10 was a less traumatic transition for me than the move from elementary school to junior high. My grades started to improve, my peer group changed, and I observed that more teachers connected personally with students, and treated students in a more respectful manner. My own sense of academic confidence was developing, and my academic record was improving but still mixed, with an assortment of As and Ds on most of my report cards. I was a voracious reader outside of school, but continued to spend little time reading assigned texts in school. I had some teachers who were passionate about their subject areas, and more of them built relationships with their students than did teachers in junior high school. What I most clearly recall from senior high school was my encounter with one teacher—Mr. Kirby—who seemed to enjoy his subject (English) and his students, and who provided me with a certain amount of academic encouragement. Once again, it was the personal relationship with a teacher that made a difference in my self-beliefs about my learning. Mr. Kirby taught in a way that was inspiring to me—he connected literature with current events, he discussed the universal and important themes in literature and adolescent life, and he spoke to his students not only about their academic flaws, but about their academic strengths and potential. One afternoon after class, we were walking down the hall, talking about an assignment I had handed in, and he commented, "You're a good writer, Rob. You should really consider..." at which point he was interrupted by another teacher walking by, and he entered the teachers' staff room with me left hanging onto his last phrase "I'm a good writer? I should really consider...consider what? What was he going to say?" His off-the-cuff comment awoke in me the idea that maybe, just maybe, I had the talent to do something—anything—intellectual in nature. His words stuck with me, and not because of their content (I know my limitations as a writer), but because of the beliefs his words instilled in me that I had the capability to do...well, something anyway. The confidence those words gave me helped me to move beyond my academic self-doubt and amotivation, and led me to start thinking about academic possibilities beyond high school.

ANALYSIS

Reflecting on my adolescent school experiences, I can see one event and two teachers that helped change my early adolescent amotivation into more functional motivation beliefs. Until I was able to develop a sense of personal agency, that is, an understanding that my actions could influence outcomes, and that I was responsible for my own social and academic functioning, my self-beliefs were vulnerable to every mistake or failure that I experienced. As a result, my academic self-efficacy was low, with few instances of successful performance, and minimal positive verbal persuasion or modeling of success. My rugby field epiphany helped me understand that my actions led to consequences in my environment, and especially that I could positively influence my own outcomes. The two teachers I described—Mr. Campbell and Mr. Kirby—increased my enjoyment of formal academic learning, and helped me believe that I was capable of achieving at a higher standard than I had previously. Most of my junior high school teachers offered little in the way of positive feedback, verbal persuasion, or what Legault et al. (2006) call "competence suppport," in which students' capabilities are reinforced and highlighted by teachers' comments and actions. The two teachers that made a difference to my adolescent self conveyed the sense that they took pleasure in teaching, in interacting with their adolescent students, and in forming guiding and supportive relationships with their students. This relationship-building with students, and perhaps especially with the disaffected, under-achieving adolescents who seem especially populous in many junior high schools, makes a difference to the students who are alienated from mainstream school society and who do not feel connected to other teachers or to the school ethos.

My motivation beliefs were influenced by family and social contexts, but the academic support provided by my family, peers, and teachers in early adolescence did not result in strong academic motivation or striving (although my parents reveled in my later academic accomplishments). The two teachers who had an impact on my adolescent academic development shared one thing in common—they made the effort to establish a bond with me, a bond that was built through mutual respect and even affection for their less-than-likeable adolescent students. Motivation researchers suggest that low academic self-efficacy is a primary feature of academic disengagement. My own early adolescent self-efficacy trajectory mirrored the oft-cited decline in motivation that occurs during the transition from elementary school to junior high school, and this lack of confidence in my own academic capabilities influenced my academic interest, my choice of friends, the subjects I studied, and the tasks I chose to complete. Most importantly, the building of my academic self-efficacy did not occur in a social vacuum, and my growing sense of academic confidence was enhanced by feedback from trusted important individuals, namely two teachers who made an effort to build a personal connection with an underachieving student. I was receptive to the opportunity for enactive experience in my science class with Mr. Campbell, and I was receptive to the verbal persuasion in Mr. Kirby's English class only after a friendly and respectful student-teacher relationship was built. For teachers of early adolescents, it is important to provide relevant content and high quality instruction, but it is *critical* to build positive and functional relationships with students. The value of building strong relationships with adolescents should not be underestimated when attempting to understand how academic motivation functions in adolescence.

CONCLUSION

Now I'm a parent of adolescents, and although not surprisingly I can see myself in some ways in my children, I'm pleased (relieved) to see that their academic motivation is far more functional than my own when I was their age. In fact, all three show a genuine interest in and aptitude for learning, and are actively engaged in school in a way that I would have disdained. I attribute their relative success to support from academically aspiring parents, stronger connections with teachers who are willing to build relationships with their students, and a more functional and supportive peer network. These foundational supports do not directly influence academic achievement, but rather work through motivation beliefs, such as self-efficacy, wherein opportunities for success are carefully considered and offered, positive academic role models abound, and successful experiences are noted and verbally encouraged. Consequently, the academic confidence, academic achievement, and social adjustment of my adolescent children are, thankfully, stronger than mine at the same stage. Motivation beliefs are "internal" self-beliefs, but the social context—family, peers, and especially teachers—plays an important role in influencing how students participate in learning in childhood and adolescence.

REFERENCES

Legault, L., Green-Demers, I., & Pelletier, L. (2006). Why do high school students lack motivation in the classroom? Toward an understanding of academic amotivation and the role of social support. *Journal of Educational Psychology, 98*, 567–582.

Wigfield, A., & Eccles, J. S. (2002). *Development of achievement motivation*. Academic Press: San Diego.

CHAPTER 9

MR. WEBB'S ZOOLOGY CLASS

How One Teacher Motivated and Transformed High School Students

David A. Bergin
University of Missouri

In the Spring of 1973, I drove to Powell Slough on Utah Lake with some high school buddies to meet Mr. Webb. We were about to go bird watching, which seemed a strange and even unmanly activity. Even stranger was that we were about to meet our high school zoology teacher in the middle of a marsh in the evening of a school day. What teenagers do things with their teachers outside of school? It was the time of year when snow was gone and the earth was warming. The landscape was becoming green, a contrast with the coming brown of summer and passing gray of winter.

We parked on the edge of the dirt road and greeted Mr. Webb, who had his bird book tucked in the back of his pants, like a detective's handgun in some movie. We hiked through several farmers' fields, through mud that sucked at our heels, and into the marsh, each student carrying a borrowed Golden bird book and a pair of borrowed binoculars. As we walked, Mr.

The Ones We Remember: Scholars Reflect on Teachers Who Made a Difference, pages 77–86
Copyright © 2008 by Information Age Publishing
77

Webb called out the names of birds that he heard (red winged blackbird, meadow lark) or saw (pintail, red tailed hawk, avocet).

When we reached the water's edge, we hunkered down and watched. We looked out upon muddy carp-churned shallows, cattails, reeds, and 40-foot dead trees capped with massive piles of sticks. We spotted killdeer, curlew, white pelicans, mergansers, and all sorts of ducks. Once I could identify a great blue heron, I realized that the treetop piles of sticks were great blue heron nests.

We were amazed at Mr. Webb's skill at spotting and identifying birds. He could usually identify at a glance or from a partial song. His modeling inspired imitation. I tried to see what he saw, studied the bird books, and listened carefully to bird songs. I struggled to pick out color, song, beak shape, and wing shape simultaneously.

I have had many influential teachers. At the risk of insulting others, Mr. Webb stands out as the teacher I remember most. He went by Merrill, his middle name, and his first name was George. We always called him Mr. Webb to his face, but occasionally Merrill or George Merrill behind his back. Mr. Webb was demanding, a bit irascible, and utterly passionate about his subject. He loved learning and teaching about botany, entomology, ichthyology, ornithology, and other related fields. He could go on about how elevation, the direction a slope faced, latitude, and other aspects of geography affected wildlife, vegetation, soil moisture, and invertebrate life. When we completed his course, he expected us to be able to think in those terms.

I felt that he was training us to be zoologists, and that he would be disappointed if we went into other careers. When I talked with him while preparing this chapter, he said, "I thought that everyone I taught would become a zoologist. That was my intent." He was disappointed early in his career when he met a former student who was studying accounting at the university. He later realized that most students probably would not go on to study zoology. After that, he backed off a little in his expectations.

My first class with Mr. Webb was Vertebrate Zoology, and the content included massive (to us) amounts of zoology, vertebrate anatomy, ecology, and biome analysis. The zoology class was known to be advanced and difficult, like an honors or AP class but without the label. Based on Mr. Webb's offhand comments, we thought that he preferred our class to his remedial classes; he loved teaching and challenging our class, which made us feel elite.

HOW DID MR. WEBB GET STUDENTS INTERESTED?

How did Mr. Webb get teenage boys to traipse through a marsh observing birds when they could have been pursuing other activities? There are several answers. First was Mr. Webb's knowledge and enthusiasm for the subject. Some teachers give a lesson as though they are working from a script and if they got off the script, they would be lost. They may be effective at teaching the prescribed content, and enjoy teaching, but they do not exude confidence. In contrast, Mr. Webb seemed to know all about whatever we studied, and when we got out in the field, he amazed us with the breadth of his knowledge about trees, grasses, fish, birds, and mammals.

Second, Mr. Webb was very demanding. He wanted us to know all the material in the book, and to learn from lecture, and to do projects, and to dissect fish, frogs, and turtles. He made no apologies for teaching the course at a college level and using a college level zoology text book. Today, when I study classroom motivation, I find that high school students like demanding classes *if* they feel that they are being taught the requisite skills to meet the demands, and *if* they find the class interesting.

Third, Mr. Webb taught clearly. The course expectations were clear. Lectures were understandable, and in labs we knew what we were supposed to do and to learn. He supported our learning by actually teaching the material (not all teachers do that), letting us know what would be covered on the tests, and grading fairly. Thus, students had to work hard, put in a lot of time, and study carefully, but good grades were always possible.

Fourth, students had self-selected into this elective course. A key aspect of classroom engagement is pre-existing personal interest in a topic. Many in the class came in relatively interested in the topic, and were thus primed to appreciate a teacher who could guide them to increase their knowledge of the subject. Some of the students enjoyed camping, hunting, and fishing, and Mr. Webb's class fit their desire to know more about the natural world. This was true of me, though I did not hunt. I was new to the school because my family had recently moved. I was happy because I had moved from New Jersey to Utah. I switched from catching small yellow perch, sunfish, and an occasional eel in the muddy Hackensack River to catching brown and rainbow trout in the cold, clear Provo River.

Fifth, the students generally liked each other. The school was large, so students did not necessarily know each other going into the class, but the class quickly developed a camaraderie that facilitated both fun and learning. "Community of learners" is a current term for describing effective classrooms, and we were a community of learners. The class included lots of social interaction, which responded to students' need for belongingness and relatedness. We had lab partners, but also felt free to wander the class during labs and see what other pairs were doing. We learned from each other and had fun.

The classroom was set up with the classic black science tables with two seats at each. I ended up with Tim Scheuer as my table partner. We were an unlikely pair. He was athletic, played on the football team, and threw the shot put on the track and field team. I was not so athletic. He was not necessarily college-bound, and I was clearly college bound. We shared having missed the year-long course's part one, Invertebrate Zoology, and were starting with Vertebrate Zoology mid-year. We formed a strong bond and ended up camping and fishing together and playing on the same intramural basketball team.

Finally, Mr. Webb implemented other characteristics of interesting classrooms (Bergin, 1999). For example, identification with a group can foster interest, and he influenced many in the class to identify with being zoologists. Possessing relevant background knowledge can foster interest, but many of us lacked that knowledge. However, Mr. Webb taught the material well, and I felt that as I gained knowledge, topics relevant to zoology became increasingly interesting, even outside of school. The class included hands-on activities like labs and animal dissection, which were also novel and thus attention grabbing. The demandingness of the class was balanced with autonomy support. That is, the material on the classroom exams was highly prescribed, but students had considerable autonomy in how they approached class work during labs, how they accomplished projects like bird watching and insect collecting, and what they did on the field trips.

THE OUTDOOR CLASSROOM

Mr. Webb was a bird watching maniac. I thought, and I perhaps speak for other classmates, that bird watching was not cool. However, Mr. Webb required us to go bird watching and to identify a specified number of birds in varied habitats. He required us to go into the field with him and demonstrate identification skills so that we could not scam the requirement. That was why we met him at Powell Slough. At first, when I spotted a bird and picked up the field guide, I would have to flip through the entire book, page by page, as I attempted identification. Soon I realized that the book was organized into families of birds like raptors and finches, and that if I could generally categorize a bird, I would only have to examine a small section of the book.

To facilitate our bird knowledge, Mr. Webb took the whole class on a yellow school bus to the Farmington Bay Wildlife Refuge by the Great Salt Lake. This is another example of the hands-on, novel, social sort of activity that made the class fun and interesting. It was a chilly and gray day. The school bus drove on the dirt road atop a dike. We hiked along dikes and levees, surrounded by dead, brown vegetation, black water, and gray skies. I was surprised to find myself excited to see grebes, egrets, cormorants, ibis, plovers, and black-crowned night herons. There is something about seeing a bird for the first time and being able to identify it that I, and many others, find satisfying. I had heard of ibis and pelicans, for example, but thought that they were exotic birds that existed in National Geographic television shows and maybe in California. I was surprised to identify them in the field guide and realize that they live in Utah.

In May, at the end of the school year, Mr. Webb scheduled a four-day, three-night field trip to Southern Utah. We met at Provo High School with sleeping bags, backpacking stoves, coolers of food, and jackets, loaded into a yellow school bus, and were off to the Little Sahara sand dunes. We cooked, ate, flirted, examined the dunes for insects and rodent sign, and slept—a little, maybe. Mr. Webb guided us in setting live traps that caught kangaroo rats and pack rats. After examining them in the morning, we released them back into the wild.

Then we drove farther south. We stopped at Cove Fort, a Mormon historical site, where we observed the juniper-sage ecological community. Cove Fort was high enough in altitude that the weather was still cold. We overnighted at much lower and warmer Snow Canyon State Park, where the film *The Conqueror*, in which John Wayne played Genghis Khan, was partially filmed. The area was covered with atomic fallout after bomb tests in Nevada, and some claim that exposure led to the cancer deaths of John Wayne, and many other members of the cast and crew. I did not know any of this at the time, and we climbed around the red rock looking for pot holes filled with water that we could examine for insects and small shrimp. Mr. Webb helped us understand how the insects and crustaceans survived, and their place in the food chain.

In the morning, led by a park ranger, we hiked across the valley floor that was covered with black volcanic basalt. The ranger led us to an unmarked lava tube cave whose entrance was an opening in the ground. Lava tubes are formed when lava begins to harden on the outside while the inside continues to flow. As the interior molten lava flows out of the hardened shell, it leaves a cave. At the opening in the ground, we chose buddies. When it came my turn, I was too scared to lower myself into the dark hole in the ground. When I protested that I could not do it, my buddy, Tim Scheuer the shot putter, said that if I didn't go, he would not either. I thought that he might be as nervous as I was, so I lowered myself into the hole. He followed, and we had a fascinating trip into the underground world. Mr. Webb led us in looking for signs of life below the ground.

We visited Ash Creek, LaVerkin Creek, Red Cliffs, Beaver Dam Wash, and Smoot's Hill. We seined a creek—two students held poles attached to the net and ran down stream with the net stretched. We thus caught various dace and chubs that Mr. Webb identified.

The outdoor classroom was much different from the school classroom. In school, Mr. Webb expected us to memorize a lot of facts in addition to thinking about their relationships. In the field, he expected us to think much more deeply about the interconnections among life forms in the desert. We measured things like stream water pH, hardness, and CO_2. We figured out the positions of different organisms in the food chain. We used kick nets to collect and observe leeches, water mites, caddis fly larvae, clams, shrimp, and other organisms. We classified organisms into their taxonomic classes. I constructed a deeper understanding of the influence of latitude, elevation, and time of year on weather, vegetation, and wildlife than had been possible through book learning alone. I observed why juniper-sage, sagebrush-creosote, willow-cottonwood, and Joshua tree-black brush communities existed where they did.

The field trip revolved around Mr. Webb. We students would go off and observe or collect the assigned forms of life, and then we would return to him for verification, classification, or clarification. I did not know what I was doing, but gradually built up schemes and scripts for observation, analysis, and record keeping. We were like toddlers clustering around the parent, going off to explore, and then returning for affirmation. I still have the trip report that I made, and 35 years later I admit that I now view my records as pitiful, not college level (maybe that is why I earned a grade of B).

One of the highlights of the trip was catching lizards and snakes, a high interest activity. We had brought telescoping car antennas and old fishing poles equipped with monofilament slipknot loops for catching reptiles. We would spot a lizard sunning on a rock and quietly approach until we could slip the loop over the head and pull it tight. This was quite exciting. Some of the lizards were vicious and would bite one's gloved finger and not let go. At one point, Tim and I were startled by the sound of rattling. I had caught rattlesnakes before, but in those cases I had startled the snake. This time I was startled. We were relieved to find it was just a big grasshopper rattling its wings against dry, stiff grass stalks. I don't recall that we caught any rattlesnakes, but we did catch a number of other desert snakes, some of which were big enough to nearly break the thin fishing line we were using. After examining the reptiles, we let them go.

On the bus drive home, after four days without showers, we were on a dirt road and spotted a round cattle watering tank that was about 3 feet deep. Mr. Webb called for the bus driver to stop. We piled out. The first one in was a 7 foot student who was also an outstanding basketball player. Soon everyone was in the tank, fully clothed, enjoying the cool water. No cattle were within sight.

My experience in the course was so outstanding that in the fall of my senior year, I signed up for Invertebrate Zoology, part one of the course sequence. The experience was again memorable. Mr. Webb had us do projects, but they did not feel like busy work or wasted time. We did not make silly posters or displays. Mr. Webb required us to make an insect collection. We were supposed to collect insects using killing jars, correctly mount the insects on pins that we stuck into Styrofoam in cigar boxes (we had to spread the wings of butterflies and moths and dry them), and label the insects with name, date, and place of collection. The assignment required us to present around 15 different orders, and to hand in a minimum of 100 insects. We got extra points for more precise identification. On my own, I never would have considered collecting, mounting, and identifying insects. I turned in several boxes that contained rows of insects and a few alcohol-filled vials that contained insects too small or too delicate to pin. I had those boxes for many years (well, they were actually in my parents' basement). I had put in so much time and effort that I was loathe to throw them away, though I did eventually. I can still imagine the musty, dead scent that the cigar boxes gave off when opened. To this day, when I am at a rummage sale and see empty cigar boxes for sale, I am tempted to buy a few in case I ever want to start an insect collection. (I don't.)

As we collected the insects, we learned a lot about observation, record keeping, insects, and the interconnectedness of organisms. The task was the sort of complex task that each person can adapt to his or her own strengths and interests. One could spend time in a corn field, on a river bank, or in a suburban back yard and complete the assignment. Thus the task was multifaceted, difficult, and inherent with feedback. These attributes made it interesting. I dug into bushes, dirt, dead leaves, and stream beds and noticed tiny organisms that the casual observer never sees. It was a new and more detailed level of observation for me.

The last semester of my senior year, I had no course with Mr. Webb, but I knew that he would be going on another four day field trip to southern Utah. I wanted to go on that trip, but I was not technically eligible because I was not in the class. Tim Scheuer was in the same situation. We started early lobbying to go. Mr. Webb did not object, nor did my parents, but getting the school administration to agree was a bit of a trick, especially because Tim had just medaled with third place in the regional shot put competition. The coaches and administrators wanted him to represent the school at the state track and field meet, though he said that he had little chance of placing. They eventually allowed us both to go. It is noteworthy that Tim, the athlete, preferred a zoology field trip over a state-wide athletic competition. Once again, we had a fascinating experience and visited some of the same places. One new stop was Zion National Park.

Those two field trips were two of the best learning experiences that I ever had, and the most fun. They provided an opportunity to construct new, deeper understanding of all that we had learned about habitat, diet, identification, food chains, and the interconnectedness of life. Some of us formed deep friendships. Plus, the trips were exciting. Catching snakes and lizards on poles, fish in seines, and rodents in live traps was pretty exciting.

Much of what we did is now illegal, like catching lizards and snakes, or ill-advised, like catching rodents that could spread hantavirus.

SCHOOL-PROMPTED INTEREST

One reason why I remember Mr. Webb's class so fondly is because of the way that it has informed my thoughts on school-prompted interest, one of my research areas. School-prompted interest exists when you become so interested in something in school that you learn more about it on your own outside of school (Bergin, 1992; Pugh & Bergin, 2005). It occurs, but not at the rate that one might hope if schools are accomplishing their task of teaching the skills for life long learning. As a result of Mr. Webb's course, several of us went bird watching on our own. Tim Scheuer and I rented telephoto lenses and went to a duck pond in Payson, Utah to photograph ducks. While my photos mostly turned out rather badly, I learned new things about ducks and about photography. Fellow student Bruce Barrett and I went birding with Mr. Webb in Provo Canyon. Bruce later earned a PhD in entomology, and traces his interest in the subject to Mr. Webb's course. Tim ended up earning a PhD in geophysics. He says that Mr. Webb's class opened his eyes to the natural world and how one might understand it.

McKay Platt and Pam Woodbury had an extreme case of school-prompted interest—they married each other. They both said that they probably got married because of Mr. Webb and his class. Pam and another female student in the course had become birdwatchers as a result of the course, had joined the local Audubon chapter during college, and were elected officers. They were sent to a national conference at Asilomar in California and invited McKay to come along. He did, and he and Pam became engaged at the conference. They continue to birdwatch today. Pam, McKay, Tim, and Bruce were dramatic cases of school-prompted interest. My own case is less dramatic, but still potent.

My school-prompted interest in bird watching lay dormant for a time, but re-surfaced. After I graduated from high school, I did not go bird watching at all. I did not own binoculars or a bird book. I married and started graduate school. One winter day during Christmas vacation, my wife and I were in Chico, California, visiting her parents. At some point I was foraging in the house and came across the classic Golden field guide to birds (first published in 1949 and still in print) and a pair of binoculars. Chico is the home of Bidwell Park, a huge park that lies across the street from the in-laws' home. Soon I was out hiking along the creek, viewing acorn woodpeckers, white crowned sparrows, and dippers and learning to spot the unique flight pattern of woodpeckers. After that, I acquired my own binoculars and bird books (Golden, Petersons, and National Geographic, in that order). On a subsequent Chico visit, I drove to nearby Gray Lodge Wildlife Refuge to view snow geese. It was quite a turnaround for someone who thought that bird watching was strange and unmanly.

During graduate school, when we lived in the San Francisco Bay area, I went birding in the Palo Alto Baylands, Marin Headlands, or Stanford hills fairly often. When I heard that Mr. Webb was bringing a group of high school students on a field trip that would include an open-water trip out of Monterey, I met them at the boat and went birding still again with Mr. Webb. However, when my wife and I began to have children, I largely quit formal bird watching. We took our firstborn birding in controlled areas like the Palo Alto Baylands boardwalk. After the second child, we had trouble keeping track of the birds and the kids. We still watch for birds while driving or hiking, but seldom use a bird book or binoculars.

TRANSFORMATIVE EXPERIENCE

A construct that overlaps with school prompted interest is transformative, aesthetic experience (Pugh, 2002; Pugh & Girod, 2007). These are experiences that change the way one perceives and experiences the world, that lead to an expansion of perception. Pugh and Girod (2007) point out that science can be particularly transforming. They state that teachers can help students "re-see" by "explicitly teaching students to look at ordinary objects from a new perspective" (p. 20). Before Mr. Webb's class, I ignored birds and did not even see insects; after Mr. Webb's course, I noticed birds and considered whether they were in an environment where I would expect to see them. Pam said:

> He introduced me to the broader world. You live in the world but don't really see anything. He made you see new things. All of a sudden I realized that there were insects around me and birds in the sky and a world around me.... This class was one of the major events of my life. I can't say enough good about Merrill Webb. He changed everything for me. I'm more aware of the world now because of him.

Pugh and Girod also point out that teachers who foster transformative experience model a passion for their subject. McKay said, "Mr. Webb was one of the two or three people in my life who most impressed me with their enthusiasm for a subject. ... He knew so much about his subjects. You can't help but be drawn into it." In sum, Mr. Webb generated more school-prompted interest and transformative, aesthetic experience than any instructor I have experienced.

Thirty-five years later, I continue to have fond memories of Mr. Webb's classes and field trips. To this day, he is a prominent birder in Utah. You can find his work featured on Utah birding websites.

REFERENCES

Bergin, D. A. (1992). Leisure activity, motivation, and academic achievement in high school students. *Journal of Leisure Research, 24,* 225–239.

Bergin, D. A. (1999). Influences on classroom interest. *Educational Psychologist, 34,* 87–98.

Pugh, K. J. (2002). Teaching for transformative experiences in science: An investigation of the effectiveness of two instructional elements. *Teachers College Record, 104,* 1101–1137.

Pugh, K. J., & Bergin, D. A. (2005). The effect of schooling on students' out-of-school experience. *Educational Researcher, 34,* 15–23.

Pugh, K. J., & Girod, M. (2007). Science, art, and experience: Constructing a science pedagogy from Dewey's aesthetics. *Journal of Science Teacher Education, 18,* 9–27.

AUTHOR NOTE

Thanks to Christi Bergin and the fabulous Leigh Bergin, who gave constructive feedback on this chapter, and to Tim Scheuer, Bruce Barrett, Pamela Woodbury Platt, McKay Platt, and Merrill Webb, who reminisced with me by phone.

CHAPTER 10

ON RELATING TO A SPECIAL TEACHER

Lyn Corno
Teachers College, Columbia University

Relate\ *vb* [L *relatus* (pp. of *referre* to carry back)…]

—Webster's Dictionary

The teachers of my own adolescence are far removed from aging memory, but having just gone through the college application process with our daughter, Carter, I have fresh reflections on her high school Latin teacher, who made a real difference in this child's life.

BACKGROUND

Our daughter began taking Latin as a language in the sixth grade at her local public school. When she moved to Dana Hall School in seventh grade, she just continued. Located in Wellesley, Massachusetts, Dana Hall is an all-girls', private preparatory school originally founded in 1881 as a "feeder" for Wellesley College. The school now places students broadly and serves those from a wide array of backgrounds in both the U.S. and abroad. Upon entering the Upper School in grade 9, Carter placed into Ms. Jacqui Bloomberg's Latin III course, and thus began a relationship of great sig-

The Ones We Remember: Scholars Reflect on Teachers Who Made a Difference, pages 87–94
Copyright © 2008 by Information Age Publishing
All rights of reproduction in any form reserved.

nificance. Before I explain this relationship, however, some background on Carter is in order.

Carter had qualms about attending an all-girls' school in seventh grade. We, her parents, had offered her the opportunity to be educated at Dana Hall, but allowed her make the decision, fraught as it was with all the angst of pre-adolescence—what it would be like with "no boys" in a new place? In retrospect, Carter's decision to go to Dana Hall was perhaps the best thing she did for herself in her adolescent years. In one of Carter's college essays she wrote about the kind of teaching she received at her all-girls' school:

> My teachers at Dana Hall began to mold me before I knew what was going on. No one had ever told me I was good at math or science, but I found myself in Honors Algebra in eighth grade. By the end of that year I not only thought that I could succeed, but I was enjoying it! When I placed into Honors Chemistry as a sophomore, I thought, 'I'm not sure I can do that,' but a teacher, Mr. Fadden, convinced me I could, and I stayed on the honors science track....So girls aren't good at math and science? Don't ever say that in the halls of Dana.

Carter has become quite a Latin student since she moved to Dana Hall. One of her favorite Latin quotations is from the *Aeneid*: "Dux femina facti" (Book 1, line 364), "The deed was done by a woman." It is unlikely that when Vergil wrote this line, he was thinking about the issue of gender equality. As a seventh grader beginning at an all-girls' school, Carter hardly considered empowerment of women either. But looking back on the switch to a single sex school illuminates the path she took, at least academically, and Carter feels that path would have bent another way had she not gone to Dana Hall. She now defines herself boldly as a "Latin and math nerd," with dueling passions for the ancients and for Calculus. She says, "When I don't do math or translate Latin, I miss them."

Now in college, Carter continues to pursue her interest in Latin and the study of Classics. She hopes to attend a center for Classical studies in Rome during her junior year, and is contemplating a major, or minor, in Latin. Carter recently told her Latin professor at Duke University that:

> Two female, Latin-crazed teachers at Dana gave me such an understanding of Latin, it enabled me to love a subject that few people do, especially not women. The day I sat at my desk and translated Book 1 of the *Aeneid*, I realized the full impact of my attending an all-girls school.

THE SPECIAL TEACHER AND THE RELATIONSHIP

With this background, I can speak specifically of the influence of Jacqui Bloomberg, the one teacher who is the central focus of this paper. Jacqui is a 1988 graduate of Tufts University, where she majored in Classics. While attending Tufts, Jacqui also completed her Bachelor's degree in French Horn Performance at the New England Conservatory. She received a Master of Arts in Teaching from Tufts in 1989. For the past 18 years, Jacqui has been teaching Latin at Dana Hall; before that, she taught Latin at the Boston Latin School. Ms. Bloomberg is currently Head of Dana Hall's Language Department; she also works with and advises the school's Cum Laude Society and the Gay/Straight Alliance.

Again I begin by quoting what our daughter has said about Jacqui Bloomberg. Carter wrote in another college essay as follows:

"If I open this book to any page and pick any line, I could give it as life advice for any circumstance."

Ms. Bloomberg held up a light green book with some obscure painting on the front. A few students in the class rolled their eyes; some chuckled skeptically. At the time, I hardly believed my AP Latin textbook could be useful either. I decided to settle any looming argument right then and there.

"Prove it!"

I would soon learn that Ms. Bloomberg had more faith in Vergil than anyone. Without hesitation, she cracked open her worn, scribbled-over copy of the *Aeneid*.

"One of my favorites…"

She read the Latin aloud with a melodious rhythm and a dreamy look on her face:

"Spem vultu simulat, permit altum corde dolorem" (Book 1, 209). ["He feigns hope on his face and controls the grief deep in his heart."]

I did not understand the line when she read it; nor did I grasp the influence that same book would have on me as I hunched over my desk every night that year translating Vergil's famous words. Since that day, it has been a source of amazement that the words of a "dead language" from centuries ago could relate so directly to my life in that moment and the modern world in general. Aeneas faces war, endures the deaths of loved ones, falls in love, fills his father's shoes, and finally dies a hero, all in one journey to fulfill his destiny. Through each trial, Aeneas matures in ways we all must at some point, so whether I was translating Book 2, immersed in the trickery of the Trojan horse, or Book 4, shocked at Dido's suicide, I was struggling to understand Aeneas' responses and reflecting on what my own would be under similar circumstances.

Ms. Bloomberg's assignments required us to translate the original text of the *Aeneid*, and this made reading the book a whole new adventure. When I worked through a complex string of clauses to a final translation, I'd look back at my own interpretation of Vergil's words, and be as proud of giving it my own flair as I was of making sense of the multi-layered text. In discussing the translations, Ms. Bloomberg made it clear that I could extract much more from the reading of a text in its original language, where aspects such as word order, figures of speech, and scansion add depth and intensity to the words.

I looked forward to my nightly translations of the Aeneid during junior year; I would even find myself saving them for breaks between other classes, eager to hear more about my hero, Aeneas. When certain lines called to me, I'd neatly write them out on a stickynote to post above my desk. "Forsan et haec olim meminisse iuvabit" (Book 1, line 203). ["Perhaps someday it will please us to remember even this."] Not only do I know that line by heart, the florescent pink stickynote still hangs on my bedroom wall.

It has been months since I last translated Vergil, yet I think about the light green book and what its pages hold nearly every day. It will always sit on my bookshelf among all the other novels I have read 'just for pleasure,' distinguished by its torn binding, excessively marked pages, and curling edges.

In addition to the challenges Ms. Bloomberg provided the students in her classroom, she gave our daughter what can only be called a wide-ranging level of support and direction throughout high school. When Carter applied to attend a program at Brown University in the summer of her sophomore year, Ms. Bloomberg wrote a letter on her behalf. She told Brown that Carter was not well placed in her class as a freshman because the three-year language requirement at Dana means that inevitably some students in a level-three class are hoping simply to get through the year to the point where they can stop studying the language. "Carter's skills and abilities far exceeded those of her classmates, and the class didn't provide the challenge she deserved; however, there was only one Level III class." In Carter's sophomore year, she was one of nine students in an Advanced Placement class studying Vergil's *Aeneid*. Five of these students were in their second Latin Advanced Placement class, and four were from Latin III. Ms. Bloomberg described that class as "dynamic, vocal, motivated, and craving challenge," and said that "Carter more than met" the standard.

Another example of her caring for Carter is the time and effort Jacqui Bloomberg took each term with her comments on report cards. For example:

She completes thirty lines of poetry without pause, and her translations are accurate, fluid, and representative of her ability to apply grammatical and syntactical rules. The seniors in the class who have already had a year of poetry under their belts admire Carter's ability and respect her excitement and interest in the course. While some students occasionally struggle to understand a translation explained in class, Carter's ease with translation allows her to delve more deeply into the subject, inquiring about literary analysis, word studies, and historical background. Although she is discerning and doesn't immediately trust what is presented to her, Carter's excitement and interest in knowledge is truly infectious. She accepts her "Latin nerd" status with pride, but in truth, she is anything but that. Her abilities extend beyond the classroom, making her choices about what courses to take very difficult. I am one of many teachers hoping Carter will take my class next year, so that I can learn with her, next year reading the Latin poets Catullus and Ovid. Since she frequently brings knowledge from outside sources into my classroom, I know that as a teacher, I benefit from any course in which Carter participates.

Ms. Bloomberg was also an advocate for Carter when her name came up for induction into the school's Honor Society as a junior. At the end of junior year, at "Class Day," when academic and extracurricular awards were announced, Ms. Bloomberg gave Carter the Latin prize. She shared with me the comments that she read that day:

> Only every other year are there two awards for Latin. As this is a year in which we teach Vergil, I am proud to be able to award the Beryl Wilbur Prize in Vergil. Generously donated by a former Dana teacher Dorothy Farmer in honor of another former teacher, this prize marks a Latin student particularly for her spectacular ability in reading the Latin poet, Vergil. Usually it takes students years to appreciate Vergil's style, but for this student it didn't even take one year. She enthusiastically took on the task of translating multiple lines of poetry for each night's homework, never complaining about the difficulty or amount, always willing to share her translations with the class, sometimes as the only one prepared to do so, and often 100% accurate at first reading. However, on those occasions when a line did give her trouble, she worked hard to figure out any irregularities, and she would remember that if it appeared again later in the poem. When Dorothy Farmer was alive, she would always tell me, pick an outstanding graduating senior for this prize, but if a junior stands out, she should be more than outstanding.

One of the most interesting encounters I had with Jacqui Bloomberg was, when upon entering her senior year, Carter had to make a decision about whether or not to take yet another course in Latin (her second at the AP level). It seemed like overkill to her Mother—all this work in Latin—I thought she might better spend her time that year in European History. Carter had clearly mastered the basics of this language, so now it seemed time to move on. But Carter was not deterred by my argument; indeed, she colluded with Ms. Bloomberg to mount a defensive case about the value of continued study of Latin and the Classics.

The three of us met together one day after school to discuss this. Ms. Bloomberg was prepared; she gave me copies of news stories she clipped on how knowledge of Latin can be useful in today's world, as well as statements from prominent scholars on the importance they attached to their studies of Latin. Jacqui explained to me that a child with this sort of talent for the language comes along only now and then, and how having Carter in her class had made her a better teacher. I left convinced; Carter and Ms. Bloomberg had made their case, and none of us ever looked back. In the end, the essays Carter wrote on what being "the Latin girl" in her class had meant to her helped open doors to some wonderful opportunities for her post-secondary education.

Finally, I want to note that, just before Dana Hall's graduation ceremonies in the Spring, Ms. Bloomberg hosted a dinner at her home for all the senior girls she had worked with. She presented each of them with antique volumes, texts written in Latin, that she received as a gift from a closing library on the Wellesley campus. They spent the evening comparing their books and discussing future plans.

ANALYSIS AND CONCLUSION

So what is this teacher story about? It is not so much about the empowerment of women in a high school without male students. Rather, it is about the kind of relationship that can develop between a teacher who has a strong intellectual passion for her subject, and an adolescent with both a keen interest and the potential to get the most from the material to be learned. Psychologists say such students have a "mastery orientation;" they learn in order to understand and make meaning, rather than to get good grades or to look "smart" in front of their peers (see Pintrich, 2000 for discussion of this and related terms in research on academic motivation).

This story is also about what some might call zealous encouragement by a teacher of a talented student, an extraordinary example of how caring for a student extends beyond the classroom—to advocacy, to prizes, to reference letters—even to a gratitude for having had the student in class! Some years ago curriculum theorist Nel Noddings (1984) wrote eloquently about the deeply caring relationship than can develop between teachers and their students. Noddings speaks of "feeling with" (p. 24) the other—relating, as in the Latin sense of carrying some of oneself over to another.

Perhaps most importantly, there is a lesson in this story for other teachers to discern. An astute reader can see the amount of specific information and performance feedback that Jacqui Bloomberg communicated to both Carter and her parents over the course of their relationship through high school. Writing long and detailed explanations for report card grades, taking time to meet with Carter and her parents outside school (doing research and providing material on the topic to be discussed), offering to write letters of reference in support of related academic pursuits, and sharing (allowing the family to "own" copies of) the written versions of thoughts that Jacqui expressed when she gave an award—these efforts took a good deal of Jacqui Bloomberg's time, probably time beyond what the teachers union would encourage in a public school. Perhaps, however, if more teachers made the effort to communicate in these ways with students and their parents, the quality of life would be different in many schools, both public and private. This is a hypothesis worth testing.

In closing, I have to confess that when I first thought about what to take as the focus for this paper, my mind went quickly to teacher classroom behavior—after all, I have made much in my career of the combinations and sequences of instructional activity that teachers use to affect what students learn. I could have provided sufficient examples of excellent classroom teaching to fill the necessary pages of text, and just as much to say about what I might include as analysis (e.g., Randi & Corno, 2005). But something drew me back to Jacqui Bloomberg and to Carter instead, to the entirety of this child's high school experience. Perhaps because the college application process requires students to be so self-reflective, and Carter is one who shares her reflections, I had a clear awareness of what her Latin teacher meant to her.

Yet, when one of my friends said, "Carter is one of the few kids I know who loves her school because she got a great education there," I realized that I could not say that about my own high school. Nor would our son (just two years older than his sister), be likely to say that about his secondary years in our local public school. For me, I think that is what, in the end, this story is most about. When there is synergy between a special teacher and an adolescent student, it is magical. That relationship carries the student over, even when other relationships they have at school are not so good, and even when the work requires all you can give. The experience broadens beyond the one teacher to affect the whole educational experience. Our family knows how fortunate we are to have had Jacqui Bloomberg be such a part of Carter's adolescent life. We wish her many more students in her teaching career with whom she can *relate* (trans: *carry back*) in such a myriad of ways.

Nota Bene: As I was completing this chapter the phone rang—it was Carter wanting to be sure the email address she had for Jacqui Bloomberg was correct. Carter's professor for her first Latin course at Duke ("Transition to Advanced Latin") had asked all of the students who received a term grade of "A" to give him the email addresses of their high school Latin teachers. He said he was going to write their teachers to tell them what a good job they had done. When Carter told her professor that her Latin teacher's name was Jacqui Bloomberg, he smiled and said, "She was my advisee at Tufts back in the eighties!" Jacqui, of course, was thrilled; exclaiming, "I love that man!" And so the relationship between a receptive adolescent and a passionate teacher wraps around and across generations.

REFERENCES

Noddings, N. (1984). *Caring: A feminine approach to ethics and moral education.* Berkeley, CA: University of California Press.

Pintrich, P. (2000). An achievement goal theory perspective on issues in motivation terminology, theory, and research. *Contemporary Educational Psychology, 25*(1), 406–422.

Randi, J. & Corno, L. (2005). Teaching and learner variation. In P. Tomlinson, J. Dockrell, & P. Winne (Eds.), *Pedagogy—Learning for Teaching, British Journal of Educational Psychology Monograph Series II* (3), 47–69.

AUTHOR NOTE

I would like to thank Jacqui Bloomberg and Leigh Carter Herbert for their contributions to this chapter—I could not have written it without their words.

CHAPTER 11

I DARED TO PROCLAIM

The Influence of African American Women Teachers

Jacqueline Jordan Irvine
Emory University

In my high school yearbook, next to that unrecognizable picture of me trying to look like Diana Ross of the Supremes, I stated that I would one day be
a college professor. In retrospect, I can't believe that an African American
sixteen-year-old living in the segregated South in the 1950s and '60s dared
to proclaim such an illustrious career goal. Moreover, my parents were not
college educated, and my Father did not receive his GED until I was in
the ninth grade. I had never had a conversation with an African American
female (or male) professor or, as a matter of fact, never been in the same
room with one.

In one of my earlier publications (Irvine, 1996) I wrote about growing
up in the segregated South in Phenix City, Alabama. Phenix City, formerly
a busy factory town, is located in eastern Alabama bordering Columbus,
Georgia, the third largest city in the state, and Fort Benning, Georgia, a
large military base where my Father was stationed. Phenix City during the

The Ones We Remember: Scholars Reflect on Teachers Who Made a Difference, pages 95–101
Copyright © 2008 by Information Age Publishing
95

'50s and '60s was like so many small southern towns that African American people like to forget—segregated, oppressive, poor, cruel, abusive, and dehumanizing.

Not surprisingly, the quality of the all-Black public schools reflected these dismal conditions and years of discrimination and neglect. My parents knew that the inadequate and crowded facilities and half-day school sessions in Phenix City's public schools could never prepare me or my sisters for a world outside the provincial constraints of our existing environment. Consequently, their choice was to stretch their meager income and pay the tuition and fees so that we could attend the local segregated Catholic school where White Vincentian Sisters of Charity and Salvatorian Fathers of Milwaukee taught African American Protestant children. My parents' decision to send us to a Catholic school was certainly an enormous sacrifice both financially and emotionally. Emotionally, my parents must have worried about our religious socialization. My family has a long and distinguished history of leadership in the African Methodist Episcopal Church (AME), and I remember Mother's frown when I told her the nuns and priests said we would all burn in hell if we didn't convert to Catholicism. My family was unrelenting, no Catholics in this AME household.

Consequently, I attended Mother Mary Mission Catholic School from grade three through eleven. The curriculum was far superior to the curriculum of the Black public schools. At the Catholic school, we took music classes and were exposed to major European and White American classical compositions. All students had four years of high school math and science as well as language classes in French, Spanish, Latin, or Greek. One of my most memorable experiences was the arrival of Father Austin Martin who opened the world of theater to me through the work of playwrights like Shakespeare and Moliere. We constantly recited poetry, lengthy Biblical and literary passages, diagramed sentences, and spent endless evenings doing homework. These grueling learning activities, however, instilled a love of literature, music, and poetry. I even wrote poems and essays that were published in a national high school Catholic literary magazine.

The high expectations were motivated by the religious teachers' missionary calling to minister to all the African American students in the school, not just to the best and the brightest. As students, we were motivated to leave segregated, apartheid Alabama, which offered two alternatives for African American children—escape through academic achievement or face a life as a maid or laborer for Whites. These were the only two options. Consequently, we complied and worked hard because the options for noncompliance and non-achievement were too harsh and unbearable.

This classical, "no frills" college preparatory curriculum excluded subjects like home economics, shop, typing, and the state required Alabama history. Mother Mary Mission students benefited from our teachers' national and international perspectives. Unlike the public school teachers of Black and White children of the South, these nuns and priests had lived, studied and traveled in diverse and international settings. Father Gregory studied in Rome and the eccentric Father Romuald, our history teacher, had a Ph.D. in history from a European university and is the author of a seminal book on Cardinal Newman.

During the summer of 1964, the summer before my senior year, my schooling was abruptly derailed when the school closed because of lack of financial support from the Catholic Church. With less than two months notice, my parents had to find a suitable school for my senior year of high school. The public high school in Phenix City, Alabama, was not an option. Mother acted quickly and contacted an acquaintance, Miss Elmira Parker, a counselor at George Washington Carver High School in Columbus, Georgia, about transferring me to a school where I knew no one and had never seen. The idea of going to a school across the state line was not a novel idea to Mother who had attended William Spencer High School in Columbus, Georgia, the nearest high school for Blacks at the time. Each day she walked 6 miles to high school, thus my concerns and protestations about getting up at 6:00 AM and riding two city buses for nearly an hour fell on deaf ears.

Therefore in September 1964, under the watchful eye of Ms. Elmira Parker, I hesitantly enrolled at Carver High School, where my schooling took a dramatic and unexpected positive turn. It was this African American woman, Miss Parker, who opened up the window for these reflections on the influential teachers in my life. Miss Elmira Parker, the counselor who advised Mother to enroll me at Carver, was a no-nonsense, take-no-prisoners educator whose stare sent the most insubordinate student running for cover. It was Ms. Parker who enrolled me in the most selective college prep classes with the schools' most stellar teachers and students.

Mrs. Rosa Stanback was certainly one of these stellar teachers. She taught Government and was known for her keen intellect, high expectations, and care. No student dared to come to class unprepared because Ms. Stanback would be disappointed. She was excited about social studies and Black History and her enthusiasm was contagious. I majored in Political Science at Howard University because of Mrs. Stanback's influence. One of my fondest memories of this teacher was preparing for the 1964 high school Social Studies Fair at Fort Valley State College. I decided to construct an oversized Black History Scrapbook of famous African Americans in various fields. Mrs. Stanback stayed after school helping me with this project. (She routinely stayed after school to help students.) She recruited the shop teacher to help with the construction of the poster-size wooden boards for the scrapbook's cover. The home economics teacher gave advice about covering the boards with red velvet fabric. I researched the topic in the library and Mrs. Stanback found old magazines and books so I could find photos of my subjects. When the project was completed, I was so proud of myself because Mrs. Stanback was pleased. Unfortunately, I had to tearfully break the news to Mrs. Stanback that I couldn't go with her and the other students to Fort Valley State College because my Father would not allow it. A few days later, I was shocked to see Mrs. Stanback at our house. She talked to my parents and assured them that she would take care of me. My Father agreed to let me make the 80-mile one-day trip; no small feat given my military Father never changed his mind. Later that year, before I made the decision to attend Howard University, Mrs. Stanback took me to her alma mater, Tuskegee Institute, with application in hand, and introduced me to some administrators and faculty. A few weeks later I had a full tuition scholarship.

Mrs. Stanback's willingness to visit my home and advocate for me with my parents and expose me to African American intellectual life was repeated with Miss Eula Battle, a young teacher at Carver. Miss Battle taught journalism and recruited me to work on the school's newspaper and yearbook. Since I lived far from Carver High School, my parents did not allow me to routinely stay after school. Because I was so interested in these extracurricular activities, Miss Battle, like Mrs. Stanback, came to the house to talk with my Father. She told him she would bring me home on those days I stayed late for yearbook and newspaper activities. Miss Battle even picked me up from home and took me to Carver's athletic events. Perhaps the greatest coup of all was Miss Battle's visit to my home to gain permission for me to stay two nights on the campus of Savannah State College for Georgia's Black high school newspaper conference. This was the first time I had ever been away from home without my parents or sisters.

My descriptions of these unforgettable and profound African American female teachers explain why at sixteen, I had the confidence to proclaim that I wanted to be a college professor. My countless conversations with these women, their hugs and encouragements, my trips to Black college campuses, and their willingness to come to my home to speak with my parents made all the difference in my life. Although I have mentioned only three powerful educators I encountered my senior year, I can attest that other African American teachers who taught me that year had similar influence. Mrs. Thelma Robinson introduced me to African American literature. Mr. Elijah Pitts helped me to conquer my fear of mathematics and I turned out to be one of the best trigonometry and calculus students in the class. Mrs. Della Gray patiently taught me how to sew, and the dress I made in her class won first place in the Muscogee County Fair. More importantly, Mrs. Gray's constant directive to "Rip that seam out and do it again until you get it right" has served me well in the academy. Although I would like to think that I was special, the teachers displayed these same behaviors with other students at the school. I will be eternally grateful for these African

American women who touched my life, believed in my intellectual ability, and envisioned a future that I could not imagine for myself.

IMPLICATIONS FOR CONTEMPORARY
EDUCATIONAL ISSUES

I believe that my experiences at George Washington Carver High School and my memories of the African American women who taught me have implications for a number of critical issues facing education. According to recent figures, 90% of teachers are White and only 6% of teachers are African American. In spite of national efforts to desegregate schools and teaching staff, segregated schools are on the rise and African American teachers continue to teach mostly African American students. These data suggest questions for researchers and policy makers. Why should special efforts be made to recruit African American teachers? Do these teachers interact with and instruct their African American students in culturally specific ways? If so, how? Do African American teachers motivate and increase the achievement and aspirations of African American students?

Although I spent ten years in a parochial school with all-White nuns and priests, it was my brief nine months at Carver High with African American female teachers that significantly influenced my life. There are a number of explanations that come to mind. First, although our White Catholic teachers were obviously aware of the racial differences, they never acknowledged our African American heritage except for the one statue in the courtyard of the Black saint, Martin de Poores, to whom few references were made, and an occasional Negro spiritual we sang when the school's White benefactors came south to visit. On the other hand, the African American teachers were keenly aware of the racism we encountered everyday and directly assisted us in dealing with these challenges.

Second, the White teachers were well trained in their subject matter content. I cannot, however, remember any instance where African American culture and history was integrated in the curriculum. On the other hand, the Black teachers at Carver were similarly competent in the content they taught, but they also captured my attention with their knowledge and pride for African American history.

Third, these teachers cared for me in demonstrable and obvious ways as I have indicated in the stories above. I suspect that the White nuns and priests cared for the African American students they taught; however, it is difficult for me to remember specific instances or examples. What I can remember are the harsh punishments they metered out and their "holier than thou" dispositions that made them unapproachable and distant. I remember a particular incident in elementary school where, by some minor miracle, I hit a baseball home run. So excited by this unbelievable feat, I ran toward one of the nuns and grabbed her hand. She recoiled and pushed me away admonishing me to never touch her because she was " a bride of Christ." Like the White nuns and priests, the African American teachers at Carver High were stern disciplinarians. I was known as a talker and joker in school and received my fair share of reprimands and punishments. However, it's not these more negative encounters with these Black teachers that I recall. What I recollect is their care, concern, and warmth.

Fourth, neither the White nuns nor the priest ever visited our home and rarely left the confines of the school grounds. My parents often could not remember their names. More importantly, my parents' interaction with the White administrators and teachers was mostly negative and related to some misbehavior by my sisters or me. It was always that perennial "C" or "D" in conduct that got me in trouble. The research is conclusive that a positive relationship and seamless connection between school, home, and community are essential components of school success for students of color. Mrs. Parker, the counselor, was an acquaintance of my Mother. My Mother knew Miss Battle's family. My parents did not know Mrs. Stanback. What these African American teachers knew was how to approach my parents, and how to talk to them in culturally relevant ways. Also, they felt comfortable in our home and my parents were not intimidated by their presence.

Finally, the African American teachers shared with me both a racial and gender identity. For obvious reasons, I did not identify with the White nuns and priests. They did not share my ethnicity, culture, religion, or geographical origins. The African American female teachers, conversely, identified with me and I with them. They were smart, articulate, confident, had a sense of humor, and were respected in the school and the larger community. Not inconsequential was the fact that I admired the cars they drove, the way they dressed (particularly those spike heel shoes with the pointed toes) and wore their hair, and how they juggled their personal and professional lives. Put simply, I wanted to be like these "other Mothers."

Toni Clewell, Puma, and McKay (2005) raised the question: Does it matter if my teacher looks like me? Research findings suggest that African American teachers positively influence the school achievement and aspirations of African American students. The presence of effective African American teachers appears to positively affect African American students' scores on standardized achievement tests, attitudes toward school, graduation rates, college attendance, and placement in gifted and talented programs. Additionally, African American teachers decrease the likelihood that African American students are tracked in low ability classes, special education, and expelled or suspended from school.

Other findings suggest that gender matters, concluding that the teacher's gender has a significant effect on teacher-student interactions and student achievement. This line of research suggests that students who share the gender identity of the teacher are more engaged and have fewer discipline problems.

As I approach the end of my academic career at Emory University, it is amazing to realize that the University's first regular, full-time African American students were two graduate students admitted in 1963. The first African American professor arrived on campus in 1970, only nine years before I became the first African American professor in the Division of Educational Studies. I credit my success at Emory to many individuals, including my parents and the nuns and priests at the Catholic school; however, the African American female teachers were the mirrors on which I could see my future and myself. Their influence was not lost on me as I tried to model their attributes with my own students. Parker Palmer (1999) got it right: Whoever our students may be, whatever subjects we teach, ultimately we teach who we are.

REFERENCES

Irvine, J. J. & Foster, M. (1996). *Growing up African American in Catholic schools.* New York: Teachers College Press.

Clewell, B. C., Puma, M. J, & McKay, S. A. (2005). *Does it matter if my teacher looks like me? The impact of teacher race and ethnicity on student academic achievement.* Paper presented at an Invited Presidential Session of the Annual Meeting of the American Educational Research Association, Montreal, Canada, April 2005.

Parker, P. (1998). *The courage to teach.* San Francisco; Jossey-Bass Publishers.

CHAPTER 12

A TEACHER'S INFLUENCE

A Conversation

Avi Kaplan
Ben Gurion University of the Negev, Israel

Again and again I have observed in the lives of especially gifted and inspired people that one teacher, somewhere, was able to kindle the flame of hidden talent.
—Erik Erikson

What can I do, I'm only a figment of your imagination.
—Augusto Cousteau, in the film, *Ratatouille*

Dear reader,

This is not an ordinary essay for an academic book. It is different in both the style and the message from what a reader might expect to find in a book that concerns "influential teachers." The difference is deliberate, and is intended to challenge what might be commonly held assumptions about the meaning of teachers' "influence" and the means by which such influence is affected. I invite you to engage in a dialogue with this chapter, for that is what it is primarily about—dialogue!

The Ones We Remember: Scholars Reflect on Teachers Who Made a Difference, pages 103–109

PROLOGUE

The editors' invitation to write about the most memorable and influential teacher of my adolescent years came at a perfect time. I had just returned from AERA, stimulated by the apparent need for new ideas and methods for understanding motivation in education, and here was a request that seemed to imply such a direction—going straight to the core of the educational experience, the root of the (interactive) matter, the foundation of the facilitative relationship. Moreover, in light of Erikson's statement above, the request kindled a hope that I might find myself, after all, to be gifted and inspired. Happily setting to the task, it occurred to me that if a search for such a formative experience was required, then the application of analytical and reflective skills—skills, I'm afraid to say, that I had little possession of during my adolescent years—would be the wrong strategy to start with. Arriving at such a foundational experience of influence would require reaching for my emotional associations with my teachers—it would call for the use of..."imagery!" I should relax, close my eyes, and allow the image of my "Influential Teacher" to appear. And so, excited by this innovative idea, I sat comfortably in my chair and summoned the figure to emerge...to no avail! "But, can this be?" If no such associative memory came to mind, then did it mean that there was no such Influential Teacher that had kindled my hidden talent? Regrettably, this might confirm my long-held suspicion that I am, after all, not gifted nor inspired. Well, being somewhat self-regulated at this point in my life, and determined to locate an influential teacher no matter the efforts she or he might exert to avoid my quest, I reflected on my failure and decided to replace the strategy I had taken with one of proactive methodical search. I attempted to recall who my teachers were, chronologically, naming those who I remembered from the early grades on. Knowing intellectually that teachers in the early grades can indeed cast long-lasting influence on students' lives, I was dismayed to realize that eliciting the names of my elementary school teachers did not do much to stir hope for discovering meaningful influences. Yet, suddenly, to my surprise, my thoughts lingered on one peculiar figure: my history teacher from 7th grade. For reasons soon to be clear, I chuckled, dismissed the possibility that this teacher was in any meaningful way influential to who I am today, and continued to go through the list of teachers I remembered. But, in a somewhat annoying way, my thoughts kept returning to the image of this odd-looking man in his checkered jacket, untidy shirt, disheveled hair and perplexed gaze—the rather comical figure of Shraga Firshtman. I stopped to consider, and after brief contemplation, decided that ignoring this associative sign might indicate incoherence with my original contention about where "influence" is fundamentally located. And so, while feeling rather hopeless about the matter, I decided to explore: Was Shraga Firshtman influential to me?

What followed was a surprising and eye-opening conversation I had with Shraga. The conversation was surprising, firstly, in the most mundane sense, since Shraga has been dead for about two decades. Secondly, it was surprising to Shraga himself, who seemed never to have considered it a possibility that long-forgotten students would employ a semi-intellectual necromancy in order to question him on his influence as a teacher. But, thirdly, and most importantly, the conversation was surprising in the new light it threw on the relationship between an obtuse and rather immature early adolescent and an odd-looking, scatter-brained, quick-tempered, literary-oriented, and often ridiculed history teacher. Indeed, the discovery (or should I say "construction?") of the meaning of that relationship to who I am today might hold some surprising implications to the varied ways by which teachers could be thought to influence their students. I invite you, reader, to engage in a conversation with the following words as you think of the meaning of "a teacher's influence."

A CONVERSATION

Avi: (somewhat apprehensive) "Excuse me?"

Shraga: (sitting in an armchair with a book, looking about confusedly) "What...ahh, who is it?"

Avi: "Hello Mr. Firshtman. My name is Avi Kaplan. I was your student in A'had Ha'Am elementary school many years ago."

Shraga: (still confused, lifting his reading glasses to his head) "What... where...what did you say? One of my students in A'had Ha'Am? (A sudden partial focus) Oy...have you come to disturb my peace again? I thought I got rid of the lot of you when I passed from the world years ago."

Avi: "I'm sorry; I have no desire to trouble you. I was just wondering if I could talk to you a bit about your teaching?"

Shraga: "After all those years...you come to ask me about my teaching... Aahhhch...well... (a long pause) ...where are my...? (patting his jacket pockets) ...I (finding his glasses on his head, and putting them on to look at his interlocutor; realizing he does not need them and raising them back to his head) ...I...hmmm... OK... (leaning back and folding his arms on his belly) ...I thought I would love teaching...History! History is a story to be explored and imagined. I really thought that I could ignite this passion in the young...Ahhh...the disillusion."

Avi: "Disillusion?"

Shraga: (annoyed a bit) "You need to ask? You were there, you said. Were the students listening? Were they imagining? Were they constructing their own story out of the history? I don't need to tell you about the petty and tormenting treatment the students gave me. I would lose my temper, it was so infuriating. Young minds with so much potential occupied with imagining how to harass a teacher instead of with the fascinating weaving of personal and collective lives and stories. But they would get to me... to my shame... (shaking his head)... I remember chasing and grabbing a child who threw a paper ball at me in the middle of class... aye, aye, I broke his arm grabbing him (holding his head)."

Avi: (sympathetically) "Yes, I know, I was there."

Shraga: (looking up) "...and the time I was sick, and I coughed and spat blood and the girls shrieked and ran out of the classroom screaming with disgust..."

Avi: "I remember that too. This too happened in my class."

Shraga: (annoyed) "Of course you remember! This whole conversation is a figment of your imagination. So, why did you summon me like this... to ridicule me?"

Avi: (apologetically) "NO, NO. I admit that we laughed at these events at the time, but... I, at least, also felt sorry... very sorry. I also want to apologize for the time I wrote the material for the test on the blackboard before the exam, knowing that you would be too absent-minded to notice."

Shraga: (still annoyed) "So you summoned me to make an apology for your appalling behavior as a student?"

Avi: (trying to change the mood) "Well, actually, I summoned you because I wanted to find out how you influenced me by being my teacher."

Shraga: (surprised) "How I influenced you?... (turning glum but also annoyed)... well... probably by giving you an example of how not to be a teacher... I'm afraid to say that I don't have many fond memories of teaching. I guess that with all my desire to pass on my love of history to the students, I was not able to reach them. I guess I lacked the talent."

(silence... the two just sitting there, looking down)

Avi: (raising his head) "Aahemmm... Do you know that while I was your student, I read the book about Hassidism that you wrote for youth? It was one of my favorite books. I loved the Hassidic stories and the way you told them. You definitely had a talent for writing."

Shraga: (astonished) "You read one of my books?! (looking straight now) What is your name again, you said? Wait a minute... (observing and mumbling)...without the beard...quite a bit shorter and skinnier...thirty years younger...(voice rising), yes, I think I remember you. You were one of the two or three kids who used to come to my apartment on Tuesday afternoons to prepare for the skits I wrote for the school's Friday-morning ceremonies."

Avi: (remembering) "Ahhmmm...yes, I did do that for a couple of years...during seventh and eighth grade I think."

Shraga: (smiling softly) "The kids who did the skits were pretty good... well, (looking a bit malevolent), not the greatest actors, but with some performing talent. (Looking somewhat hopeful) Do you remember those weekly Friday ceremonies?"

Avi: (thoughtful, but also wanting to please) "Yes...Admittedly, my memory is a bit vague. I do remember that the whole school would gather at the beginning of the day on the basketball court facing the stage, which was actually the roof of the bomb-shelter, and each class would be arranged in one long line, short kids at the front and tall kids at the back... (pausing, reflecting slowly)...I have an image of the principal addressing the students...and I remember the teacher who was the emcee calling us to come up... we were acting the skits while reading from papers...that...you dictated to us in your apartment. (With more excitement) Now I remember, we would come to your apartment and sit at the kitchen table, and you would pace and dictate to us our roles. We would rehearse then once and perform on Friday morning in front of the school! I remember—I enjoyed it a lot. The skits were very often funny. (With interest) Were you inventing those skits on the spot?"

Shraga: (smiling, but reflective) "Well...yes...I guess. I mean, I had an idea about the theme—you know, something related to the time of year, historical event, or holiday that was relevant—and I used to think of a scene that I thought would highlight an important issue or moral. It was in the meeting with the kids that I would imagine the figures and give them words, affect, mannerisms... (laughing) you kids were not very good at taking-on the roles during the rehearsal at my apartment, but you were pretty good on stage."

Avi: (admiringly) "...I'll admit to you that back then, I didn't think twice about the ease with which you came up with these skits:

the different roles, matching the words to the historical personality—and from such different periods of history! I just had fun performing on stage. Looking at it now, for you to make-up a new skit every week, and dictate it to us on the spot...this is remarkable."

Shraga: (thoughtful) "Yes...well...making-up these scenes was a way for me to enact my imagination of history. I liked history, and I always liked to tell stories. I guess that I was always better doing it, either on paper, or through others' performances. Yes! For me, connecting with history is about imagining what historical figures were feeling and thinking when they were alive, how they interacted with each other, and what we can learn from them today. (Sadly) I guess it was hard for me to relay this to the children...particularly with the history national curriculum...(more angrily) particularly when the children were such pests! (Sighing), well...but this in itself is now history. Now (straightening to look at Avi), did you get what you came for? Did you figure out how I influenced you?"

Avi: (embarrassed a bit) "Well...no...I'm not sure that you did influence me...but it was nice talking to you...thank you!"

Shraga: "...So, tell me a bit...what happened to you after A'had Ha'Am elementary; did you like history in high-school?"

Avi: "Ahhmm...no...not really, I'm afraid. I can't say that I "enjoyed" any of my lessons in high-school. Some were OK. What I mostly enjoyed was writing for the school's newsletter backpage. My friends and I had a comic-strip there. We had great fun inventing the stories and then writing and drawing them."

Shraga: "Aha...so you write?"

Avi: "Well...yes, I guess that I've been writing a little bit since high-school. Mostly humorous stuff—short funny poems, satirical essays, stuff like that...Well, actually, I write a lot these days...I'm an academic."

Shraga: "An academic?!"

Avi: "Yes,...I'm teaching, and conducting research...and...I... write."

Shraga: (laughing cynically) "What do you teach? Anything interesting?"

Avi: "I teach educational psychology. I find it very interesting to understand...and help the students see...how educational theorists developed their ideas within their historical milieu, how they interacted with each other, and what we can learn from them today...how we can...develop our understandings...or...stories. I guess that what I do is create a story and perform it in different ways that would encourage the students to construct their own story of certain aspects of the world that touch on education. Yes, I like to plan, write my lessons, and perform them. It gives me pleasure to make students passionate and reflective....Come to think of it, that is a big part of what I do also as a researcher: use different methods of getting to know the world in order to write a story about it...I like telling stories...of different kinds."

Shraga: (sarcastically) "And what about writing skits?"

Avi: (confidently) "Skits? No, I never write skits."

Epilogue

Avi: "So, what do you think?"

Shraga: "Well, I'm not going to grade you on this, but...I'm not sure that your portrayal of me was very accurate."

Avi: "Eeehhhh...Does it matter?"

Shraga: "Hmmm...No...No...I guess it doesn't."

CHAPTER 13

"I WILL NOT LET THIS BE AN INTELLECTUAL WASTELAND"

The Legacy and Limitations of an Inspiring Teacher

Michael Middleton
University of New Hampshire

"WHAT WOULD HE THINK?"

Teachers often revel in the last weeks of summer trying to squeeze every last minute out of long sunny days. In a few weeks I'd be starting my fourth year of teaching high school math. To avoid adding to the challenge of the first few days of school, I spent one day in early August setting up my new classroom. Driving home, I thought about the coming year, the new students I'd be working with, and the lesson plans and activities that I'd use to start the year.

As I arrived home the phone was ringing. "Hey Mike. It's Steve." Steve and I had been best friends in high school almost ten years ago. We listened to music, studied, and talked about our futures together. I was surprised to

The Ones We Remember: Scholars Reflect on Teachers Who Made a Difference, pages 111–125
111

hear his voice since we had rarely spoken after our sophomore year of college. "I just heard that Mr. C died last week."

The news was a shock. Mr. C had been our English teacher sophomore and senior years. At that time he was in his 30s and always seemed so vigorous and animated. It was hard to imagine that he was gone.

The funeral had already occurred, but Mr. C's death led a small group of high school friends to meet for a long overdue lunch later that week.

On my way to lunch I drove to the high school that had once been the focus of my daily life. Set on a hill, the campus was like a small college—red brick buildings, an imposing spire, lush green fields. I parked in a lower lot and walked up the hill past the tennis courts and community service building where I had spent countless hours after school. I followed the path from the gym toward the main buildings and recalled making that walk after gym class with my friend Jim listening to his stories about the girls he dated and hiding my secret crush on him.

St. John's is a Catholic, all-boys, preparatory school with a mission since 1907:

> ...committed to educating the whole person, Our rigorous academic and co-curricular program encourages students' to develop their spiritual, intellectual, moral, physical, and creative potential and inspires them to honor the diversity that enriches both our school community and the world beyond...

In the early 1980s, this mission took on the character of the times. Reagan was President. Gordon Gekko with his motto "Greed is good" was a movie icon. The first cases of AIDS were being reported with resulting scorn toward gay men.

To an adolescent entering an achievement-oriented high school in which almost everyone went on to college, "developing my potential" and "making a difference in the world" meant getting good grades, admission to a good college, choosing a suitable profession, and assuming my role in society. As the son of working class parents who did not graduate from college, my family equated intellectual pursuit with professional training and status.

I continued my walk through campus. At the school's main academic building I could glimpse into the second floor windows of Mr. C's old classroom. Memories of his classroom rushed back to me. Mr. C was short, even by the standards of a high school sophomore, and impeccably dressed in a jacket and tie every day. He wore round wire-rimmed glasses that added to the perception of his heavy intellect. Mr. C was legendary in our high school. In freshman year, we would hear about the amount of work we'd have to do but how much we'd learn if we were lucky enough to be in Mr. C's honors English class. The reviews of his class were a mix of praise and survival tactics:

"You have to read a book every week and he knows if you haven't done it."

"The research paper in his class is 20 pages. He makes you rewrite it over and over if it isn't right."

"Be ready for getting grilled during class discussions. Everyone will get called on. There's no escape, and you better be prepared."

Mixed with the sense of dreaded learning were more personal asides:

"He's in his 30s and not married. You know what that means."

During class, Mr. C spoke loudly in short bursts as he moved around the classroom that he had arranged in rows. The 25 or so boys sat quietly, not daring to speak while he spoke. There was an anxious air of anticipation during recitations in class. His questions rapidly probed our understanding of the text we had just read. He was masterful at drawing our attention to important passages, eliciting our understanding of the connection to underlying themes, and pressing us to form conclusions based on evidence from the text. It was not uncommon for his passion to edge on contempt if our class seemed unprepared or uninspired on a particular day. We were prepared for him to scold, "I will not allow this to be an intellectual wasteland!"

I remember one particular tirade the day after February vacation when our fifteen year-old minds were still half-asleep and my friend Rob tried to bluff his way through a question about symbolism in *Beowoulf*. That was a mistake none of us would attempt again.

Similarly, Mr. C did not hold back when he led peer reviews of our papers. He would read a model paper from one of our class members to serve as an example for us. I can still remember the feeling of pride when my paper about creating a mythical story was chosen. During these classes, he would demand our critique of other students' work. This activity created personal anxiety and social tension. No one wanted to be critical of a classmate or friend, but those concerns were no matter to Mr. C who pushed us to examine classmates' work as a way to improve their writing as well as our own.

It was clear in our school that academic achievement in all classes was important but there were subtle messages that some classes held more importance than others. Success in math and science was the gateway to college. However, in Mr. C's class, nothing was more important than thoughtful reading of quality literature and clear, logical writing. He saw writing as a powerful tool to express ideas, argument, and beauty. Writing for Mr. C went beyond the formulaic five paragraph essay to constructing arguments with supportive text and illustrative examples.

On the surface Mr. C was a perfect fit for this achievement-oriented prep school. A school mission existed, but his personal mission for me was clear—turn a timid boy into an educated man.

Back in our reunion lunch, the conversation alternated between our current lives and reflections on the man who had influenced all of us:

"How'd he die?"

"Pneumonia? At least that's what I heard."

"Do you think he was gay?"

"I don't know. Does it matter?"

"No, I guess not."

I sat in silence and shame. Did it matter? It did to me. Years later I still found it difficult to come out as a gay man to this group of high school friends. In high school I felt as if every word and action was being scrutinized and the slightest slip would doom me to being ostracized through verbal harassment, such as "fag," or worse. I remembered looking for clues in a teacher like Mr. C, who was also scrutinized because he was nearing middle age and unmarried. Did we share a secret? Most of the images I had of gay men were negative—drag queens in gay pride parades, AIDS patients wasting away. If a dynamic and respected teacher like Mr. C might be gay, perhaps I had options for the future beyond shame and isolation. But, overlaying that hope was an understanding that even if he were gay, he could never be open about it. Whispers and speculation would continue.

Our small group talked about the success we had in college and beyond. Each of us could trace back our accomplishments in some way to sophomore English class. At times we focused on the challenges of his class as if his sole purpose was to prepare us to perform well in college:

"His AP English class was much more demanding than my Freshman English class in college."

"He was a challenging teacher who also had a sense of humor. His standards were high, and he made sure you were doing the best you could. He was a teacher that really seemed to enjoy what he was doing."

However, we also realized that his purpose went beyond critical thinking and preparation for college. He inspired a love of literature:

"He opened new perspectives on literature and turned us all into writers."

"Mr. C taught me to love my language and was flexible enough to change his syllabus to fit in more Shakespeare because somehow he got ALL of us to love it."

"I did not actually do very well in his class. However, what he taught did catch up to me. He did encourage my writing, and he also reinvigorated my love of reading, which had taken a few hits due to too much crap being assigned. Mr. C had good taste in reading assignments."

Upon reflection, we began to realize how he changed us as young men, not just as students. Having Mr. C as a teacher was initially a daunting prospect, but, in retrospect, it changed our lives:

"(This is) exactly the word he used…I gave him too many opportunities to say it to me: 'Don't be an ass'…Anyone who was in his class will understand how it was meant."

"Mr. C was a tough teacher and wouldn't let me be a slacker. It's a cliché, but he didn't just teach me English lit, he taught me how to be a decent, honest, stand-up adult. I wouldn't put my integrity up against his, but I still think of him, 'What would he think,' when I find myself going the easiest way or the superficially beneficial way instead of the right way."

I drove home feeling sad for the loss of this man who influenced my life but whom I never truly knew. I had no doubt that he understood the impact he had on all of us as students. His former students went on to succeed in college and in their professional lives. However, did he understand how he might affect an adolescent like me, not only his student, but also a future teacher, and a gay man?

STAGE-ENVIRONMENT FIT

For decades and across epistemological perspectives, psychologists have described an individual's behavior as a result of both personal characteristics and opportunities afforded by the environment (e.g., Lewin, 1935). The theory of person-environment fit suggests that when there is congruence between individual needs and environmental opportunities, favorable motivational, affective, and behavioral outcomes should result. However, Lewin's theory did not include a description of how successful growth may be dependent on meeting different needs at different stages of life.

Hunt (1975) suggested a revision of person-environment fit theory to consider developmental changes and implications for long-term growth:

Maintaining a developmental perspective becomes very important in implementing person-environment matching because a teacher should not only take account of a student's contemporaneous needs by providing whatever structure he currently requires but also view his present need for structure on a developmental continuum along which growth toward independence and less need for structure is the long-term objective. (p. 2221)

Subsequently, person-environment fit theory was revised into stage-environment fit (Eccles & Midgley, 1989) based on "the assumption that if changes in needs are aligned with changes in opportunities at a certain stage of life, positive outcomes will result" (Midgley, Middleton, Gheen, & Kumar, 2002, p. 110).

Since adolescence seems to be an important "turning point" in development, considerable research on stage-environment fit has focused on this time of life. Adolescents who experience positive patterns in the environment are more likely to report positive changes in their academic expectations and value (Midgley, Eccles, & Feldlaufer, 1991; Midgley, Feldlaufer, & Eccles, 1989). More recent examinations of stage-environment fit have shown perceptions of school and family psychological environment related to both mental health outcomes such as depression and self-esteem (Gutman & Eccles, 2007) and school related outcomes such as engagement and peer relationships (Zimmer-Gembeck, Chipuer, & Hanisch, 2006).

Previously, we provided an overview of our research on stage-environment fit during early adolescence as students moved from elementary into middle schools (Midgely, Middleton, Gheen, & Kumar, 2002). Using the work of Eccles and Midgley (1989), our overview focused on three potential developmental needs of adolescence: a) academic challenge or demand, b) a motivational focus on developing competence, and c) a strong positive student-teacher relationship. We examined how changes in the classroom environment related to changes in students' report of these educational needs.

The guiding perspective for our study was achievement goal theory (Ames, 1987, 1992) which provides a conceptual framework for understanding the nature of motivation and the learning environment. The theory suggests that in addition to having personal achievement goals, students perceive the goals that are emphasized in their learning environment, referred to as classroom goal structures (Ames, 1992; Ames & Archer, 1988; Kaplan, Middleton, Urdan, & Midgley, 2002; Meece, Anderman, & Anderman, 2006).

Considerable research has focused on the teacher's role in creating a developmentally appropriate learning environment that enhances a stage-environment fit. Based on the work of Epstein (1989), Ames (1990) identified features of the classroom that could serve as a focus for building a positive motivation climate. These classroom qualities have been assessed through observation (e.g., Patrick et al., 2001) and aggregated results from student self-report surveys (e.g., Midgley et al., 2000). In a series of qualitative studies, Turner and her colleagues (Turner, Meyer, Midgley, & Patrick, 2003; Turner & Meyer, 2004; Turner & Patrick, 2004) examined the relation of teacher behavior and discourse in support of student motivation and learning. Instructional approaches, motivational messages, and academic support were associated with different student participation patterns (Turner & Patrick, 2004). Teachers who consistently and explicitly supported student autonomy and intrinsic motivation for learning had students who reported more beneficial patterns of educational beliefs and behaviors (Turner et al, 2003). It is clear that teachers' behaviors, including instructional practices and explicit messages to students, relate to students' perceptions of the learning environment and their own educational beliefs and behaviors.

Motivation research has provided a deep understanding of the role of teachers in creating environments that meet the developmental needs of adolescents. Although, most prior work has provided insight into a teacher's interaction with a whole class, the developmental needs of an individual student may or may not reflect the general needs of adolescents. Additionally, the teacher-student relationship exists in a social/historical context that may provide opportunities and limits on the potential fit of developmental stage and environment. Using the understanding we have developed about stage/environment fit and the adolescent needs of academic challenge, facilitative motivational goals, and positive teacher-student relationships, Mr. C's story illustrates:

- Ways a teacher might contribute to the psychological environment experienced by an adolescent; and,
- Possibilities and limitations of a teacher's contribution to a stage/ environment fit for adolescents.

ANALYSIS: CAN A TEACHER CREATE A STAGE/ENVIRONMENT FIT FOR EACH STUDENT?

Using the framework of adolescent educational needs described earlier in the chapter (Midgley et al., 2002), the short story about Mr. C reveals his strong contribution to stage/environment fit in the areas of academic challenge, adaptive motivational climate, and teacher-student relationship. However, the story also reveals the limits that individual differences and social/historical context place on the contribution of a teacher to the development of a student.

Academic press. If a need of adolescent development is to experience challenging academic work, the level of challenge or demand can be described as an "academic press." A press for understanding requires students to engage in higher-order thinking skills, such as linking understanding to previous knowledge, checking answers against what they already know (Stevenson, 1998), and demonstrating conceptual understanding (Shouse, 1996). Others (Blumenfeld, 1992; Henningsen & Stein, 1997; Meece, 1991), describe instructional practices that support press for understanding, such as attention on the main point, checking for understanding, asking high level questions, demanding justification or clarification, encouraging connection making, and sustaining an expectation for explanation. Academic press has been related to short-term achievement outcomes (Shouse, 1996) and may work in combination with instructional pacing and support (Stone, Engel, Nagaoka, & Roderick, 2005) and scaffolding (Kempler, 2007) to support learning. Moreover, press also has been associated positively with self-efficacy, self-regulation (Middleton & Midgley, 2002), and school belongingness (Ma, 2003) and negatively with avoiding help-seeking (Middleton & Midgley, 2002).

As Mr. C's student I experienced a strong academic press for understanding. His class was demanding and challenging. Mr. C did not only expect quality work from his students; he demanded it. His focus on widespread participation in recitations put every student on notice to be prepared and attentive. His emphasis on critical thought led me to read more carefully and thoughtfully. I learned that drafting writing projects wasn't a sign of inability but the key to progress. As suggested (Kempler, 2007; Stone et al., 2005), his level of demand was met with a high level of support. Mr. C was a master at asking the right questions to scaffold student thinking. His questions provided prompts and guidance about how to find the answer, and he used both teacher and peer feedback to guide the improvement of our work.

However, the highly competitive school climate provided a sometimes harmful setting for Mr. C's demands. Knowing that in the short-term our grades and in the long-term our admission to college were at stake raised the level of anxiety about Mr. C's demands. His class was only one of several that placed high level demands on us. The academic press that was a hallmark of Mr. C's class at times easily slipped into pressure for performance with its corresponding anxiety and self-doubt (Middleton, 2004).

Mastery classroom goal structure. A second adolescent educational need is to learn in a supportive motivational environment. Patrick (2004) describes mastery goal structures as "involv(ing) a perception that students' real learning and understanding, rather than just memorization, are valued and that success is accompanied by effort and indicated by personal improvement" (p. 234). Mastery classroom goal structures have also been associated with a variety of beneficial educational beliefs and behaviors (Ames & Archer, 1988; L. Anderman, 1999; Kaplan & Midgley, 1999; Meece et al., 2006; Roeser, Midgley, & Urdan, 1996) creating an "adaptive pattern of learning"

(Midgley et al, 2000) in the classroom. In contrast to mastery environments, students may also perceive a performance goal structure in which the classroom emphasis would be on demonstrating or proving competence.

The relation of mastery goal structures to patterns of adaptive learning suggests that teachers should try to establish mastery-oriented classroom environments. Based on the research of Epstein (1989), Ames (1990) identified features of the classroom that could serve as a focus for building a positive motivation climate, concentrating on the acronym TARGET (task, autonomy, recognition, grouping, evaluation, and time).

Mr. C's class was clearly aligned with a mastery goal structure. He wanted each student to develop and improve his academic work and wanted to instill a respect and love for literature and writing. These dual purposes of developing competence and interest reinforced each other. As my work in his class improved and my thinking became more sophisticated, my appreciation for literature and writing were enhanced. After dissecting a Shakespeare play, my classmates and I were eager to read more, and Mr. C was glad to alter his syllabus for us to accommodate that desire.

Although some might argue that his demand for quality work supported the development of performance goals, to me Mr. C emphasized improving our competence above all else. A fallacy about mastery goal orientation is that it does not emphasize quality work. In Mr. C's class, mastery involved working hard, reflecting on feedback, and improving competence.

However, Mr. C was not operating in a vacuum. I also experienced the motivational environment of our school culture. In addition to perceiving the motivational emphasis of a classroom, students also experience the motivational goals of their school (Ciani, 2007). An interesting question for educators is how these two goal structures operate together. Does a mastery classroom goal structure act as a buffer to the more distal school goal structure or does the more pervasive school goal structure overwhelm the efforts of an individual teacher? I know Mr. C wanted me to develop and improve my literacy skills and to gain an appreciation for literature; however, I also know that the pervading school performance goal led me to do my work to get good grades at times. It is difficult to disentangle the two levels of context, and I'm not certain that Mr. C could resolve this conflict or even viewed it as a conflict of goals.

Student–teacher relationship. During adolescents, the organization of schools often presents an obstacle in developing student-teacher relationships despite adolescents' desire for a connection to their teachers. In younger grades, students are with the same teacher all day and there is a strong emphasis on teachers getting to know each child. However, in most secondary schools a student will have multiple teachers during the day and each teacher will have at least 100 students across all her classes. Adolescents report the desire to have a connection to teachers, and those positive connections are beneficial to classroom engagement (Patrick, Ryan, & Kaplan, 2007) and to coping with problems (Zimmer-Gembeck & Locke, 2007). A positive relationship with a teacher may take the form of both academic and personal support.

Mr. C was not the type of teacher who attended after school activities or had students in his classroom before or after school for informal conversations. My relationship with him was based on his knowledge of me as a student. He knew my strengths and areas that needed improvement. His personalized feedback on my work showed that he cared about me as his student and wanted me to achieve my personal best.

As the above story suggests, Mr. C also had a relationship with his students as a role model. He had high personal standards and expected no less of us. He taught us lessons of personal integrity and hard work.

However, for me the relationship was more complex. Although Mr. C did not disclose personal information or let us into his life beyond the classroom, we speculated what his life might be like outside of school. In particular the questions about his sexual orientation helped shape my understanding of what it meant to be gay. To be gay in a 1980s all boy high school meant being "in the closet"—whether you were a teacher or student. Research on male development has referred to this "policing of masculinities" (Martino & Frank, 2006) in single sex schools that acts in opposition to knowledge about guiding gay youth in developing a "viable social identity" (Cote & Levine, 2002). Creating a "viable social identity" necessitates learning to manage a stigmatized identity (Cote & Levin, 2002). In fact, through observing Mr. C and others' reaction to him I received the message that managing my emerging identity as gay meant hiding that aspect of myself if I wanted to be part of accepted society.

CONCLUSIONS: SOCIOCULTURAL PERSPECTIVES AND STAGE/ENVIRONMENT FIT

Although promoting a challenging classroom that motivates students for learning and provides a supportive relationship may constitute a "positive press" for learning (Middleton, 2004), the short story presented illuminates the limitations of this perspective.

As a teacher Mr. C helped meet some important needs of my adolescent development but because of who I was and the social context of our school at that time, his contributions were limited. He helped develop my interest in literature and writing by emphasizing its importance and by pressing me to improve in my academic work. However, the school culture that emphasized grades and college admission sometimes led to anxiety and a focus on performance rather than learning. He provided a strong ethical model of the importance of integrity and hard work but at the same time the suspicion that he might be gay in a homophobic school and culture contributed to my sense of shame and isolation as a young gay man trying building my own identity.

Our developing notions of stage environment fit (e.g., Eccles & Midgley, 1989; Midgley et al., 2002) have provided a solid compass for creating contexts appropriate for adolescent development. However, as psychologists our understanding of context may need to acknowledge greater complexity if we want to work toward meeting the needs of each student in a particular place at a particular time.

Prior work in motivation, especially achievement goal theory, "characterizes engagement in terms of the individual's sense-making activity" (Hickey, 2003, p. 407). Although researchers acknowledge the influence of classroom conditions on individual motivation, "their analysis of motivation and context implies a rationalist characterization of knowing and learning and uses aggregated individual-level constructs to characterize broader contexts" (p. 407). In other words, social cognitive conceptions of stage-environment fit have depended on theoretical generalizations made from successful individual student participation in schooling. These theories have overlooked how adolescents' motivation is tightly interwoven with school and community as a particular context in which learning occurs (Sinha, 1999). In response, Nolen and Ward (in press) encourage greater empirical "analysis of the social meaning systems in which motivation arises."

Sociocultural theorists, in particular, may provide a helpful lens to view the complexity of culture and context and to promote an understanding of situated learning that can be incorporated into psychological theories such as stage/environment fit. Our educational community and each school within it embody a community of practice (Lave & Wenger, 1991) which includes the customs, social norms, and ways of operating. In a community of practice, our actions may be viewed as mediated by culture (Cole, 1998). As a result, people develop not as a result of the environment but "as they participate in and contribute to cultural activities that themselves develop with the involvement of people in successive generations" (Rogoff, 2003).

The contribution Mr. C made to my development did align with the mission of my high school. His demand for quality work, encouragement to see value and beauty in literature, and support for developing competence helped me develop my potential. However, those contributions were made in the social context of a performance-oriented school and a society that often devalued diversity and difference. I've wondered what Mr. C might be like as a teacher in today's society. His early death denied a generation of students the unique experience of Mr. C's English class, a class which he would not allow to be "an intellectual wasteland" and a class where young men were taught to be "decent, stand-up, honest adults."

REFERENCES

Ames, C. (1987). The enhancement of student motivation: In M. Maehr, & D. Kleiber (Eds.), *Advances in motivation and achievement Vol. 5: Enhancing motivation* (pp. 123–148). Greenwich CT: JAI Press.

Ames, C. (1990, April). *Achievement goals and classroom structure: Developing a learning orientation in students.* Paper presented at the annual meeting of the American Educational Research Association, Boston.

Ames, C. (1992). Classrooms: Goals, structures, and student motivation. *Journal of Educational Psychology, 84,* 261–271.

Ames. C., & Archer, J. (1988). Achievement goals in the classroom, students' learning strategies and motivation processes. *Journal of Educational Psychology, 80,* 260–267.

Anderman, L. (1999). Classroom goal orientation, school belonging, and social goals as predictors of students' positive and negative affect following the transition to middle school. *Journal of Research and Development in Education, 32,* 89–103.

Blumenfeld, P. C. (1992). The task and the teacher: Enhancing student thoughtfulness in science. In J. Brophy (Ed.), *Advances in research in teaching* (Vol. 3, pp. 81–114). Greenwich, CT: JAI Press.

Ciani, K. D., Summers, J. J., & Easter, M. A. (in press). A "top down" analysis of high school teacher motivation. *Contemporary Educational Psychology.*

Cole, M. (1998). Can cultural psychology help us think about diversity? *Mind, Culture and Activity, 5,* 291–304.

Cote, J. E., & Levine, C. G. *Identity formation, agency, and culture: A social psychological synthesis.* Mahwah, NJ: Erlbaum.

Dweck, C. S. (1986). Motivational processes affecting learning. *American Psychologist, 40,* 1040–1048.

Eccles, J. S., & Midgley, C. (1989). Stage/environment fit: Developmentally appropriate classrooms for early adolescents. In R. E. Ames, & C. Ames (Eds.), *Research on motivation in education* (Vol. 3, pp. 139–186). New York: Academic Press.

Epstein, J. L. (1989). Family structures and student motivation: A developmental perspective. In C. Ames & R. Ames (Eds.), *Research on motivation in education* (Vol. 3, pp. 259–295). San Diego, CA: Academic Press.

Gutman, L. M., & Eccles, J. S. (2007). Stage-environment fit during adolescents: Trajectories of family relations and adolescent outcomes. *Developmental Psychology, 43,* 522–537.

Harackiewicz, J. M., Barron, K. E., Pintrich, P. R., Elliot, A. J., & Thrash, T. M. (2002). Revision of achievement goal theory: Necessary and illuminating. *Journal of Educational Psychology, 94,* 638–645.

Henningsen, M., & Stein, M. K. (1997). Mathematical tasks and student cognition: Classroom-based factors that support and inhibit high-level mathematical thinking and reasoning. *Journal for Research in Mathematics Education, 28,* 524–549.

Hickey, D. T. (2003). Engaged participation versus marginal nonparticipation: A stridently sociocultural approach to achievement motivation. *The Elementary School Journal, 103,* 401–429.

Hunt, D. E. (1975). Person-enviroment interaction: A challenge found wanting before it was tried. *Review of Educational Research, 45,* 209–230.

Kaplan, A., & Middleton, M. J. (2002). Should childhood be a journey or a race? A response to Harackiewicz et al. (2002). *Journal of Educational Psychology, 94,* 646–648.

Kaplan, A., Middleton, M. J., Urdan, T., & Midgley, C. (2002). Achievement goals and goal structures. In C. Midgley (Ed.), *Goals, goal structures, and patterns of adaptive learning* (pp. 21–53). Mahwah, NJ: Erlbaum.

Kaplan, A., & Midgley, C. (1999). The relationship between perceptions of the classrooms goal structures and early adolescents' affect in school: The mediating role of coping strategies. *Learning and Individual Differences, 11,* 187–212.

Kempler, T. M. (2007). *Optimizing students' motivation in inquiry-based learning environments: The role of instructional practices.* Dissertation Abstracts International Section A: Humanities and Social Science.

Lave, J., & Wenger, E. (1991). *Situated learning: Legitimate peripheral participation.* Cambridge: Cambridge University Press.

Lewin, K. (1935). *A dynamic theory of personality.* New York: McGraw Hill.

Ma, X. (2003). Sense of belonging to school: Can schools make a difference? *Journal of Educational Research, 96(6),* 340–349.

Martino, W., & Frank, B. (2006) 'The Tyranny of Surveillance': Male teachers and the policing of masculinities in a single sex school, *Gender and Education 18,* 17–33.

Meece, J. L. (1991). The classroom context and students' motivational goals. In M. L. Maehr & P. Pintrich (Eds.), *Advances in motivation and achievement: Vol. 7. Goals and self-regulatory processes.* Greenwich, CT: JAI Press.

Meece, J. L., Anderman, E. M., & Anderman, L. H. (2006). Classroom goal structure, student motivation, and academic achievement. *Annual Review of Psychology, 57,* 487–503.

Middleton, M. J., (2004). Motivating through challenging: promoting a positive press for learning. In P. R. Pintrich & M. L Maehr (Eds.), *Advances in motivation and achievement, Vol. 13.* Elsevier.

Middleton, M. J., & Midgley, C. (2002). Beyond motivation: Middle school students' perceptions of press for understanding in math. *Contemporary Educational Psychology, 27(3),* 373–391.

Midgley, C., Eccles, J. S., & Feldlaufer, H. (1991). Classroom environment and the transition to junior high school. In B. J. Fraser & H. J. Walberg (Eds.), *Educational environments: Evaluation, antecedents and consequences* (pp. 112–139). Elmsford, NY: Pergamon Press.

Midgley, C. Feldlaufer, H., & Eccles, J. S. (1989). Student/teacher relations and attitudes toward mathematics before and after the transition to junior high school. *Child Development, 60,* 981–992.

Midgley, C., Kaplan., A., & Middleton, M. J. (2001). Performance-approach goals: Good for what, for whom, under what circumstances, and at what cost? *Journal of Educational Psychology, 93,* 77–86.

Midgley, C., Maehr, M. L., Hruda, L. Z., Anderman, E., Anderman, L., Freeman, K., Gheen, M., Kaplan, A., Kumar, R., Middleton, M., Nelson, J., Roeser, R., & Urdan, T. (2000). *Manual for the Patterns of Adaptive Learning Scales (PALS)*. Ann Arbor, MI: University of Michigan.

Midgley, C., Middleton, M. J., Gheen, M., & Kumar, R. (2002). Stage-environment fit revisited: A goal theory approach to examining school transitions. In C. Midgley (Ed.), *Goals, goal structures, and patterns of adaptive learning* (pp. 109–142). Mahwah, NJ: Erlbaum.

Nicholls, J. G. (1989). *The competitive ethos and democratic education*. Cambridge, MA: Harvard University Press.

Nolen, S., & Ward, C. (in Press). Sociocultural and situative approaches to studying motivation. In T. Urdan (Ed.), *Advances in motivation and achievement (Vol. 15): Social psychological perspective on motivation and achievement*. Amsterdam: Elsevier.

Patrick, H. (2004). Re-examining classroom mastery goal structure. In P. R. Pintrich & M. L. Maehr (Ed.), *Advances in motivation and achievement* (Vol. 13, pp. 233–264). Amsterdam: Elsevier.

Patrick, H., Anderman, L. H., Ryan, A. M., Edelin, K., & Midgley, C. (2001). Teachers' communication of goal orientations in four fifth-grade classrooms. *The Elementary School Journal, 102,* 35–58.

Patrick, H., Ryan, A. M., & Kaplan, A. (2007). Early adolesents' perceptions of the classroom social environment, motivational beliefs, and engagement. *Journal of Educational Psychology, 99,* 83–98.

Roeser, R. W., Midgley, C., & Urdan, T. (1996). Perceptions of the school psychological environment and early adolescents' psychological and behavioral functioning in school: The mediating role of goals and belonging. *Journal of Educational Psychology, 88,* 408–422.

Rogoff, B. (2003). *The cultural nature of human development*. Oxford: Oxford University Press.

Shouse, R. C. (1996). Academic press and sense of community: Conflict and congruence in American high schools. *Research in Sociology of Education and Socialization, 11,* 173 - 202.

Sinha, C. (2000). Culture, language and the emergence of subjectivity. *Culture & Psychology, 6,* 197–207.

Stevenson, J. (1998). Performance of the cognitive holding power questionnaire in schools. *Learning and Instruction, 8,* 393–410.

Stone, S. I., Engel, M., Nagaoka, J., & Roderick, M. (2005). Getting it the second time around: Student classroom experience in Chicago's Summer Bridge program. *Teachers College Record, 107*(5), 935–957.

Turner, J. C., & Meyer, D. K. (2004). A classroom perspective on the principle of moderate challenge in mathematics. *Journal of Educational Research, 97,* 311.

Turner, J. C., Meyer, D. K., Midgley, C., & Patrick, H. (2003). Teachers' discourse and sixth graders' reported affect and achievement behaviors in two high mastery/ high performance mathematics classrooms. *The Elementary School Journal, 103,* 357–382.

Turner, J. C., & Patrick, H. (2004). Motivational influences on student participation in classroom learning activities. *Teachers College Record, 106,* 1759–1785.

Zimmer-Gembeck, M. J., Chipuer, H. M., & Hanisch, M. (2006). Relationships at school and stage-environment fit as resources for adolescent engagement and achivement. *Journal of Adolescence, 29*, 911–933.

Zimmer-Gembeck, M. J., & Locke, E. M. (2007). The socialization of adolescent coping behaviours: Relationships with families and teachers. *Journal of Adolescence, 30*, 1–16.

AUTHOR'S NOTE

The author would like to acknowledge that some character quotes in this chapter come from online discussion forums regarding favorite teachers at www.stjohnsprep.org and www.dailykos.com and have been recreated as conversation.

CHAPTER 14

F EQUALS YOUR MOTHER AND THE CONTINUING SAGA OF SHERMAN AND MR. PEABODY

Or What I Learned in High School Physics

Allison J. Kelaher Young
Western Michigan University

Ask most people about their high school physics class and more often than not, they will have a horror story about it. Notorious for awful teachers, and esoteric material, physics is not known for its pedagogical charms. High school science teachers in general are either terrific or terrible, with very few in between. However, my high school Physics I and II classes transformed me as a person and as a learner. I learned that I was capable of more than I thought and that I could trust myself to get there. I learned that I understood mathematics, more as a language than a field of study, even if my grades in trigonometry did not bear this out. I learned to solve problems systematically and thoughtfully. And I learned that good teaching was

The Ones We Remember: Scholars Reflect on Teachers Who Made a Difference, pages 127–137

based on theory. My work in this class ultimately may have led to my interest in educational psychology as a field of study.

I took physics in my junior year of high school. I had been in the honors track in most of my classes, so I had taken biology and chemistry already. My goal was to take anatomy and physiology in my senior year so that I would be poised to take on a pre-med program in college. I wanted to be a medical doctor at the time and I knew that I needed chemistry and physics, but my heart had always been in biology.

The first day of school, I walked into a science room at the end of the hall on the second floor to find a large, bearded man with dark tinted glasses standing at the front of the room behind a lab bench. This was Mr. Fazzino, or "Fazz," as we called him outside of class. He had a reputation for being tough and this first day was confirming that reputation. Right away, he seated us in a semicircle around the lab bench, starting with the seniors alphabetically, followed by the juniors. I took my seat just to the right of his desk area, the last junior to be seated.

As soon as we were seated, Fazz began to talk about his expectations for the class. We watched as he methodically erased the board, walking back and forth holding the eraser in long, horizontal sweeps so that his back was never to us. In a booming, even voice, he explained the conditions under which we would be operating, the upshot of this entire discussion being that he would not tolerate any kind of lateness or misbehavior. For instance, if you were coming through the door threshold as the bell was ringing, you would earn yourself a detention. I had been nervous to take physics as a junior in the first place. By the time it was over, the tone and content of this monologue had me terrified. As an anxious kid who earned As and Bs, who had never had a detention, who was "a pleasure to have in class," I asked myself whether I would be able to handle this class. I had never run into a class as challenging as this one, both academically and emotionally.

One of our units of study for the first marking period was to be mechanical equations, the only things he expected us to memorize in the entire course. He said that we would be able to look up almost anything else, but that these equations for speed, velocity, and acceleration, were the basis of everything else that we would study, so we might as well commit them to memory. And with that, Fazz introduced us to Newton's second law. "Given a frictionless surface, F equals your mother," he said, writing the equation "$f = ma$" on the board. We all laughed. It was the first time this gruff man had tipped his hand to show us his sense of humor and I began to see him as a person.

To Fazz, the point of physics was being able to think and to solve problems. Aside from the mechanical equations, rarely did we memorize. We had to approach a problem by following a process that I still use today. We learned to set a problem up by identifying the givens, drawing a diagram, and explaining our thinking. In homework and on tests or quizzes, we got credit for setting up the problem. The process was as important as getting the right answer. Sometimes there were multiple ways to get to the answer, so it was important to show all our work. I began to see writing out the steps as a way for Fazz to "see" what I was doing and to be able to help me figure out my mistakes.

Most of our problems were written from the perspective of two popular cartoon characters of the time, Sherman and Mr. Peabody. "Sherman and Mr. Peabody are at the top of a twenty story building where each story is twelve feet high. If Mr. Peabody throws an apple from the building at an angle of twenty-five degrees how far away from the building will it land?" Starting with what I knew, I would identify the "givens" and any constants involved; for example, gravity is $9.8m/sec^2$, a number I still remember, though I have no immediate use for it in my daily life. I would also draw a diagram of what I thought the problem looked like. I then would identify the equations that would solve the problem. In this case, I would have to use trigonometry and vectors. Then I could go on to solve the problem. Of course, this was before I took calculus. It was only after an introductory calculus course in college that I realized how much *easier* physics is with that particular language.

At the end of the first marking period Fazz handed out a worksheet with all of our assignments listed on it, blanks next to each waiting for grades. He announced that he would read each score aloud and we were to write it in the slot and then calculate our own grades. Again, this was the first time I had been asked to do such a thing. He went through each member of the class, reading each name and then a stream of numbers. I was the last in the class to hear my list. I quickly calculated my grade as a C+. I knew I had been trying as hard as I could in this course, but it would have been my first C ever, and I had to keep from crying. Each of us individually brought our worksheets up to Fazz at his desk. When it came my turn, I quietly approached his desk and said "I calculated a C+." Fazz studied my worksheet for a moment before turning to me and saying in a low voice, "This score is close, so I'm calling it a B−, but can you do me a favor and try to relax?" A wave of relief spread over me as I returned the two steps to my desk, but I was left to ponder the comment about relaxing. My guess was that he had noticed my anxiety and that it was in the way of my learning.

For our final assignment in Physics I, our class was assigned to find an example of something we had studied that year in a short story, and explain it in terms of whether or not it was viable or realistic. We would be presenting our story and concepts to the class. I found a story called "The Billiard Ball" by Issac Asimov. This story involved two rival scientists, Priss (a theoretical physicist), and Bloom (a billionaire inventor who applies Priss' ideas in an effort to show him up). Bloom builds a billiard table where one of the pockets has an electro-magnetic field that is designed as an anti-gravitational device. One thing leads to another and Priss is killed by the billiard ball that he taps into the anti-gravity pocket. The story leaves the reader wondering whether this was accidental or a murder.

I had already noticed that there were similarities between the equations for the gravitational field of the earth, magnetic fields, and electrical fields (see Table 14.1) and I began to consider the idea that these forces could be related. A week or so of library research and I came across the idea of a unified field theory that had not been resolved and I remember the excitement I felt at making this discovery. In 1982, it seemed like something that scientists were still working on.

TABLE 14.1   A Unified Field Theory?

Earth's gravitational field	Magnetic field	Electrical field
$F = g\dfrac{m_1 m_2}{d^2}$	$F = k\dfrac{mag_1 mag_2}{d^2}$	$F = k\dfrac{elec_1 elec_2}{d^2}$

Source for equations: Genzer & Younger (1969)

I couldn't wait to present my work in class. I had organized my notes, I knew that I knew my stuff. I was presenting on something that was meaningful and real, because it still was an ongoing discussion in the scientific community. It was only a fifteen minute presentation delivered to half of the class (the seniors had left by that point), but it felt like a conference presentation. I felt like I had made a real discovery as opposed to just formulating an answer to a question. Having a teacher who held high expectations was the beginning of my transformation as a learner.

The August before my senior year, I went into school to check on my course schedule. The guidance office had made a habit of producing incorrect schedules for me, so I wanted to smooth the start of my busy final year in high school by making sure things were in order. I met Fazz in the main office where he asked me why I wasn't taking Physics II. "I signed up for anatomy and physiology because I want to do pre-med. Besides, I don't think I'm cut out for it, too much math," I said. I had come quite close to failing trigonometry the year before, and the anxiety I felt around math had become more intense. "Really?" he said, "Because I think you are one of about three kids who I feel like I could give the book to and you'd pretty much teach yourself. Well, I'll see you later." And he left the office. I didn't think too much of this conversation until a few minutes later when I got a copy of my schedule. Right there, during seventh hour, was Physics II. To this day, I can't be sure whether anatomy and physiology just wouldn't fit in my schedule or Fazz fiddled with it. I like to think it was the latter.

Thirteen students found their way to Physics II senior year; ten boys and three girls. It was during this course that I began to notice some of

Fazz's instructional strategies. When someone had difficulty understanding a problem we were discussing, Fazz often started all over from the beginning again, yet taking a different route. One day in class, we were discussing a problem that I understood fairly well. Fazz turned and looked around the room in order to judge where we were as a class. Without any of us having to say anything, we would often hear Fazz say "Okay, Carl and Tammy, where did you get lost?" Fazz would read the looks on our faces to determine where we were. This astounded me—it was like having a clairvoyant for a teacher.

At this point, it was up to the students to talk Fazz through to the point where they got lost. That gave Fazz an idea of where the misunderstanding was, and then Fazz would start the problem again. Fazz would attempt to see what strategy the student was using and then direct his instruction toward that strategy. Often the second solution would look markedly different from the first, demonstrating that there was usually more than one way to approach a problem.

REFLECTION AND REFRACTION

The summer before I went to college, my best friend Carl and I were visiting with the Fazzinos at their home. Mrs. Fazzino had been our chemistry teacher, so we'd been with them for three years of high school. I told Fazz about my experience in his class, and he explained that his instructional practice had been informed by the work of a theorist named Ausubel. Without knowing it, what I had witnessed in his classroom was the application of Ausubel's maxim, "The single most important factor influencing learning is what the learner already knows. Ascertain this and teach him accordingly" (Ausubel 1968, prologue). The effectiveness of emphasizing prior knowledge in instruction was obvious to me as a learner.

Nearly twenty-five years later, my work with Mr. Fazzino remains a critical juncture for me. I went off to college, prepared to think about things logically as well as flexibly. I had learned how to learn. I had learned to organize my thinking in a logical way, to persevere and look for multiple avenues to solve problems, to look for connections between different ideas. I also learned that I could do what most people perceive as difficult work and that I liked it. I learned that mistakes helped me to learn. I learned how to work with others and I learned to be confident in myself.

During my education coursework as an undergraduate, I learned about theories of learning, development, and motivation that explained what I had experienced in my two years of physics. In fact, during that time I wrote the first draft of this chapter. Work by theorists such as Rogers, Vygotsky, Piaget, and others informed my reflection on this experience of relationship and relevance. Later, my graduate work focused on more contemporary research on learning, motivation, and self-regulated learning which allowed me another level of reflection on this critical experience. My current work as a teacher educator has further fostered my thinking about my relationship with Mr. Joseph Fazzino.

PRINCIPLES OF PRACTICE

Adolescence is the second of two fantastic developmental periods in the human lifespan, the first being toddlerhood. Remarkable brain growth facilitates socio-emotional changes and the development of new cognitive abilities, such as flexibility of cognitive structures and reflective capacities needed for making effective judgments. Because of this, adolescent learners want to participate in instructional practices that are both meaningful and authentic.

I have always seen this narrative as an example of the humanist perspective of learning and development. As an undergraduate, I effectively applied Rogers' work to this experience. And while I never formally studied Ausubel's work, I never forgot the conversation I had with Fazz about his application of this theoretical framework. Because of this, I wanted to explore Ausubel's work for this story. What is striking to me is that, for both Ausubel and Rogers, meaningful learning, cognitive or socio-emotional, is an integrative, relational process designed to enable learners to become more self-regulated. While they use different terms, they are essentially arguing for similar principles.

Three principles dominate my thinking about this narrative. The first is that the learning process and relationships around it need to be perceived as *real*, whether these are termed "meaningful" or "authentic." The second principle, *connectivity*, is important in the learning process, whether that be in terms of "relatability" or "empathy." And finally, the learning process requires *intentionality* through which we express what it is that we value, whether it be people or ideas.

Realness

For Ausubel, *meaningful* learning comes as a result of cognitive structures that are relatively stable, clear, and orderly. This allows the learner to more easily bridge his or her prior knowledge with new material to be learned. This is evident in the narrative where Fazz would stop at the end of discussing a problem and check to be sure we were all with him. Anyone with a quizzical look would be asked to talk about how he or she understood the idea. He would listen to a student's explanation for clues to the student's existing cognitive structure. From there, it seemed to be a process of re-mapping ideas and sometimes presenting a completely different perspective in order to help the learner make the new knowledge his or her own.

Facilitating this kind of learning requires a teacher to be *authentic*. This means that the teacher should present himself as he is, "not a façade, or a role, or a pretense" (Rogers, 1961, p. 282). The teacher is present to herself, to her thoughts and feelings. She accepts herself, with an awareness of her reactions and their consequences. She is able to listen to herself. Teachers who are authentic can laugh at things that are funny, admit when they make a mistake, and be vulnerable. Authenticity also allows students to be more real as well. As Rogers (1969) argued:

> such a teacher can accept the student's occasional apathy, his erratic desires to explore by-roads of knowledge, as well as his disciplined efforts to achieve major goals. He can accept personal feelings which both disturb and promote learning—rivalry with a sibling, hatred of authority, concern about personal adequacy. (p. 109)

Because he was able to be real himself, Fazz was able to take *us* as *we* were. He could laugh at his jokes as well as at ours. He could be angry with us without being mean. And mostly, he always started where we were.

In my experiences in Fazz's class, realness did not mean simply "real world problems," though certainly this is not a problem in physics. It also involved the learning process itself. For instance, the idea that our work was a use-ful part of the learning process, something for which we were given credit helped me see the meaning in our work. Realness to me now implies that the learner accepts herself and her ideas more fully, that she comes to see herself and her ideas differently, and that she is capable of recognizing any beliefs (i.e., motivational beliefs) or behaviors about learning that get in the way of achievement. Realness is a function of awareness and openness to change.

Connectivity

To facilitate learning, teachers must introduce concepts and principles in such a way that the learner can see them as *relevant* and *relatable* to ex-isting cognitive structures. Relevant ideas are ones that are generalizable to concepts and principles, so that the learner can make sense of his or her experience with respect to the context of a bigger picture. Likewise, relatability is an idea that suggests the nature of cognitive connections, or relationships. Ausubel (1968) argues that integration of new knowledge depends upon the number and quality of concepts in existing cognitive structures. Both of these ideas are related to the notion of knowledge in context. As a teacher, Fazz contextualized much of our work, including giving us Sherman and Mr. Peabody as referents in our problems. While it can be argued that cartoon characters may not make the problems "real world," they still gave us something with which to operate, to relate to.

Similarly, physics itself provided a context for mathematics. Things I was studying in math classes now had a purpose. I had a reason to remember sine, cosine, and tangent as well as a need to know more about how to calculate the area under a curve. As early as my junior year, I understood mathematics as the language of physics, even though trigonometry in my math class had evaded me. Effective physics teachers like Fazz can make physics and mathematics relevant because it is all around us.

To create relevant and relatable instruction, a teacher needs to approach students from a position of acceptance, or *empathy*. Empathy is the ability to put oneself in another's place; to really hear and recognize another's experience. Rogers (1969) argued that meaningful, substantive learning can take place "when the teacher has the ability to understand the students' reactions from the inside, has a sensitive awareness of the way the process of education and learning seems to the student" (p.111). Empathy is about connection and connectedness. This is evident in my own physics experience, as Fazz was willing to listen and to ask questions to determine how we saw our learning.

During my time in Physics I and II, I began to see how ideas connected to one another. My "discovery" of a unified field theory is an example of connectivity. My ability to see these relations was supported by an environment where the interpersonal relationships were solid. Connectivity implies to me that the learner becomes more flexible, less rigid in her perceptions and thinking and that she becomes more accepting of others, both personally as well as ideologically. Connectivity is a function of stability and flexibility.

Intentionality

Contemporary motivation theories argue that tasks that are challenging, meaningful, and relevant, and are assessed as a function of effort and improvement are more likely to lead to the adoption of intrinsic or task-focused goal orientation. Academic tasks that require analysis (or what Ausubel called *progressive differentiation*) as well as tasks that require synthesis (or what Ausubel called *integrative reconciliation*) create a "need to know." These tasks create a value for learning or an intention to learn. For Ausubel (1963), motivation is "not endogenous but acquired—and largely through exposure to provocative, meaningful and developmentally appropriate instruction" (p. 11). I saw and experienced this in physics nearly every day as

I began to meet challenges and develop a sense of self-efficacy with both physics as well as mathematics. This carried over into a college calculus class where I discovered how much easier physics would have been had I known calculus.

Being able to react from a position of empathic understanding requires the teacher to value or prize his students as people, rather than constantly evaluating them. I was a learner in Fazz's class, not a C+ or B-. I was, as Rogers (1961) argues "of value, no matter what [my] condition, behavior, or feelings" (p.185). Fazz made this clear in his comments to me in class as well as his attempts to get me to take Physics II. I remember this as one of the first classes where my ideas were put up on the board and discussed as possibilities. This kind of valuing led to my transformation a learner. I felt that someone else trusted me and cared about my learning, which allowed me to trust myself.

In Fazz's classes, I was able to develop as a self-regulated learner. I was provided tools which I could use to organize my experiences and knowledge. In addition, I was valued as a member of a community of learners, which gave me confidence in my abilities, even when I made mistakes. Intentionality implies that the learner adopts realistic goals for himself and becomes more self-confident and self-directed in his learning and relationships. In my mind, intentionality is a function of vision and action.

I always find it remarkable that works written forty years ago still speak so clearly to conditions of teaching and learning today. The works I have cited are set in the 1960s, post-Sputnik period in American education that was framed by an increasing emphasis on science and mathematics education. During this time we experienced social revolution as well, placing a burden on the educational system to create better scientists as well as to solve social problems like poverty and racial injustice. David Ausubel (1963, 1968) entered the conversation in education and psychology as the cognitive revolution was in full swing. His work directly refuted many of the behaviorist ideas of learning by assuming an internal cognitive process. Informed by Piagetian theory, Ausubel focused on the organization and interaction of cognitive structures was particularly instructive for science and mathematics educators. Likewise, Carl Rogers (1961, 1969), informed by his contemporaries in humanistic psychology (e.g., Bugental, Maslow), turned his attention toward education as a crucible for relationship. He recognized similarities between the therapeutic relationship experienced in psychotherapy and the relationship between teacher and student, the idea being to create a caring dynamic in the classroom.

What is striking about these theories is that one can see remnants of these ideas in contemporary educational writing. For Ausubel, the effective teacher would have an awareness of both his or her own cognitive organization of the material as well as how students might organize the same ideas.

These ideas about cognitive structure formed the foundation for practical tools like concept maps and other graphic organizers as well as the post-positivist research on conceptual change in science education (cf., Novak 1977; Posner, Strike, Hewson, & Gertzog 1982; von Glasersfeld, 1984). Similarly Rogers reasoned that experience in a relationship with a teacher who was a real, accepting adult would be liberating for students. The focus on human potential nurtured in that relationship is associated with contemporary work on the importance of emotions and the ethic of caring in education (cf., Boler, 1999; Noddings, 1984).

In looking at my own teacher education practice, I find that each of these theories is important to my philosophy of teacher education; that teaching is a specialized form of learning and that my teacher candidates must know themselves as learners before they can be teachers. I also believe that teaching and learning is all about connection and relationship. I value cognitive connections and elaboration in my teacher candidates' work, and I make every effort to provide them with meaningful, relevant learning opportunities. I try to approach my teacher candidates from a position of authenticity and to prize them as human beings, hoping to help provide them with what Rogers terms "the freedom to learn," a climate of liberation where the learner wants to learn more.

Many of these ideas about teaching and learning are recognizable as elements of self-regulated learning, which is particularly important in teacher education because it is not possible to teach someone how to teach. I tell my teacher candidates that I can't teach them anything, a statement that is always rather shocking to them. But it isn't because I am an incompetent teacher... it is because anything worthwhile has to be learned. Learning is a powerful process when self-directed and self-evaluated, and in this way I focus my pedagogical practice on the transition from *student* to *learner* so that my teacher candidates can be more effective teachers. And this is important because I made this transition in high school physics. And if teachers teach the way they were taught, then I want my students to remember these things, the things I got from Fazz.

REFERENCES

Ausubel, D. P. (1963). *The psychology of meaningful verbal learning.* New York: Grune and Stratton.

Ausubel, D. P. (1968). *Educational psychology: A cognitive view.* New York: Holt, Rinehart, and Winston.

Boler, M. (1999). *Feeling power: Emotions and education.* New York. Routledge.

Genzer, I., & Younger, P. (1969). *Physics.* Morristown, NJ: Silver Burdette Company.

Noddings, N. (1984). *Caring; A feminine approach to ethics and moral education.* Berkeley, CA: University of California Press.

Novak, J. (1977). An alternative to Piagetian psychology for science and mathematics education. *Science Education, 61*, 453–477.

Posner, G., Strike, K., & Hewson, P., & Gertzog, W. (1982). Accommodation of a scientific conception: Toward a theory of conceptual change. *Science Education, 66(2)*, 211–227.

Rogers, C. R. (1961). *On becoming a person.* Boston: Houghton Mifflin Company.

Rogers, C. R. (1969). *Freedom to learn.* Columbus, OH: Charles E. Merrill Publishing Company.

von Glasersfeld, E. (1984). An introduction to radical constructivism. In P. Waxlawick, (Ed.), *The invented reality* (pp. 17–40). New York: Norton.

AUTHOR NOTE

I would like to acknowledge that I have had remarkable "teacher karma" throughout my life and want to thank the many teachers I carry with me into my classroom. I could have easily written about any of the following: Marilyn C. and John A. Young, Mr. Schwanfelder (7th grade Social Studies) Ms. Silvestre & Mrs. Early (8th grade, Social Studies and Science), SueEllen Schwartz (11th grade English), Michelina Fazzino (10th grade Chemistry), Tahme Adnolfi (High School Choir), K. Ann Renninger (Swarthmore College), and the late Carol Midgley and Paul R. Pintrich (University of Michigan).

CHAPTER 15

TEACHER INFLUENCES ON STUDENTS' LEARNING

High School Experiences of Iranian Students

Farideh Salili
The University of Hong Kong

My high school experiences are from a radically different time and different culture, namely Iran. I started high school in late 1950s when Iran was a monarchy and the Shah was a supreme ruler. Many events since then have changed the face of high school education in Iran. Since the 1978 Islamic revolution, the school curriculum places heavy emphasis on religious education and practices in the schools. Girls are required to observe the Islamic dress code. However, even in that era of relative openness, no co-ed schools existed. I therefore, attended all-girl schools in which the climate was very different from the co-ed schools that constitute the majority of schools in the Western world.

During my high school years, I changed school three times, each time when we moved to a new house. Each time I had to adjust to the new school

The Ones We Remember: Scholars Reflect on Teachers Who Made a Difference, pages 139–147
Copyright © 2008 by Information Age Publishing

and make new friends. I have been trying to remember a teacher in these three schools who left me with a lasting impression or one who influenced what I have become today. Unfortunately, while I remember most of my teachers, none has left me with such a lasting influence. Perhaps like most Iranian students of my time, I was most influenced by my family rather than by any of my teachers. I could, however, give an account of teachers who were unpopular (bad teachers), those who were respected but feared (feared teachers), and those who were popular and respected (good teachers). But first, let me provide a foundation for understanding these teachers by describing the method of teaching and learning during my high school education in Iran before the Revolution.

During the dictatorship and autocratic government of the Shah's time, together with traditional Iranian culture, a different system of education prevailed in Iran. Although students had input in the process of learning, it was always in response to the demands from teachers, who would ask questions or give problems to solve and demand responses from the students.

When I look back and examine how we engaged in learning the subject matter taught in high school classes, I cannot find a proper term to describe it. Perhaps one could call it rote memorization, but it was not quite that simple. I must also add that I actually don't know who taught us to learn that way. Probably, like children's games that pass from generation to generation, learning styles are also part of the culture of schools that passes on to the new generation of students. In order to understand the subject matter taught in the class, we first read the material quietly and sometimes aloud while walking around. Some students would even move their heads forwards and backwards, similar to Jewish people praying at the Temple Mount, or like those reciting the Koran in the Pakistani *madressehs* seen on television. We would then close the book and try to recall the main ideas from what we just read. If necessary, we would repeat this process several times until we knew the material by heart. Some difficult tasks, such as learning the names and geographical locations of African countries, were learned by meaningful rhyming. But again, I don't know why we came to learn that way. I suspect this was inherited from ancient times when our parents were first taught alphabets and words through rhyming.

Memorization is often described as a parrot-like technique that results in surface learning or learning without understanding. Its purpose is just to get through the examinations. But our learning style was not simply memorization, as we also understood what we memorized. At least I did. Whether this method was good or bad, given some cues I can still recall the content of most things that I learned in high school. I have even been able to explain some difficult concepts in high school mathematics and sciences to my two children.

Years later, when I studied educational psychology and became familiar with theories of learning, and when I had a chance to teach subjects such as learning disabilities, I realized that our learning method was perhaps not so bad after all. The way we engaged in learning was not unlike what is referred to as the *Fernald program*, also called multi-sensory approach or VAKT (i.e., using visual, auditory, kinesthetic and tactile modalities), which is a method used with individuals who have learning difficulties. The theoretical rationale for this program is based on multisensory stimulation. Many methods used to teach children with learning difficulties involve using multiple senses and integrating various modalities. It is interesting to note that, at that stage of my education, we were using somewhat similar methods, which is to say, reading loud while walking up and down in the courtyard of the school or at home to learn and memorize the materials taught. At times, to make sure the material was learned, some students would actually write down the main ideas on a piece of paper, thus using and integrating multiple senses in learning. Indeed, our method of learning also used cognitive and metacognitive activities. It involved not only reading and memorizing the main points, but also engaging in mental activities of thinking about what was being read, conceiving, reasoning, and monitoring, as well as organizing what we understood of the reading material into main ideas to remember.

CLASSROOM CLIMATE

The classrooms in my schools were traditional, with rows of benches facing the teacher and the blackboard. The teaching method was formal and involved transmitting the teacher's factual knowledge through lecturing or, in the case of science subjects, actual demonstrations and labs. This was followed by having the students solve the given problems related to the lesson taught, often calling individual students to the blackboard to demonstrate that they understood by solving the problems in front of the class. This created a threatening situation for those students who were shy, lacked self-confidence or were lower in ability, and it brought shame to those who failed to answer the questions or solve the problems. Such methods are clearly not meant to promote creativity. Nonetheless, if writing poems and literary work is any indication of creativity, Iran has produced some of the greatest poets and writers in the world. Of course, there could be other reasons for this specific talent that is prevalent even among the ordinary people.

Students were given a fair amount of homework. The assessment of learning was done by formal examinations at the end of each semester. Whoever failed to receive a mark of 7 out of 20 in the examination was allowed to sit for another examination for the failed subject in September before the new school year started. If a student failed in the second attempt on more than one exam, the year had to be repeated. There was also a state examination for the high school diploma at the end of the 12th grade.

Of course, the classroom climate depended on who was teaching and whether she or he was perceived to be a good teacher, a bad teacher, or a feared teacher. The students could be very noisy and naughty with a teacher who was not liked or not respected, or even one who was feared. Teacher-student relationship varied depending on the teachers' personality, the way they interacted with students, their perceived knowledge of the subject they taught, their teaching skills, the standard they set for succeeding in the course, and last but not least whether they were young or old or how good looking they were. Even in all-girl schools, there were male and female teachers, with male teachers teaching predominantly sciences and mathematics and female teachers teaching the arts, literature, social sciences, and home economics. The courses at the upper levels streamed into arts, sciences, and mathematics. A second language (either French or English) continued throughout high school. Arabic language (taught to enable students to read the Quran) and religious rules (Sharia) was introduced in the 7th grade but was no longer part of the curriculum after 9th grade. We also had specific sessions on sports, which were limited in scope and were not part of the formal evaluation of the students.

Teaching, I believe, is as much an art as a science. Some of my teachers appeared to have a natural ability for teaching. They were competent and knowledgeable in the subject matter they taught, they appeared enthusiastic, and they took their teaching seriously. They could also manage the class well. This meant (in those days as well as now) making sure everyone was sitting quietly at their benches, paying attention to the teacher, and taking notes. For others, teaching seemed to be a struggle, and this was quickly picked on by the students who would then make life difficult for them.

Having examined the teaching and learning methods during my high school years, I can now describe some of my experiences of the teachers that stand out in my mind.

THE BAD TEACHER

Poor Mrs. A. She was the history teacher in my 8th grade class and was new to the school. She was a middle aged woman and rather fat. She seldom smiled and was not skillful in classroom management, or in teaching. She would read from a previously prepared lecture notes and write the headings on the board. Some students would fall sleep and others became so bored that they started to chat with their classmates. Still others would make paper planes and shoot them at other classmates when she was not looking. She was perceived by students as not knowing enough about the subject she taught and not knowing how to teach.

As we all know, high school students can be cruel, and soon the class ganged together to make teaching in our class very unpleasant for her. We would write things on the board before she entered class or make strange noises when she turned to the board. In the last session before she resigned after only six weeks into the semester, our "leader" decided that we should start the class by making the sound of bees, starting from the last row in the class when she turned toward the blackboard. As soon as she walked to the end of the class in an attempt to discover the unruly students, they would stop and the front row would start the sound of bee. She tried hard to locate the culprits unsuccessfully. In the end, the whole class made the sound until she stormed out of the room, telling us that we would all pay for this. This was the last we saw of Mrs. A. We were of course all punished by being detained after class to write a line of apology 100 times.

THE FEARED TEACHERS

Mr. B taught us fairly advanced mathematics in Grade 10. He knew his subject well and could teach, but he kept order and managed the class by creating fear of bodily harm. He would bring a pocket knife and would show it to unruly students, saying that he would not hesitate to use it on the palm of the hands of any noisy or unruly student. He was well known among the students for being a bit crazy and unpredictable. Mr. B was a tall man in his late forties, but in the eyes of a young teenage student in the 10th grade he was an old man. He wore spectacles with black rims and had untidy muffled hair. Of course, he never used his knife, and he managed to teach the subject quite well, making sure we understood it by calling us to the board to solve problems and giving us many exercises. Looking back, I remember that even though his method of classroom management was unusual and by today's standard even unlawful, most students, especially those with a good ability for mathematics feared but also liked him. One thing that was going for him was the subject he taught—10th grade mathematics is not easy. In the case of history, we knew that we could probably do better ourselves reading the history book than attending the history class with an incompetent teacher. But the nature of mathematics requires a knowledgeable teacher who can teach, and Mr. B. was quite good at it. He also made mathematics interesting to most students by relating it to problems in everyday life. His occasional jokes also kept students alert, but we all knew when to laugh and when to be absolutely quiet. Here I must add that telling jokes is a cultural characteristic of Iranians. It is a way of entertaining in social gathering, and Persians are very talented in making jokes about everything. Jokes allow us to express ourselves rather freely without getting into trouble. For example, jokes are common these days about religious and government leaders and, in particular, about the President of the Islamic Republic of Iran, Mr. Ahmedinejad. These jokes nowadays are accompanied by funny and creative videos circulated through the Internet. I receive at least one or two such emails every day from fellow exiled Iranians. Many of us were also motivated to learn mathematics and get a good grade for the course so that we could be admitted into the "science stream."

I recall another feared teacher in my 12th grade with a different method of classroom management—the all powerful *Dr. H*, the geology teacher. In 12th grade, students are prepared to take the state examinations for the high school diploma, and grades were very important to students who wanted to enter university or graduate from high school. Dr. H was a university professor who had been asked to also teach us in preparation for the university entrance exam. Having a university professor, and a well-known one for that matter, was rare in Iranian high schools. That sort of thing happened only in elite and prestigious schools. My school had a high standard for achievement and only top students who could also afford to pay the high fees managed to get in. Some were accepted through the influence of their families, and so my classmates were mostly the daughters of the rich and famous families. Most of them were well behaved and serious students, thus classroom management was not a problem. The school was called *Reza Shah Kabir* (great) after the Shah's father, who was the founder of the Pahlavi dynasty and credited for liberating women by ordering them to take off their head covers (known as *hejab*). He was deposed due to his support for the Nazi regime during the Second World War and was replaced by his son, Mohammed Reza Shah, the last Shah of Iran. Despite the fear factor, the course was very interesting to me and I learned a great deal about geology, not just from reading the school books, but from the wealth of knowledge Dr. H was able to share with us in an interesting way.

Dr. H. was extremely knowledgeable in his field and used maps and other materials, such as different types of stones with layers of sediments and fossils, to make sure we understood geology and how the earth evolved. He was also one of the most feared teachers. He was a stern looking man in his 50s with short stature and piercing eyes. He would set an extremely high standard for success, and his grades would never go above 12 (out of 20).

In Dr. H's class no one dared smile or look anywhere except at the front of the room and what was being written or drawn on the board. He would not hesitate to ask a student to leave the class for coughing or talking, or give a grade of zero, which would bring the student's mark down for the class very low or to a failure. Students who failed in a course were not eligible to sit for the state examinations. To make sure everyone read or prepared for the class, he would call a few students randomly to the blackboard, one at a time, and ask them questions about what he had taught in the previous session and about the reading assignments. Students had to respond accurately, sometimes by drawing or calculating the age and stating the mineral composition of a piece of stone he brought with him. I remember I would always put my head down and tried not to have eye contact with Dr. H at the start of the class, fearing he might call on me to answer his questions. However, I did not escape and was called to the board several times. I remember that I always prepared for this course particularly well, but when I was called to answer questions my heart would pound rapidly and my voice would get very low, out of fear of humiliation or receiving a zero.

GOOD TEACHERS

Mrs. F taught the history of Persian literature in 12th grade. In Iranian schools, Persian literature and poetry are important subjects and are emphasized to a lesser or greater degree depending on the student's academic track. I was in the science track, which meant that we had to study advanced mathematics and sciences. The literature taught in this track, although important, was only one course as opposed to a few in the arts track. We were asked to write essays on given topics, interpret difficult pieces of literature, and learn about different prominent Persian poets, reciting some of their poems by heart and interpreting them in simple modern Persian. Some of the literature from the Islamic era contained Arabic verses or words that made them very difficult to understand.

Mrs. F was very popular with students. She was a young woman in her early 30s with a friendly and approachable disposition. She was very knowledgeable in Persian literature and poetry and could interpret them without difficulty. Here I must add that Persian poets use many metaphors and imagery in their poems, and literary Persian, which is somewhat different from the spoken language, is difficult to understand even for a native Persian. Some poets from the Islamic era used Arabic verses or passages together with their Persian lines. During that time, using Arabic (the language of the *Quran*) in writing Persian literary work was a sign of knowledge and prestige.

With poetry being part of Persian everyday life and culture, we paid special attention to it and memorized the famous pieces. Some I still remember even to this day. Our teacher could recite the poems herself with contagious enthusiasm. She always encouraged students for their efforts regardless of their ability. I respected and liked our literature teacher, not only because of her caring and approachable style of teaching, but also because I enjoyed the poems. The love of poetry runs in our family, and many members of my maternal family and ancestors were themselves poets.

DISCUSSION AND CONCLUSION

Looking back, it is clear that several factors influenced my perceptions of what it meant to be a good or bad teacher. When I was a high school student, it was extremely difficult to get admitted into the only existing university in Tehran. Tehran University accepted very few students, and there was a competitive entrance examination conducted in two stages. In stage one all students had to successfully pass the Persian literature and a foreign language exam (either French or English). Passing the entrance exam at this level was necessary to be allowed to participate in the second set of examinations, which focused on subject matters related to the field of intended study. My perceptions of effective teaching were therefore primarily influenced by how well teachers could prepare me for the university entrance examinations. In my case I needed to excel in mathematics, sciences, Persian literature, and French language. Teacher knowledge and teaching style for these subjects were therefore the most important quality.

There are of course differing ideas about what constitutes a good teacher. But there are many similarities between what was considered a good teacher in Iran and what is considered a good teacher in the United States. For example, in both cultures, knowledge of subject matter, teaching skills, enthusiasm, and love of teaching are important characteristics of effective teachers. Also, teacher personality, approachability, charisma, and politeness are much appreciated by students in both cultures. Another important factor was how important it was for us to succeed in a particular subject matter. These factors affected our judgments about the teachers who taught the courses and whether they were good teachers.

Even today, high school education in Iran is very different from that in most American high schools. Compared to high schools in Iran, American schools have a more open and relaxed atmosphere and are student centered. Teachers appear to be more approachable and allow students to actively contribute to their own learning. The learning environment in Iranian high schools is teacher centered. The style of teaching is authoritarian and one-sided. The teacher teaches, and students listen and take notes. There is little interaction between teachers and students except when the teacher asks questions or allows a student to ask a question on aspects of the lesson that may not have been understood.

Despite these differences, students like me who had been educated in traditional Iranian high schools and then emigrated to the United States have generally done well in American universities. Adolescent Iranians are also very similar to their American counterparts. We had similar concerns as adolescents everywhere have and could be just as naughty and noisy as teenagers in American high schools when the opportunity presented itself.

We had our own style of learning which seemed to be effective and was not unlike the multisensory approach used for individuals with learning disabilities. We liked and respected teachers who were knowledgeable in the courses they taught, could teach well and were enthusiastic, and were approachable and fair in grading students' work. We would also make life difficult for teachers who did not have these qualities.

Looking back at my own high school experiences has made me realize that high school days were some of the best times in my life. However, by emphasizing the role of teachers in influencing student achievement, we tend to ignore other important factors, such as the role of parents, peers, school environment, the political system, cultural tradition, and, last but not least, the students' own ability and what they bring with them into the classroom.

CHAPTER 16

TOO GOOD TO LAST

The Short But Inspiring Career of an Autonomy-Supportive English Teacher

Richard M. Ryan
University of Rochester

When it comes to motivating students to learn, the current climate of education often favors power tactics, and pressure from without. The ambient talk is about "high stakes" evaluations, sanctions, rewards, and accountability. "Tough" educators are celebrated with presidential awards, and schools are increasingly becoming places for drill and testing rather than discovery and growth. Perhaps some find emotional satisfaction in thinking one can "make" unmotivated students work merely by exerting adult control and power. But in reality, controlling, strong-arm tactics are typically a fast track to losing rather than retaining students, and while at best they can foster surface compliance, they have clear costs in terms of the quality of students learning (Ryan & Brown, 2005; Ryan & LaGuardia, 1999).

In my consultations with teachers I am often asked, "What can an individual teacher, or principal, or superintendent, do under this political climate?" There is no easy answer to this. But a fundamental task of the teach-

The Ones We Remember: Scholars Reflect on Teachers Who Made a Difference, pages 149–159
Copyright © 2008 by Information Age Publishing
All rights of reproduction in any form reserved.

ing professionals is to protect all those beneath them from those harmful outside influences; in the midst of the storm to provide an umbrella under which authentic learning and growth can still occur.

My story is about a teacher who was, in his own quiet and revolutionary way, truly talented at motivating students from within. He found methods to connect and encourage, even with students who viewed his classroom as a joke or a burden. Kids like me. He did not win any presidential awards. Indeed, he was fired from his position in the English department in my high school. Yet for me, and for many other young alienated souls, this soft-spoken teacher of literature was a critical figure in our development. Personally, he was a key player in transforming me from a disruptive, wise-cracking, self-handicapping student, into a person who believed he might have something to say, and could put it down on paper. Though my school counselor had, perhaps accurately suggested that I was "not college ma-terial" and that I should look into vocational training, this man opened up possibilities to me that others, including myself, couldn't see. My life changed because of him, though he couldn't know the extent of that. His name was Mr. Gregory.

OPTING OUT OF MR. GREGORY'S ENGLISH CLASS

Donald Gregory was the chair of the English department in my high school, a large suburban school not far from New York City. He was not a figure who drew attention to himself: no booming voice, no wildly stylish actions in class, and no teaching "tricks." At a time when many teachers tried to dress like the students they taught, and were called by their first names, Gregory came to school each day in a white shirt with a tie, and was ad-dressed as "Mr." I was unhappy when assigned to his class. Rumor had it that he was a "great" teacher, but one who made people work. I didn't much like the sounds of that, and I entered his class ready to test his mettle.

That first day in Gregory's class was a strange one for me. I did my best to be disruptive. I made a couple of wisecracks in the first few minutes, sat with my feet up on the desk, but I received little or no attention from Gregory, who simply kept on track with his discussion. It was, I remember, a discus-sion about *us*, about young people having a voice, and about the power of words. Everyone seemed engrossed, except me, who felt a bit disempow-ered by the power Gregory's words seemed to have over the others.

The class was held first period. Relatively unsupervised, I was able to meet my friends most mornings before school. We typically went cruising for a half hour or so, getting high, staying away from cops. By the time we entered school we were usually feeling rowdy and full of teenage swagger. I took that attitude into Mr. Gregory's class for the first week of that year, but each day found that my attempts at undermining the class were ineffective. The other students liked this class, and I resented them.

The first day of the second week of classes Mr. Gregory called me aside after class. I thought, "alright, now I will get yelled at." This was a satisfying idea—finally some sense of efficacy. But that is not what happened. Mr. Gregory asked me to take a seat. He asked me in a quite but curious tone whether I really wanted to be in class. I thought the question was nonsensical. "I gotta be here," I said, "it's required." But he said something that surprised me. Basically, he said that I was conveying everyday that I didn't want to participate in class, and he asked if he was right about that. When I said "for sure" he smiled and said, "I understand." He said we should discuss alternatives. In my mind this meant he was going to punish me. Usually "alternatives" meant you could either toe the line or face some bad consequence. But in fact, he meant it. He offered me the option of not coming to class. Instead, he said that on any day I wished not to attend, I could go to the lunchroom for a study hall first period. He would provide assignments for me to do on my own so I could pass, and in this way he said, "You won't have to be coerced into a class you really may have no interest in." I was shocked and giddy. I'll accept that deal. Mr. Gregory then requested that I stop by and get a pass each morning. But he added, the door is always open to return to the class, and he hoped I would. Fat chance, I thought, and I left feeling victorious.

The next two weeks were somewhat confusing for me. Every day I expected Mr. Gregory to renege on this offer. But instead he would ask me, "How is it going?" He inquired about my independent work, and he treated me with a manner and tone I had never experienced (and probably had never deserved either), namely *respect*. It was as if he viewed this refusal to be in class as an adult decision on my part, a true choice.

In the lunch room I found a few friends, ate snacks, laughed, and kicked back. Sometimes I slept with my head on the table, or wandered about looking for distraction. This was kind of boring, but better than being in class, I imagined. But then I would run into the students from Mr. Gregory's class. Contrary to my fantasies, none of them appeared to be the least bit jealous of my "arrangement." Only one other kid had even asked for the same deal, and whatever happened in his conversation with Gregory, he changed his mind. I alone had escaped. But I was getting curious about what was happening within that class. I was feeling left out, and having a hard time admitting it.

I turned in my first assignment to Gregory. It was an essay on a novel I had chosen from a long list he provided. I read only the cliff notes, and wrote a short piece attacking the characters as unrealistic, the writing outdated, and the message irrelevant. It came back to me the next day. It was remarkable. I had expected to get some ire from Gregory. Instead, attached to my essay was a couple of handwritten paragraphs in which Mr. Gregory explained that he found my perspective interesting, and though he did not agree, he cited several ways in which I could have made my critique even more compelling. And he mentioned specific passages relevant to my argument, which I had to crack the actual book open to find. He had climbed into the *inside* of my argument. In the essay he also inserted a few alternative phrasings that I had to admit did make my points clearer and more engaging. He did nothing to defend the book, or dispute my rejection of it. This guy was bizarre.

Face saving. I couldn't help it. I was starting to like him. Gregory was giving me choices, treating me with respect I had never experienced, and giving me nothing to rebel against. More importantly, he had taken my essay *seriously*. It was as if he had actually cared what I had to say. I was also feeling less happy each day as I went down to snack and sleep, as I watched the others excitedly head off to class. I wanted back in, but didn't know how to ask. I think Mr. Gregory sensed that, and he found a way for me.

On a Tuesday I went in for my pass, and I asked him what was up. He told me what the class was working on, and I said "interesting." He said, you know, I have been meaning to ask you if you had considered giving this class another shot. He said he was feeling a little pressure from others to get me back in class, but he would withstand that if I really didn't want to be there. He looked at me with a kind of sincerity I had not felt from a teacher, and said he really wanted it to be my decision. He invited me to at least experiment with it. I now see that he was giving me a face saving chance at re-entry, and it worked. I told him I'd give it a try—as if I were doing him the favor. As he handed me my last lunchroom pass he said, "I look forward to having you in class tomorrow."

WHY THEY WERE EXCITED

I can say that I cannot remember ever looking back on that decision to rejoin my senior English class. From the moment I returned I was engaged, right in the mix with the other 27 students in that group. What had them, and me, so excited?

The classroom style. Mr. Gregory was not charismatic in the sense that he wore costumes or jumped on desks to grab attention. But he was clearly enthusiastic about literature and more so, about our opinions about literature. He loved to hear, form, and refine criticisms of literature, unveiling the structure, the meanings, and the tools of fiction. He understood that criticism of literature required the critic to find a voice, and he understood that this was a challenge for us as adolescents. He took it as a mission to help us be articulate about what we thought. This was a stark contrast to the rest of school as I had experienced it. In the rest of school one regurgitated, and one complied. A student's opinions were irrelevant and distracting. Not in Gregory's class. Our opinions were authentically welcomed and respected, but never left unclear. They were reflected, elaborated, restated, and by the end of that process we could experience the genius of a thought. He taught us that style and message are inexorable, a message that would reverberate throughout life, because it applied whether one was teaching, talking politics with a friend, or arguing with a traffic cop to get out of a ticket. In addition, it was clear that Mr. Gregory *enjoyed* the class, and you almost felt weird if you couldn't partake of that joy. He expected us to love this stuff, and somehow that made it easier to do so.

A sense of choice. Part of the reason class was easy to embrace is that we students had a hand in constructing it. He had a booklist to begin with. It was long but had on it some of the most controversial yet relevant novels and essays of the time. Authors such as Eldridge Cleaver, J.D. Salinger, Phillip Roth, Doris Lessing, and Kurt Vonnegut populated that list. These works had youth appeal, and provided plenty to argue about.

And we did. Part of what the class did daily was to debate books, and choose what was next. We also discussed and negotiated paper assignments, and what criteria we should be using to judge them. We felt a sense of ownership of what we were doing in class. Such empowerment could dampen the alienation of even the most rebellious.

Connectedness. The respect Mr. Gregory had for each one of us was also something that came to characterize our treatment of each other. Mr. Gregory had a way of modeling respect for even the most lowly persons or opinions. The quite nerdy kid who everybody ignored had an opinion that *mattered* to Mr. Gregory. The girl with the bad stutter was given time to speak without interruption, and her words reflected. It felt good to witness, and it also set a norm. Occasionally, Mr. Gregory even made that norm explicit. He talked about the importance of hearing everybody, and making sure we really understood another's opinion before judging it. Often he found gold in what might start as a seemingly inarticulate jumble. It made everyone freer to speak.

Competence. I know that the class was graded, but truthfully, I cannot recall what grades I received in this class. I do remember, however, really looking forward to my papers coming back, not for the grade, but for the comments. I came to expect and know that Mr. Gregory would actually read what I wrote and say something thoughtful. It would not be either an endorsement or rejection of my position, but rather a comment on where my argument was strong, and where there were gaps in logic or vagueness. The fact that he really picked up on the crucial issues, and was nearly always correct in his diagnosis, gave him tremendous credibility to me. He really did know something, especially bout how to write! But importantly, it was not being passed *down* to me. He instead took the role of an engaged and interested critic. His comments led me to think about my strategy of writing, and to see new possibilities, providing a kind of intimate and authentic feedback that no rubric-driven templates could ever yield.

Structure. The class was, objectively, demanding. There was a clear set of goals to be accomplished, and lots of books to read. But how we reached those goals was always, and explicitly, a matter for debate. What books we read, and the criteria for judging what we wrote about them, was most often chosen by us students. This facilitated our "ownership" of the work, and enhanced our investment in what we were doing.

Valuing an activity is also made a lot easier when one has a reason. The purpose of this English class was to increase our knowledge of literature and our skills in writing. That was true of all my high school English classes. But in Gregory's class the purpose of our activities was much more proximal and personal. It was the task of expressing one's own opinions. There was therefore an inherent relevance and "press." Everyone seemed to want to better express what they authentically thought, and Gregory saw his task as helping each of us be as articulate as possible, both in spoken language and in writing. In fact, Gregory was explicit in saying that this was his task. He often discussed why learning the craft of self-expression would be an abiding asset in life. As plausible as that is, no teacher had really explained that before.

Removing barriers. This was not an easy class. I wrote more in this class than in any prior, and that was true of all of us. I struggled at times, and others did too. Mr. Gregory intervened, with a definite style. Usually it began with his "one-on-ones." During small group discussions he would call individuals aside to check in. He had their portfolio with him. He would ask how it was going, where was the going toughest, and what barriers, personal or academic, were in the way. He always seemed to sympathize with barriers, yet he did not seem to excuse people because of them. Indeed, he accepted the barriers as real issues, and was open to problem solving.

As an example, Fred B. was a 17 year-old guy in my class. He was a brooding, often disengaged kid. His father had recently died, and I am sure his family was in turmoil. One day I saw him, as he shuffled from class, place a very brief essay, shoddily thrown together, on Gregory's desk. I thought to myself, "Fred is a mess." Mr. Gregory must have thought so too. I saw them later that day talking alone. And over the next while, I noticed a subtle kind of extra support cast in Freddie's direction. Small smiles, an extra hand on the shoulder. Maybe I was just attuned to it because I knew Freddie, but my guess is most students felt somehow especially understood by Mr. Gregory, just as I had. Gregory was oriented to helping us stay on task despite obstacles, which he treated as genuine, and formidable, rather than as excuses or cover-ups. He showed interest and caring for that which was in our way as learners.

Setting limits. Discipline was a big task in most of my classrooms, and its dynamics often dominated the classroom atmosphere. In some of my classes most of the energy was focused on the battle between teacher and students, on who could gain the upper hand. It made the day pass faster. As frequently the focus of discipline, I mostly found teachers' attempts to control or punish me kind of annoying, but wimpy.

Yet discipline was just not much of a focus in Mr. Gregory's class. As I said previously, we felt kind of weird if we were not engaged there. It was, after all, OUR class. Or it felt that way. When people got out of hand, Mr. Gregory actively moderated that, but usually he could accomplish that with a clear statement. He might say, "Let's make sure we get everybody's voice in here" when somebody was dominating. Or when somebody would say something dumb, and people would laugh, Gregory might laugh too, but then he would reframe the question as it might have been intended. The student laughed at would feel supported, understood, and sometimes even vindicated. When we could be stupid and still feel safe from humiliation and judgment, we were also freer to be smart, creative, and risk-taking.

In any case, students were connected enough to not want to act out, and because everybody was "into" this class, it was perhaps the only class I had where it wasn't cool to be disruptive, or to go after Gregory. In our adolescent mindset, we'd save that for the teachers we hated! But even if the group was off task, that was not for Gregory a moment to exert power. It was instead a moment for understanding, and for discussion.

MR. GREGORY AS A MODEL OF MOTIVATION: A SELF-DETERMINATION THEORY PERSPECTIVE

I did not know at the time that I would ever become a motivational theorist in the distant future. Having now studied teachers' styles and classroom practices over many years through the lens of self-determination theory (SDT; Ryan & Deci, 2000; in press), I have come to appreciate factors in classrooms associated with self-motivation, quality learning, and well-being. I see in retrospect that Mr. Gregory embodied a number of principles of motivation that are now at the core of the SDT approach.

The facilitating environment. As a theory of motivation, SDT is concerned with the conditions that foster volitional engagement, optimal learning, and well-being in students. SDT is specifically focused on factors within classroom climates that are conducive to both *intrinsic motivation*, or finding tasks to be inherently enjoyable, and *internalization*, or the finding of value in those tasks that are not so inherently enjoyable. When students find interest, value, or both in their learning activities they engage them more fully, as manifest in greater performance and persistence.

Although there are many specific tenets to SDT, in broad strokes the theory argues that students' intrinsic motivation and tendency to internalize are fostered by environments in which their *basic psychological needs* are supported. Specifically, in a learning atmosphere where there is support for feelings of autonomy, competence, and relatedness, optimal motivation results. Indeed, literally hundreds of empirical studies have supported the SDT view concerning what constitutes a facilitating environment. In what follows I do not attempt to review those findings, but rather to simply suggest how Mr. Gregory's English class represents such a need-supportive environment.

Autonomy-supportiveness. According to SDT, autonomy support concerns those elements in classrooms that support a student's sense of initiative, choice, and volition. The idea is that people are most motivated when they experience the motivation for acting as coming from within—from interest or value. In theory, many factors can facilitate the experience of autonomy, but the foundation for all of them is that a teacher takes the internal frame of reference of the learner—that is, he or she understands the students' own experience of events. On top of an appreciation for the students' perspective, factors such as interest, value in the material, opportunities for choice, absence of controlling interventions, and provision of rationale for uninteresting tasks, are all techniques for supporting autonomy.

Mr. Gregory used all of these techniques. First and foremost he showed all of us that he cared about our perspective. He was always interested in our views, and of the obstacles as we saw them. In addition, he provided choice wherever possible. He even gave me the ultimate choice—whether to attend or not. In class we had choice over what we read (within limits) and what our work should aim for. Supporting that sense of choice even further was a reading list clearly designed to appeal to our interests and culture. Furthermore, he always had a reason for the tasks we assigned, beyond the idea that we would be graded or tested. Indeed, he played down the evaluative components of class, and played up the relevance of what we were doing, and its potential value. He also did not compare students' performances or abilities, implicitly or explicitly. Finally, Mr. Gregory rarely used discipline. He didn't need to. If there was a problem, he wanted to talk with us about it, understand it from our viewpoint, and find a way to circumvent it. Rather than trying to overcome barriers to learning with more control or evaluation, he seemed to think grappling with the barriers was a part of the learning process, one in which he was a partner rather than adversary.

These autonomy-supportive strategies of perspective taking, provision of choices and rational, minimal use of controls and maximal promotion of interest, all facilitated ownership and volition in this class, and for writing more generally.

Competence support. According to SDT, support of competence comes by providing feedback that is effectance relevant, generally positive, and focused on specifics. Effectance relevance specifically means that any feedback or evaluation given is clearly directed at helping a person improve. Feedback is never itself treated as a reward or punishment.

Mr. Gregory's feedback was always specific and effectance relevant. As I said, I cannot really remember grades, as they were not very salient. What was salient is that the written feedback we received was focused on the betterment of our writing. It was personal, targeted, and explicit. This stands in contrast to the evaluations one gets in most classes, which typically consist almost exclusively of a normative grade. Research has of course shown that whereas relevant comments enhance intrinsic motivation, grades and normative evaluations, on average, diminish intrinsic motivation. Mr. Gregory must have implicitly understood that principle, and he applied it daily. In the classroom on a daily basis Gregory always tried to hear the best in people's verbal contributions. He treated no input as valueless, and he struggled to make each input as clear and articulate as possible. This was more than just helpful, it was also freeing. People were not afraid to try out an opinion, knowing it would be respected.

Relatedness Support. I felt cared about and significant in this class. From the very beginning I had a sense Mr. Gregory was invested in me, and wanted me to grow. I think we all felt that. He demonstrated this in his individual discussions with us, his way of dealing with our issues, and his respect for our ideas and choices.

The sense of relatedness was not just between teacher and student, however. Something magical went on in that class. Somehow the respect Mr. Gregory had for each one of us set the norm for us to respect and care for each other. He built that community not just with group discussions and projects, but more importantly by modeling mutual care and respect in the class. We internalized that model, and felt at home, and safe, in first period English.

According to SDT, when a student experiences support for autonomy and relatedness, the tendency to internalize ambient values, and make them his or her own, is potentiated. I know that I somehow underwent that internalization. From seeing school as a burden and threat, to seeing it as exciting and meaningful, did not seem possible, but it happened in this context. I came to see myself as someone who could write, and moreover, that writing and taking a stance was important. I started to think about the relevance of learning in a different way, and suddenly, I was college bound, with a sense of mission and confidence. Again, I was not alone in this transformation.

In sum, Mr. Gregory's English class created an exemplary climate of basic need supports. Students in his class experienced autonomy, competence, and relatedness, and these fueled a sense of excitement, vitality, and motivation. That this would be so is now supported by a voluminous empirical literature, but in Gregory's case he already had this wisdom incorporated into his practice. I am thankful to have been exposed to it.

EPILOGUE: MY FINEST TEACHER WAS FIRED

Although some of these talents may have been latent, in my view it was in Mr. Gregory's class that I first learned to write. Perhaps even more importantly it was the first place where I learned that it was possible, and in fact essential, to think critically about anything written by others. I learned to question, to recognize what was, and what was not, a compelling argument. I also learned that I, a heretofore class rebel and clown, could constructively express myself. That fall I decided to go to college (despite my counselor's assessment) and there was a snowballing course of development for me after that. I was excited by my studies and loved the labor of writing, and that developing sense of interest and confidence served me well. I even engaged in politics and public speaking, something no one would have expected B.G.—before Gregory. After graduating college I worked for a time, but returned to graduate school, not being able to leave the intellectual life behind. Ten years later I became a teacher myself.

It was around that time that I returned for the first time since my high school days to my hometown, for a class reunion. On that weekend, walking the streets of the town, I encountered Mr. Gregory by chance. He had moved away, and was only in town to visit an old friend. I felt buoyant. I wanted to tell him about the impact he had had on me, and probably before he had a chance to speak, I rattled off my progress, and expressed my gratitude, albeit awkwardly I am sure. Mr. Gregory was quiet, but had a poignant look on his face, a bit touched and sad. He was no longer teaching English. He had been fired from my high school because he refused to take books off of his reading list that had been banned by the school board. Among the offenders: Salinger's *Catcher in the Rye* and Cleaver's *Soul on Ice*. I was outraged. But Mr. Gregory stated that he had, in essence, brought that fate upon himself. He had been aware of the consequences. For him it was a matter of principles, and he felt at peace with the outcome. I still am not. Those book banners, trying to keep young minds away from controversy, and "protect" them from diverse and "dangerous" ideas, had deprived hundreds of students of the riches of this man's approach. Lucky for me they got to him too late. I was already infected and inspired.

REFERENCES

Ryan, R. M., & Brown, K. W. (2005). Legislating competence: The motivational impact of high stakes testing as an educational reform. In C. Dweck & A. E. Elliot (Eds.) *Handbook of competence* (pp. 354–374) New York: Guilford Press.

Ryan, R. M., & Deci, E. L. (2000). Intrinsic and extrinsic motivation: Classic definitions and new directions. *Contemporary Educational Psychology, 25*, 54–67.

Ryan, R. M., & Deci, E. L. (in press). Promoting self-determined school engagement: Motivation, learning, and well-being. In K. R. Wentzel & A. Wigfield (Eds.), *Handbook on motivation at school.*

Ryan, R. M., & La Guardia, J. G. (1999). Achievement motivation within a pressured society: Intrinsic and extrinsic motivations to learn and the politics of school reform. In T. Urdan (Ed.) *Advances in motivation and achievement* (Vol. 11, pp. 45–85). Greenwich, CT: JAI Press.

NOTE

For articles and resources on SDT visit www.selfdeterminationtheory.org.

CHAPTER 17

A TEACHER'S SON

The Learning-Instruction Process
Up Close and Personal

Barry J. Zimmerman
Graduate Center of the City University of New York

I grew up in a small town in Wisconsin as the son of a very special teacher. My father, Victor, was the type of instructor who left a lasting impression on his students. I recently attended a high school reunion after having lived for many years in the East, and one of the most frequent subjects of my conversations with classmates was their experiences with my deceased father. Former students from other graduating classes also sought me out to ask about my father and to recount specific instances of his impact on their lives. In some cases, they mentioned the importance of the skills he taught them that served them well later in life. In other cases, it was a humorous incident or motivational discussion they remembered. My father retired far from Wisconsin to live in the Southwest, but despite the miles and years, he received regular correspondence from former students, a number of whom had gone on to careers in an area in which he had taught them.

The Ones We Remember: Scholars Reflect on Teachers Who Made a Difference, pages 161–170
Copyright © 2008 by Information Age Publishing
161

PERSONAL QUALITIES OF AN EXEMPLARY TEACHER

Although my father never studied psychology during his teaching career (which lasted from 1935 to 1972), he intuitively used instructional methods that involved influential sources of learning, such as goal setting, modeling, emulation, strategy use, and self-monitoring. As an adult looking back, I can point to several qualities that served him well and distinguished him from his colleagues. First, he was a very successful student himself. Although he did not attend college immediately after high school, when he did, he excelled. In high school, he nearly dropped out because he was a precocious musician during the halcyon days of the "big bands" (1930s and 1940s). He played the trumpet and sought to follow the career paths of such greats as Bix Beiderbecke and Bunny Berrigan, both of whom grew up in small Midwestern cities like my father's. Fortunately, his father interceded and insisted that he graduate from high school before pursuing his music career, and my father relented. Being a musician in that economically depressed era had the allure of fame and fortune, but it also had significant liabilities. Although the financial compensation for musicians was good for the time, the itinerant quality of the life style and unpredictability of work eventually convinced my father that he could not support himself and a family very well. Because teaching was a stable source of white collar employment, even in the depths of the depression, my father decided to attend college. Despite his passion for music, he chose to major in English as an undergraduate, in part because of his reverence for the spoken word. Fortunately, the tuition at the college was low, and he could survive monetarily by playing professionally while attending school. However, his nocturnal employment typically meant facing early morning classes with little more sleep than a "cat nap." His father, who was a factory worker with little education, could offer only limited financial assistance, so my father's academic fate lay mainly in his own hands.

He managed to succeed despite these obstacles, graduating at the top of his class with membership in an elite national academic fraternity. He attributed his success to his intense level of effort and his development of effective study skills for organizing and recalling information. Class notes were diligently recorded and organized into outlines. He prepared meticulously for exams, memorizing key terms from his notes. He was steadfastly committed to attaining the high academic goals that he set for himself. In short, he could be described in contemporary psychological terms as a *self-regulated learner*—a student whose self-initiated thoughts, feelings, and actions are planned and adapted to the attainment of personal goals. These self-educative skills would prove to be of particular importance when he sought employment after graduation because he found that the market for his instructional skills in music (i.e., as a band director) was greater than for

A photograph of Victor J. Zimmerman circa 1952.

his instructional skills in academic subjects. As a result, he began his career as a History teacher (his academic minor) and band director, an instructional area in which he had no formal training.

A second quality that served my father well as a teacher was his *leadership*. As class president in college, he was responsible for planning and organizing many activities and events at the college. He attributed his success in these endeavors to managerial skills he gained as a musician who organized and delivered bands to venues. These skills included choosing the right combination of instruments for a particular dance job and ensuring that the sound equipment that was operative, a piano was tuned, orchestral arrangements of appropriate songs were available, and payment of the fee at the completion of the "gig" was prompt. In my father's view, leaders are effective not only because of their organizational skills but also because of their enthusiasm, self-confidence, and, of course, successful outcomes. The latter personal qualities would be labeled as *self-efficacy* in contemporary psychological terms.

My father's initial teaching position was in a village of less than 3,000 residents, but eventually, he returned to his hometown, a city of approximately 40, 000 residents, where he was hired as a History teacher. However, during his first year, the junior high school band director was incapacitated by a stroke, and the senior high band director died suddenly of a heart attach. My father was approached to take over the music program, and he agreed to this request. He jokingly said to my mother perhaps he should ask for hazard pay! With the onset of World War II, he was drafted into the Army. After a tour of duty playing in a military band on the West Coast, he returned to Wisconsin where he was hired as a band director in a small town of approximately 6,000 residents. His position involved teaching band at the elementary, junior and senior high school levels. The music program in that town was in a moribund state, and my father realized to succeed, he would need to create community support for the program.

His leadership skills served him well as he planned the development of a music program. One of his first goals was to establish a Music Parent's Association. The Association raised money for purchasing new band uniforms and renting buses for trips to inter-city band contests. The band members' subsequent successes at band contests became a source of civic pride in this small town, much like athletics. The Music Parents Association also supported the formation of a dance band, which played for school dances after sporting events as well as during an annual "club night." The latter involved decorating the school gymnasium to resemble a night club, with a floor show and spotlighted acts, such as comics, singers, and magicians. It became a key event in the school calendar, and a major source of revenue for the Music Parents Association. Membership in the dance band, which featured prominently in the club night festivities, was highly sought after.

Another event that comes vividly to mind involved a band-sponsored float in the homecoming parade. My father learned that a farmer on the outskirts of town had a horse and an old surrey that was gathering dust in the back reaches of his barn. With a little prodding from my father, the farmer relented, and the surrey was resurrected and restored. The horse was cleaned and put through training in preparation for the parade on main street. As it turned out, the horse and surrey, manned by students dressed in 1890s period costumes, was the hit of the parade—much to the band members', music parents', and farmer's delight! After the parade, the surrey was brought to the athletic field during the half-time festivities at the football game to participate in formations with the band. Needless to say, photos of the event were prominently displayed in the local newspaper. All of these activities happened because my father exerted leadership that extended well beyond the school day, and they greatly enhanced the credibility of the music program among the students and parents.

A third quality of my father that made a major impact on his students was his *respect for the discipline* that he taught. For example, when my father took the podium in front of the band to begin the daily practice session, he would pick up the director's baton and then would wait without saying a word. He would not begin until there was complete silence, and then he would tune the various instruments in the band to ensure proper intonation. Tuning took extra time, but he wanted to stress the importance of the students' *self-monitoring* of their intonation during the practice session. My father's efforts to teach self-monitoring to band members extended beyond intonation. For example, he would give a short description of how the musical piece should sound, such as loud and soft sections, fast and slow sections, unusual rhythms, and so forth. If a student played without following my father's direction, he would stop the band and ask the student how he should be playing his or her part. The student usually did not have an answer, and my father would gently but firmly recommend that the student watch the baton more closely for guidance. My father's demeanor conveyed clearly that practice sessions were serious affairs and that, to achieve mastery, students should respect the discipline and the instructional process.

A fourth quality of my father that had a major impact on his students was the *challenging instructional goals* that were set. As director of the junior and senior high bands that ranged in size from 60 to 80 members, my fathers' willingness to provide individualized lessons, in addition to band practice sessions, represented an enormous time commitment on his part. As the spring band tournament approached, and with little additional time available in the school day, my father would assemble his band before school to drill them in marching technique. As might be expected, his ambitious goals did lead to some casualties: There were a few students who were unwilling to make this sacrifice. However, the remaining students grew in their sense of self-efficacy about their personal musical skills and in their collective self-efficacy about the competence of the band. My father's intuitive emphasis on setting challenging goals to motivate and empower his students is consistent with contemporary research on *goal setting*. In terms of his own goal setting and completion, my father decided to augment his informal musical training by enrolling in a Masters Degree program in music in Chicago, and after a number of summers of intense coursework, he graduated with honors and as president of his class.

MY INSTRUCTIONAL EXPERIENCES WITH MY FATHER

When I reached the sixth grade, the point when band was introduced into the curriculum, health problems led my father to discontinue band directing, and he returned to teaching English and History, which he felt were less arduous. However, my father began giving me individualized lessons at our home on my chosen instrument—the trumpet. Because the community in which we lived had only one junior high and one senior high school, my father was assigned to teach History to me in the 7th grade and

English to me in the 10th and 11th grades. Although being taught in a classroom setting by one's parent is ordinarily fraught with social conflicts, I encountered only a few minor problems with other students. In general, I kept a low profile in these classes, and my father assiduously avoided any favoritism.

During my individualized musical training, my father kept his lessons focused on a specific skill that he wanted me to learn, such as an advanced tonguing technique. He would *model* the proper technique with his own trumpet and would monitor my efforts to *emulate* his technique. If I made an error, he would ask me what I needed to do to correct the error in emulation. This was an effort to teach me how to *self-monitor* and *attribute causation* properly to flaws in my technique. He would then assign exercises from a practice book for me to use when I practiced on my own. If my father heard me making a consistent mistake or playing out of tune as I practiced in the basement of our home, he would poke his head in the door to the room and offer his advice: "You were flat on the high B. Remember to use your abdomen to support your air column." His emphasis on modeling, feedback, emulation, self-monitoring, and causal attributions to technique antedated research on these constructs.

My father exerted a strong vicarious effect on me even when he was not giving me lessons. For example, he practiced at least an hour a day, usually starting with slow whole notes, which was followed by scales in every key. The scales were followed by passages from difficult solos, such as the Herbert L. Clarke's classic *Carnival of Venice*, and he ended with jazz renditions of blues, dixieland, and popular dance music. He purposely *delayed the gratification* of practicing the most pleasurable works until the end of his practice episode, which is a well known method of self-motivation used by self-regulated learners in the research literature. If asked why he practiced, my father would answer that he had to "keep his lip in shape" since he periodically played professionally, but there was strong reason to believe that practicing and the sense of mastery it produces had become *self-reinforcing* or *intrinsically motivating* to him. However, my father viewed his intense passion for music as having downsides. He confided to my mother when I was born that he hoped that I would love music but not as much as he did! As one might expect, my father's passion for the trumpet also induced me to value the sound of the instrument and the type of music that one can play with it. Ultimately, it was the instrument that I choose to learn even though my father had warned me that it was difficult to master. I realized that to achieve a high level of competence, I would need to practice at least an hour per day and to structure to my practice routines like my father's. His self-directed learning methods would be classified as *deliberate practice* by contemporary researchers on expert performance, which they define as consciously monitored programmatic learning over extended periods of time.

My father used similar learning and instructional processes in his English classes. He viewed his pedagogical approach as emphasizing the role of "basics" or fundamental skills. In music, basics involved such things as the quality of students' sound, accuracy in fingering, and precision in tonguing techniques. In my father's high school English classes, basics involved semantics, grammar, and writing skills. For example, among his other assignments, such as literature interpretation, he included weekly spelling tests, not just to avoid common spelling errors but especially to expand students' vocabulary. Spelling was not usually part of the curriculum at most high schools, but my father felt that vocabulary growth was important to personal success in life, especially if the students planned to attend college. The use of spelling to teach vocabulary was an outgrowth of my father's personal method of learning. He was an avid fan of crossword puzzles, which he used to increase his vocabulary and learn linkages to other words, such as synonyms, antonyms, and examples. He viewed vocabulary building as an important form of self-education, and he would periodically assign a crossword puzzle for his advanced students.

Regarding students' mastery of grammar, my father taught sentence diagramming. He felt that this method of instruction made students more aware of how structural errors could undermine their sentences and how alternative forms of sentences could be created when writing. Although some students and some curriculum guides have questioned the need for sentence diagram training in grammar, my father was convinced of its value, and he could cite supportive feedback from college entrance tests scores for students who did well in his classes. With time, he could point also to the success of his former students in English courses at the college level.

My father taught his students a wide array of what he would term as "techniques" for monitoring and improving the quality of their writing. Many of these techniques would be recognized by contemporary educational researchers as writing *strategies*, which they define as planned sequences of activities designed to improve the effectiveness of a specific processes. Among these writing techniques was self-monitoring. My father encouraged his students to read their written prose aloud and listen to it. Not only should the meaning of a sentence be clear, but it should also sound "professional." Although this property of writing may seem elusive, my father had specific writing self-monitoring strategies in mind. For example, when unsuitable sentences were detected, students were asked to check their choice of words, the length and form of the sentence structure, and their use of synonyms instead of repeating the same word. Sentences that failed this self-monitoring test should be rewritten.

My father gave detailed feedback for each student's essay including corrections of spelling and grammar as well as substantive meaning. This required an enormous amount of time for him. One of my high school classmates' mother, who had trained as an English teacher, told me many years later that she monitored her three sons' assignments in English carefully so that she could provide additional guidance to them. She shook her head in amazement as she noted that she did not detect a single grammatical error that my father had missed. At that time (which was the late 1950s), he was the only teacher in the high school to require a formal research paper (with literature searches, citations, footnoting, etc.), and it was one of the experiences that many of his former students mentioned as invaluable to their success in college.

My father's final exams were legendary for their thoroughness, covering not only literature and writing, but also grammar and spelling. One of my father's colleagues, a biology teacher, who was well known for his multiple-choice and completion tests, confessed to me when I was an adult that he could not fathom how my father found time to grade his students' papers in such detail. But, for my father, shortcuts were incompatible with the respect he gave to his discipline.

When my father returned to English as his chosen area of instruction, he agreed to become the faculty adviser to the forensic team, which involves competitive oral presentations. The school team had been regarded as little more than a school club in which only a few students became involved. My father decided to raise the goals of the team to prepare them to enter inter-school tournaments. He encouraged student members to commit themselves to strive for first place finishes in the competitions. These public commitments antedated research on the motivational power of *goal commitment.* He spent an extraordinary amount of time helping students to select the right readings that would be advantageous for them. For example, a former student recalled with great clarity being urged to consider a short story by Ambrose Bierce (2007) entitled *The Occurrence at Oak Creek Bridge.* This was an account of a Southern saboteur during the U. S. Civil War who was captured by the Northern troops and sentenced to hang from the very bridge that he planned to destroy. The story is a stream of consciousness account of a prisoner's final moments as he awaits and then undergoes execution. The prisoner describes the hangman's rope breaking at impact and his falling into the water, from which he makes his escape downstream. As he approaches his home, yearning to see his family again, the prisoner's voice is abruptly stilled, and the audience is informed that the prisoner's lifeless body was swinging from the gallows. The student recalled being overwhelmed by the dramatic ending, and he humorously asked my father, "Is this legal?"

This student along with his fellow forensic team members competing in different categories (grade level, type of presentation e.g., drama, comedy, etc.) were meticulously prepared for competition. First, my father used modeling and emulation feedback techniques to help students master the gestures, voice tone, facial expressions as well as the articulation. Then team members made trial presentations in the regular English classes to prepare them to perform in front of audiences. Finally, my father organized the other English faculty to serve as judges at a practice tournament at the high school to simulate the experience of performing before a judge. The results were a strong affirmation for my father's devotion to the teaching-learning process as he knew it. Not only did the student who selected Bierce's short story win a first place award, the school team won the competition.

CONCLUSION

As a son of a teacher, my learning experiences with him did not seem unusual at the time of their occurrence. Although I viewed my father as a successful teacher, I did not appreciate his extraordinary dedication and teaching skill until later in life when I experienced several epiphanies regarding my father. One that had an unexpected emotional impact on me occurred when my wife and I attended a middle school band concert in which my eldest daughter participated. As I listened to the band, I was shocked by the lower quality of my daughter's musical experiences in comparison to mine in that small town in Wisconsin. I was not alone in experiencing such an epiphany. During a return trip to that place of my youth, I met two of my father's former band students who had married and remained in the town to raise their family. I recalled from conversations with my father that they both had been excellent musicians in his bands although neither went to college for further training. When I inquired about their children's musical education, they expressed their disappointment about the quality of the program in recent years. They remarked that their children's musical experiences in band bore little resemblance to theirs.

The exceptional quality of my father's instructional methods became evident to me later during my doctoral studies in educational psychology and as I began my own program of research. Interestingly, most of the research on key psychological processes, such as modeling, emulation, self-monitoring one's effectiveness, and use of powerful learning strategies, was published after my father's professional career had ended. The same was true of the methods that my father used to motivate his students, such as: setting challenging goals, instilling commitment to those goals, fostering delay of gratification, and raising self-efficacy beliefs. A contemporary researcher visiting his classes would find many advantageous motivational outcomes, such as intrinsic motivation, self-reinforcement, attributions to learning strategies, and vicarious sources of success. As a person who has conducted extensive research on students' learning from social modeling and self-regulation, I realize that my approach to and understanding of many of these important learning processes and motivational beliefs can be traced back to the most important teacher in my life—my father.

REFERENCE

Bierce, A. (2007). *The Occurrence at Oak Creek Bridge.* http://alli268.tripod.com/ id23.html

CHAPTER 18

STORIES OF TEACHING

Four Lessons

Anita Woolfolk Hoy
The Ohio State University

I have learned from a number of memorable teachers over the years. All of those years unfolded in Texas—Ft. Worth, Lubbock, and Austin. As an adolescent I attended school in a working class district just outside Ft Worth. Like the families in the community, the school was not wealthy and the classes were relatively large—but there was Miss. Guthrie and Mrs. Young. After graduation I spent my freshman and sophomore years at Texas Technological College in Lubbock, then transferred to the Universtiy of Texas in Austin where I finished my undergraduate and graduate years. Again, there were wonderful teachers, but two stand out—Mr. Adams and Dr. Iscoe. These four stories are about them and the fundamental lesson each taught me.

The Ones We Remember: Scholars Reflect on Teachers Who Made a Difference, pages 171–176
Copyright © 2008 by Information Age Publishing
171

LEARNING IS EXHILARATING: MISS. GUTHRIE

I am cheating just a bit to include Miss Guthrie in this volume, because she was my 4th grade teacher, but her memory leaps to mind when I return to those almost adolescent years. Picture a teacher in a conservative Texas school who walks in one day with bright green hair. Then, weeks later, it was lilac. She was, it turns out, not just a 4th grade teacher, but a music teacher by training and active on stage in the Ft. Worth Community Theater. Sometimes she dyed her hair for a part in a play or for the cast parties on closing night. Of course, we thought it was for our entertainment and we loved it.

The surprising and colorful hair became an image for me of her inventive teaching strategies. No other teacher had ever turned on music, then asked us to envision the words we were learning as they danced through a story, or had us imagine we were writing our spelling words in sand and could feel every stroke. The room buzzed with productive talk and even laughter. We put on a play and Miss Guthrie challenged us to learn long and complex lines. One boy played Abraham Lincoln and gave the Gettysburg address. Miss Guthrie had no doubt that a 4th grader could deliver the entire speech in front of an auditorium filled with adults. In fact, she saw in me a girl who could learn the hundreds of lines to play the murderous Rhoda in "The Bad Seed" at the Community Theater. I auditioned, got the part, learned the lines, finished the play (got pretty good reviews), attended the cast party, and saw another hair color on my teacher—exciting, exhilarating, challenging—4th grade was grand.

LEARNING IS METHODICAL: MRS. YOUNG

My senior year in high school, I had English with the legendary Mrs. Young. She would work us hard, the legend promised. We would write, and write, and write. We would memorize classic poems and recite them. She taught us how to research a topic—one we had chosen ourselves. I decided to write about the women in the life of Edgar Allan Poe (I was a big Poe fan and a believer in the power of women). Step by step, I learned to do library searches and annotate note cards, how to outline and revise, how to cite and quote sources. Ibids and op. cit.s danced through my brain at night. The final product was long and pretty good. I could not have imagined authoring such a piece at the beginning of the year. No other class had expected this quantity or quality of writing. We left the class feeling that we might be ready for college.

The hours immersed in library stacks might sound stuffy and humorless; Mrs. Young was anything but. That same year Charles Shultz of *Peanuts* fame published a book called *Happiness is a Warm Puppy*. Mrs. Young read pages to us and delighted in the good humor and simple images. "Happiness is a chain of paper clips," read one page. Students gave her a chain of paperclips that she wore with pride, sometimes twirling the chain as she spoke.

Mrs. Young was comfortable with the silly, but also with the somber. Two years before I joined her class, John F. Kennedy was assassinated in Dallas. Just hours before he was killed, our school had waved as he passed a few feet away in a motorcade on the way to the airbase where he would board the plane for Dallas. Our band played "Hail to the Chief." We saw them all—Jackie, Lyndon, Lady Bird, the Connolly's—then he was dead before we left school that day. Mrs. Young had us write about that day, and helped us to understand Whitman's, "When Lilacs Last in the Dooryard Bloomed," that speaks the ordinary details of our lives burned into memory with the death of an extraordinary person. In Mrs. Young's class, reading and writing were about living—laughter and sorrow, hard work and accomplishment. Mrs. Young prepared me for college and for Mr. Adams.

YOU CAN WRITE: MR. ADAMS

In my first year of college I entered the honors program at Texas Tech in Lubbock. The honors English teacher was Mr. Adams (he was Dr. Adams, but that is not how he introduced himself). Because it was an honors class, it was small so we wrote early and often. We wrote in class and we wrote outside. He read everything, wrote back, and then we revised. Writing became more natural—a way of thinking, but on paper. He taught us to make sense. Without ever being effusive, he recognized what was good in my writing and returned mediocre work with clear indications of what was needed. I didn't want to disappoint him.

At one point, after several classes with Mr. Adams, I told him I would probably be taking a class in technical writing the next term, as a requirement for my major in textile chemistry. His response was strangely affirming. He said, "Anita Pratt [my maiden name] in technical writing!" Then he laughed and said something like, "No, no—that's all wrong. You already ARE a writer." And I guess I was, if Mr. Adams thought so.

PSYCHOLOGY MATTERS: DR. ISCOE

I never took that class in technical writing because I transferred to the University of Texas at Austin to finish my undergraduate degree. Having changed my major several times, I left behind the most recent thoughts about textile chemistry and entered a program in social welfare studies. As part of that major, I took a class in abnormal psychology from Dr. Ira Iscoe. Quite a change from the small writing group in Mr. Adams's class, abnormal psychology met in Batts Auditorium—theater seats and a stage, several hundred students. Dr. Iscoe invaded the stage and captured the audience. His voice filled every space in the auditorium. He was sharp, funny, and different from us—a Jewish man born in New York City and educated at UCLA. He was from "The City" and most in the auditorium were from small towns or suburbs in the Southwest.

Dr. Iscoe seemed to know everything about psychopathology and the humanity of those who live with mental disorders. He communicated a remarkable compassion and commitment to using psychology for the benefit of people, particularly those on the margins. He revamped the Counseling and Psychological Center in the aftermath of Charles Whitman's sniper shooting from the top of the UT Tower. He established the program in Community Psychology. He challenged me to make psychology matter—to improve lives. Thousand of students took his courses over the years, but his message to me seemed personal. He lived his values and so should I.

So what do these four teachers tell us? I suggest that they embody at least four important concepts in educational psychology—the significance of self-efficacy, the importance practice in learning, the emphasis on value in expectancy-value explanations of motivation, and the power of passionate guides in creating an identity and a future.

LESSON 1: SELF-EFFICACY IS A SIGNIFICANT FORCE, BUT IT MUST BE BUILT ON MASTERY

Over 30 years ago, Albert Bandura (1977) introduced the concept of self-efficacy as an important factor in human motivation. Self-efficacy beliefs are defined as "judgments about how well one can organize and execute courses of action required to deal with prospective situations that contain many ambiguous, unpredictable, and often stressful, elements" (Bandura, 1982, pp. 200–201). Bandura suggested that the sources of a person's sense of efficacy for a specific task are personal mastery experiences, verbal persuasion from credible others, vicarious experiences seeing similar people succeed, and arousal—feeling anxious, excited, depressed, etc.

Running through all my stories are teachers who persuade and press. But first they teach what is takes to master. Miss Guthrie challenged us to learn long passages, but gave us tools for learning too—tools that used images and sounds and fantasy. We saw other people like ourselves do more than they thought they could—powerful models for our own efficacy judgments. Wendell became a miniature Abraham Lincoln and never missed a word of his speech in the play—maybe I could do things like that too. In Miss

Guthrie's class we celebrated mastery and it was exhilarating. Mrs. Young broke down an unfamiliar and overwhelming task—a 30-page paper—into its parts and taught us every one. She showed us what the annotated note cards looked like, what made them helpful or not, how to sort and order them into sections of a paper. The task she set was always right at the level that challenged our skill, so she already knew about flow (Csikszentmihalyi, 1990, 1997). Mr. Adams was a master of meaningful persuasions and affirmations—just enough said, just at the right time, remembered years later. He too taught how to judge good writing and made us experts on criticizing our own work.

LESSON 2: PRACTICE, PRACTICE, PRACTICE

Practice makes more permanent. All these teachers knew that we would not become masters of spelling or drama or writing without doing lots of spelling and drama and writing. Miss Guthrie made spelling and drama practice interesting. Mrs. Young and Mr. Adams made writing practice a part of every day. I tell my graduate students that writing is thinking and it gets easier the more you do. What was once overwhelming for me as a writer is now more automatic, natural, easier, and faster. To be a good writer you have to write—over and over. Mrs. Young taught me that and so did Mr. Adams. Mrs. Young made practice structured; building toward accomplishing a paper we never thought we could do. Mr. Adams made writing natural, a part of my identity.

LESSON 3: DON'T FORGET THE VALUE
IN EXPECTANCY VALUE THEORIES

Many theories of motivation suggest that to be motivated we have to expect success and value the outcome, thus expectancy × value = motivation. The expectation side of that equation has been thoroughly studied; less has been written about value. But every teacher I have described taught me to value—learning, hard work, persistence in a long job, good writing as clear thinking, a chain of paper clips, the ordinary details of extraordinary days, the possibilities of using psychological knowledge to improve lives. They taught by being powerful models of these values and passionate advocates of their subjects. Miss Guthrie brought passion to her classroom with music and also to her stage performances—she was good. Mrs. Young, in her wise way and with a Mona Lisa-like smile, showed us it was OK to care about simple things and about difficult assignments. Mr. Adams loved literature and good writing, in a part of the world that, to outside observers at least, seemed to care only about sports. Dr. Iscoe was (he would tell us) an entertainer on that auditorium stage; but he was an entertainer so excited about the power of psychological knowledge that he convinced me of its value. As I think back on these four teachers, they taught these values by being such unashamed examples of them, but also by persuading. Students came to trust them as guideposts on our path to constructing our own identities—a journey for all the adolescents in their classes. Which brings me to my final lesson.

LESSON 4: INSPIRATION, IDENTITY AND A FUTURE

There is one final lesson. All these teachers inspired me to think outside the geographic, cultural, and psychological boundaries of that small place in Texas and the immediacy of "now." They were powerful models of what someone could be—of what I could be in a future I had not even considered, so they encouraged a future-time perspective that motivated my persistence over years (Kauffman & Husman, 2004). Each teacher helped me build a possible self, a narrative of my life that seemed attainable and worthwhile (Erikson, 2007; Leondari, Syngollitu, & Kiosseoglou, 1998). Each teacher seemed to invest in me—see something in me I didn't know was there. I can't imagine what led Miss Guthrie to see in a shy 4th grader the person who could play a young murderess on stage in front of hundreds of people—not a forgiving audience of parents watching the school talent show, but real theater patrons who had paid to attend. Mrs. Young convinced me that I was ready for college courses—she was right and that helped. I came to see myself as a writer because Mr. Adams saw that in me. Dr. Iscoe knew me only as a name on the roster, but he took the time to talk with me about graduate school and opened that door in my mind.

Figuring out who you are and what you can do is a daunting task for adolescents. It helps if they have teachers who see what they could be and inspire the vision.

REFERENCES

Csikszentmihalyi, M. (1990) *Flow, The psychology of optimal experience*. Harper Collins.
Csikszentmihalyi, M. (1997) *Finding flow*, Basic Books.
Erikson, M. G. (2007). The meaning of the future: Toward a more specific definition of possible selves. *Review of General Psychology, 11*, 348–358.
Kauffman, D. E., & Husman, J. (2004). Effects of time perspective on student motivation: Introduction to a special issue. *Educational Psychology Review, 16*, 1–7.
Leondari, A., Syngollitu, E., & Kiosseoglou, G. (1998). Academic achievement, motivation, and possible selves. *Journal of Adolescence, 21*, 219–222.

CHAPTER 19

YOU MUST BE ONE OF MINE

Gio Valiante
Rollins College

It is an understatement to say that my college career got off to a dispiriting beginning. It was the fall of 1991 and I had just arrived in Gainesville, Florida to begin my unlikely life as a college student at one of the nation's top public universities. I say my "unlikely" life as a college student because my academic pedigree was neither long nor distinguished. With a father who was never shy about his disdain for formal education (the shortcomings of which were a regular topic of dinner conversation) and who insisted that I let him pull some strings to get me a job in the fire department (where I would be assured a "pension and benefits"), it's safe to say that I viewed college more as a curiosity than as a commitment.

To give you an idea of how casually I had taken my acceptance into college, I drove the 1,093 miles from my New England town to Gainesville in a U-haul the day before classes were scheduled to begin. I didn't know a single person in the state of Florida, I had not arranged for a place to live, and I had not registered for classes. I simply showed up with no expectations, like an expatriate arriving in Tuscany on a one-way ticket, figuring to come home if and when the feeling was right.

My first day in Gainesville was a Sunday, and the reason I remember that was because the tow company who impounded my U-haul was closed

The Ones We Remember: Scholars Reflect on Teachers Who Made a Difference, pages 177–184
Copyright © 2008 by Information Age Publishing
All rights of reproduction in any form reserved.

until regular business hours on Monday. In fact, my first day in Gainesville consisted of a car wreck (hence the towing), a robbery (I should've known better than to leave the U-haul unlocked), and being disinivited to a fraternity party (whose members gave fliers both to the person behind me and in front of me in line at the Bookstore). The highlight from that first day finally came when a sophomore who was looking for a roommate befriended me. He was nice enough to drive me through campus, and then to the police station to fill out my accident report. In retrospect, I should have detected the ease with which he found Precinct 7. He had been there before. Two hours into our tenure together at an apartment complex named "La Mancha," he excitedly confessed that this would be his breakthrough year as the top distributor of hallucinogens on campus. Suffice it to say, I quickly repacked my things and moved back out, ultimately landing in an area of town known to this day as the "student ghetto."

Monday came quickly and everything in my gut was telling me to get the hell out of Gainesville as fast as I could. If Malcolm Gladwell had been twenty years sooner on his book *Blink*, and I was into trusting my "snap decisions," then I would have immediately repacked all my things and headed back north with my tail between my legs; the fastest college dropout in the history of my town. But I didn't trust my instincts, probably because I was either too exhausted to repack my things for a fourth time in three days or too poor to afford another U-haul. Truth be told, I don't really remember why I didn't leave. I just know that I didn't. What I did do was collect whatever school gear I had left from my car robbery and prepare for my first day of college. My father urged me to keep a twenty-dollar bill separate from my wallet in case of emergencies, so on this day I tucked it into my notebook and headed off to class.

When I arrived at Norman Hall, I was amazed at the sheer number of students trying to funnel their way into the building. "So this is what 43,000 students looks like," I remember thinking. Like a baby penguin hesitant to take its first plunge into Arctic waters, I was reluctant to join the mass of people squeezing into the doors, unsure what might be waiting on the other side. Even as a teenager, I had an especially active imagination. I watched for a few moments to figure out the rules of engagement and then holding my breath, I made the leap and found myself caught up in the herd of adolescent humanity that swept through the hallways. In the years since college, whenever I see pictures of the crowded streets of Hong Kong or Times Square on New Year's Eve I think back to that first day when I was packed like a sardine into the hallowed halls of learning.

I quickly fell in step with the crowd, which surged at certain points near the entrance to lecture halls, and jammed at the base of the stairwells that lead to the higher floors. I had made it up the stairs on my way to classroom 219, and just as I turned the corner heading for a vacant hallway a fellow flock member bumped into me sending my books and papers flying. Apparently the fear of being late for the first day of class trumped any empathetic desire to help because everyone kept right on walking past me. I instinctively knelt to the ground to begin picking up my things. From my vantage point at ground level I saw my twenty-dollar bill attach itself to someone's sneaker. Then as the person walked, the bill fluttered up and down, as if waving good-bye to me.

Suddenly through the maze of flip-flops and suntanned legs, I saw another person scrambling on the floor picking things up. When I stood up having a tenuous grasp on my ruffled pile of pens, books, and papers I'd picked up, I saw this stranger holding out my notebook. I thanked him as I began to readjust my things. Before he could move on, I managed to stutter something to the effect of, "I think I'm lost." I hesitated. "And I don't know how to get to my classroom."

He snatched my schedule from the top of discombobulated mess I had stacked in my arms and gave it a glance. He quickly looked up from the schedule.

"You must be one of mine," he said instantly, and then, as if sensing my hardship and hassle of the past forty eight hours, he gently put his arm on my shoulder and began to guide me down the hall, shielding me from the chaos and callousness of the hurried masses, right into the classroom where he himself was the professor.

You must be one of mine. Prophetic words.

There was no way to know it at the time, but that simple act of kindness that "*Dr. P*" demonstrated was not an isolated event, but rather represented a pattern of behavior that emerged from a way he had of embracing and engaging the world like no one I had ever met. The warmth he exhibited in the hallway that day played out in various ways time and again, not only through *what* he taught but also through *how* he taught. From that day forward, Dr. P became the primary reason I enjoyed college. His passion and enthusiasm for the material and for the students made it abundantly obvious, even to a kid for whom college was a hobby, that this was not his vocation but rather, was his calling. Every time I stepped into that class, it felt as if I was entering a magical realm. He made every idea, every concept, every assignment, and every activity come alive. He was funny, profound, compassionate, and enthusiastic. It wasn't long before students began to talk, and we all felt as if we were part of something special being in this class. The way he spoke about teaching and learning was like a rising tide, and it made us feel that once our time came, we could make a difference. We stayed after class and talked. We formed discussion groups and set study hours. As the semester wore on, more and more students would wait after class to meet with him. Soon the crowds began making their way into his office, where he would spend what seemed like hours meeting with students, discussing assignments, and listening to students share all their fears, hopes, and ambitions. On more than one occasion I saw students go into his office with the teary eyes that the pressures and uncertainty of college call forth on a regular basis, only to leave smiling. As a frequent visitor myself, I remember how it felt entering that office feeling defeated yet learning to feel invincible or, at least, hopeful. He had that way about him, and it wasn't long before students began actually showing up *early* for his class, which is something I hadn't seen before, and I haven't seen since.

One assignment that he gave stands out in my memory above the others. Dr. P had asked us to write about our experiences with school bullies. I had personal experience with bullies, as much of my senior year of high school was spent finding alternate routes to class in order to dodge our school bully, Dominic. To this day I am certain that Bill Watterson used Dominic as his model for Moe, the bully in his famed Calvin and Hobbes comic strip. I'll never forget what it felt like when Dr. P returned that particular paper with the following message: "This was so good that I read it twice. I dreaded coming to the end. Excellent work. You have a real talent. Now I will expect all you work to be of this quality."

One Saturday morning later in the term, I was writing a paper for my children's literature class taught by legendary author James Haskins, whose reputation as a writer was overshadowed at the University of Florida by his reputation as harsh, critical, and demanding task-master. I was petrified of Professor Haskins, so I went to ask Dr. P if he would have a "quick look" at my paper to let me know if he thought I was on the right track. Although he was in the office deeply immersed in a project of his own, he spent twenty minutes on the first sentence identifying strengths, weaknesses, and strategies for improvement. He then took me, over the course of several hours, sentence by sentence through the entire paper. He gave up his entire morning *teaching me.* I returned home energized and eager to exercise my newly acquired skills. While he effectively sabotaged my hopes of watching college football that day (Gainesville shuts down on game day to root for its storied Florida Gators) I can sincerely say that I learned more about writing that morning than I had in the previous nineteen years of my life, or in the fifteen years since.

It was through such episodes and dedicated acts of selfless teaching that Dr. P fertilized my love of learning and illuminated the path of scholarship. It wasn't long before the library replaced the stadium as my favorite place to spend autumnal, Saturday afternoons in Gainesville. I remember one particular Saturday when I was alone in the musty stacks, surrounded by books (Dewey, if memory serves me) when my concentration was snapped by a mighty roar from the adjacent football stadium. There was a major college football game going on a few hundred yards from where I was sitting, and it occurred to me that, for the first time in my life, I didn't want to be at it. I realized in that moment how happy I felt to be right where I was, away from the crowds, a neophyte scholar in training.

That semester passed quickly and I found that I liked college far more than I thought I would. Despite my father's opposition, I decided to stay on for the spring term. Of course, my first priority was to sign up for whatever Dr. P was teaching, which in this case was educational psychology. One day he asked me to stop by his office so after class I waited as he patiently sat with student after student. I purposely let other students go ahead of me so my time with him wouldn't be rushed. Before I could even sit down, he saw me.

"Ah Gio, it's you." his face lit up. His face always lit up; not just for me, but for every student he ran in to. He continued, "I have a gift for you." He then reached across his desk and picked up an old, hard covered book. It was a copy of Will Durant's *The Story of Philosophy*. On the inside cover he'd written: "*To Gio, whose intellectual curiosity inspired me to buy him this book. I think you are ready for Durant. Actually, you were born ready. – Dr. P*"

I took the book home and dove into it. It was my first philosophy book and I was so excited that a man who I adored thought enough of me to think I was ready for it. Although I didn't understand half of what I was reading, I kept at it, certain that if I just worked hard enough, the book would reveal the lessons that Dr. P promised were contained in its tattered pages. That book delivered, and so did Dr. P, so much so that I began to take courses in both philosophy and education. Not only did I survive in college, I flourished to the point where I stayed on for a second degree at the University of Florida.

Ironically enough, I am now a college professor myself. After college I went on to teach elementary school. Dr. P remained in contact through those years, encouraging me with emails, notes, reminders and the occasional phone call.

"Gio, are you keeping a journal of your first year? You should be. You'll regret it if you don't."

"I am, Dr. P, I am," I fibbed.

Truth be told, I did keep a journal for the first few days of my first year teaching, but I fell out of the habit under the avalanche of first year obligations. As usual, he was right. I do regret not keeping one, as I would love to go back and revisit those days, which, in retrospect, seem so long ago.

Other phone calls were pedagogical. "Gio, are you finding William James relevant?" he would inquire. "Reread *Talks to Teachers*. It's an invaluable resource, even now." And so I would read and reread James, sifting out lessons the same way I'd sifted them out from Will Durant's book, five years before. Even in a modern classroom, with modern problems, James gave great council. The talks between Dr. P and me were infrequent but always valuable. He was a former principal and headmaster, and so he would teach me how to look at a school from an administrator's perspective. He was also a professor deeply immersed in theoretical research, but he always admonished me to remain practical. "Stay relevant, Gio. Let your scholarship *inform* your teaching, not *overwhelm* it. Teaching is all about *judgment*, Gio. *Situated judgment.* You're doing great." Even now, a dozen years later, I still hear that voice encouraging and guiding me as I try to teach a new generation of teachers. Not a single day goes by that I don't integrate *some* lesson that I took from the years that I spent learning from the man whose first words to me were "you must be one of mine."

LESSONS

To fully understand the "magic" of Dr. P, one can begin by exploring William Purkey's Invitational Theory, which suggests that human potential rises and falls with the messages that individuals receive from others. The primary vehicle through which to summon individual's potential is inviting messages, which tell others that they are able, valuable, responsible, and welcome to participate in their own development. Disinviting messages, on the other hand, tell people that they are incapable, not worthy, and unwelcome to participate in their own development. In school settings, teachers send messages through their attending behaviors, verbal and non verbal communication, tone of voice, and the attitude with which they approach their teaching.

Dr. P was a model of invitational education. Through both word and deed, he convinced me that I was intelligent, capable, and able to craft my own education, a point he would reinforce with his common decree, "take ownership of your learning, Gio." His messages conveyed that he believed in me, even when I didn't believe in myself. He would always assure all of us that great things lay just around the corner, so long as we were willing to work hard.

By paying the same level of attention to his students that he did to everything else, Dr. P gave me so much. By balancing continual encouragement with ever increasing expectations, he did what in retrospect seems impossible: he taught me that it is possible to become more skeptical and more hopeful, more self-critical and self-satisfied, more sensitive and less vulnerable, more afraid and more courageous, wiser and kinder. All the while, he taught me that doing even the simplest things *well* was more difficult than I ever imagined, and that I could accomplish what had seemed to me impossible.

In his book *Shadow Line*, Joseph Conrad wrote, "It is the charm of universal experience from which one expects an uncommon or personal sensation—a bit of one's own." While most aspects of human experience easily falls into identifiable patterns, it is the individuality of experience—the wrinkles in the fabrics of our lives—that provide the richness and the qualia of being a unique individual. The uncommon sensation, the chance encounter, the "bit of one's own," that Conrad wrote about all represent the variability that is inherent in the human condition. That is how I view my relationship with Dr. P. Although I know he's affected thousands of students in his life, I own those moments that he spent one on one teaching *me*, and I'll have those moments forever.

While connections can be made to the ideas of both William Purkey and Joseph Conrad, perhaps the closest connections can be traced to the ideas of Albert Bandura. In his article entitled *The Psychology of Chance Encounters and Life Paths*, Bandura argued that, "chance encounters play a prominent role in shaping the course of human lives" (Bandura, 1982, p. 747). Bandura went on to detail several stories of individuals' lives that were powerfully influenced by chance encounters, including the story of how he met his own wife. While a graduate student, he was seeking relief from an uninspiring reading assignment. After a series of events too convoluted to detail, he ended up being paired with a total stranger who would eventually become his wife. I begin this section with a serendipitous theme because it is under just such fortuitous circumstances—a chance meeting in a hallway—that I met the teacher who would powerfully influence my own life path. According to Bandura, developmental theories have largely overlooked the importance of these types of chance meetings despite the fact that they exercise a powerful influence over life paths.

According to Bandura, it isn't the encounter, *per se* that determines the course of one's life as much as what one takes from the encounter. At the root of human agency, Bandura places our beliefs in our ability to secure desire outcomes. In other words, at the core of development lies self-efficacy. While the meeting was a chance encounter, the inviting messages that Dr. P delivered every day certainly fit into Bandura's contention that "nurture shapes nature." As self-efficacy researchers have observed, "one need not wholeheartedly buy into verbal. Sometimes it is enough to just hear the right messages, and let the fortuitousness of time do the rest." I don't know that Dr. P truly believed I was smart, or talented, or a gifted teacher. In looking back on that time in my life, I'm certain that I didn't believe it. But I heard it from him enough times so that, when I did get a good grade in another class, I thought, "maybe he is right. Maybe I am smart." I heard enough times that I was going to do special things as a teacher that once the principal gave me positive feedback, it felt reassuring. In other words, his inviting messages seemed to fertilize the psychological ground such that, once a good word or a success came my way, I got a lot of mileage out of the experience. Most importantly, it was in such subtle moments that I began to *believe*.

These chance encounters become life altering when they lead to what developmental psychologist Howard Gardner termed "crystallizing experiences"—those dramatic life events that galvanize disparate aspects of experience, and set individuals down the paths that invariably define their lives. In reflecting on the arbitrary nature of developmental paths that often lead to such decisive encounters, Italian author Italo Calvino observed that:

> Opportunities of this kind are not frequent, to be sure; but sooner or later they will have to arise: it is enough to wait for one of those lucky coincidences to occur when the world wants to look and be looked at in the same instant and Mr. Palomar happens to be going by. Or, rather, Mr. Palomar does not even have to wait, because these things happen only when you are not awaiting them.

Indeed, I was not waiting for Dr. P, but perhaps as Gardner and Calvino suggest, the inherent patterns of life insure that we all have our chances to resolve the conflicts of our lives. In the fullness of time, though, the best words to describe my experience with Dr. P haven't emerged from the annals of educational psychology but rather from the pages of my other passion, running. In *The Man Who Taught Me Everything* Boston Marathon winner Amby Burfoot wrote of his mentor John Kelly;

> If you are lucky in life, you might meet someone who changes everything forever. If you are very lucky, you might meet this person when you are young and lacking direction. If you are very, very, very lucky this person might remain an influence for decades to come—a touchstone you can revisit for counsel and wisdom. I was very, very lucky. But I sure didn't see it coming.

As I reflect on my life to date, there is no doubt but that our chance meeting in Norman Hall changed the direction and focus of my life in profound ways. That's the day that Dr. P became *my* John Kelly. That's the day that he became the man who taught me everything.

CHAPTER 20

TWO TEACHERS WHO WANTED STUDENTS TO THINK

William Crain
The City College of New York

In 1961 I began my freshman year at Harvard, and I was frightened. Coming from a public high school in Southern California, I was stepping into a much more competitive world. When I saw that I was the only freshman enrolled in a social science seminar, my first thought was to switch to another course. But the instructor, George W. Goethals, taught in a manner that made me put these thoughts aside. He started each class with a question that was difficult to answer. None of us ever came up with a good answer right away. But I found the questions intriguing, and I became so focused on them that I stopped worrying about my abilities.

Goethals didn't give any answers. If none of us could get the class started on his question, he just kept rephrasing the question. Often there were long silences, but he still wouldn't give an answer. He wanted us to think.

One day he asked why a man in an indigenous society, who was caught in an act of marital infidelity, committed suicide. None of us had a good explanation, but Goethals kept the question on the table for at least half an

The Ones We Remember: Scholars Reflect on Teachers Who Made a Difference, pages 185–188
Copyright © 2008 by Information Age Publishing

hour. Then students began changing the topic. When the class was about to end, I interrupted and asked about the man who committed suicide. On this occasion, Goethals did give us his explanation. I wasn't sure I agreed with his explanation, but to this day I remember what he said and the part I questioned. I remember this class so well is because he stimulated me to put so much thought into it.

On another occasion, a young woman in the class held forth, passionately giving her views on an assigned reading. I couldn't follow all her points, but I was overwhelmed by her eloquence. For the only time in this course I had a moment of serious self-doubt.

"She is brilliant," I thought to myself. "I'll never be able to talk like that."

Then Goethals responded. "I admire your eloquence, but as I listen with my scientific ear, I don't know. On at least two points, I'd like to hear the research evidence." She smiled and nodded: "You might be right."

As a naïve freshman, I was surprised. In high school, we were constantly told about the importance of increasing our vocabularies. Latin, it was said, would help. Vocabulary was central to the SAT, and more than this, it seemed obvious that people who spoke brilliantly were in fact brilliant. But in this class at Harvard, a teacher was looking past words.

Goethals, then, introduced me to a Socratic method of teaching that put a premium on getting students to think, and he opened up the possibility that the content of thinking may lie deeper than words. I had no other teacher who demonstrated these points more strongly than Goethals—until my first semester in graduate school. I enrolled at the University of Chicago and took a course with Lawrence Kohlberg.

On the surface, Kohlberg didn't appear to be a great teacher. He certainly wasn't eloquent; he didn't always complete his sentences and his words seemed to drift off into the air. He often would begin to write on the blackboard, but he would only write a dot before stepping away to say something new. Then he would turn back to the board, write another dot, and step away again. A student's notes based on what Kohlberg wrote on the blackboard would have consisted of little beside dots.

Kohlberg struck some students as "folksie." The male professors at the University of Chicago typically lectured in a sport coat and tie—and sometimes a suit; Kohlberg preferred casual dress—usually a plaid shirt, with a tie strung loosely around his neck. He complained about scholars who built developmental theories "without talking to children," and he himself sometimes talked more like a youngster than a professor. He once referred to Albert Bandura, who had criticized his work, as "Big, Bad Al Bandura."

Nevertheless, I found that once I became accustomed to Kohlberg's classroom style, he offered tremendous insight. The more I read about and struggled with a problem, the more his thoughts—however incompletely expressed—clarified my understanding.

To get to the heart of an issue, Kohlberg often drew upon scholars he called the "old psychologists"—people such as William James, John Dewey, and James Mark Baldwin. Kohlberg's work on moral development, which built on that of Piaget, was also informed by philosophers such as Immanuel Kant and John Rawls. In Kohlberg's class, I often felt like I had returned to the days when philosophy and psychology were still united.

But Kohlberg was hardly stuck in the past. He also had a strong grasp of modern research methods, including statistics. In one class, he talked a few minutes about the conceptual foundations of factor analysis. I knew little about this difficult subject, and try as I might, this time I couldn't follow him. After class, I said to a classmate, Douglas Kimmel, "Who in the world could make sense of that?" But Kimmel, who had been working to master factor analysis for his research, said, "Actually, that was by far the best account of factor analysis I've come across. He cleared up a lot of things for me."

There was a sense in which Kohlberg's classroom style was in keeping with his academic outlook. In particular, his informality corresponded to his mistrust of verbal sophistication. Although he possessed a deep grasp of highly abstract psychological theories, he was contemptuous of what he called verbal "gobbledy gook." He repeatedly asked his students to identify the most basic issues separating scholars, and he believed the issues could be phrased in simple English. For example, he emphasized that underneath all the abstract writing about Piaget's theory, a basic issue comes down to this: "Does the child think differently than the adult?"

Kohlberg sometimes lectured, but like Goethals, he preferred to ask questions. He once referred to his teaching as "my clumsy attempt at the Socratic method." Often he asked questions that pointed to the need to read critically. For example, he asked what two behaviorists, N. Azrin and O.H. Lindsley, had demonstrated in an article titled, "The Reinforcement of Cooperation between Children." Azrin and Lindsley had rewarded pairs of children whenever one put a stylus in a hole immediately after the other had done so. Most of us initially believed that the research demonstrated just what the title said, that cooperation could be reinforced. But Kohlberg's questions prompted us to consider whether the investigators had actually measured cooperation. He asked questions such as, "What did the authors conclude? Do you agree? What did they say they measured? Is this actually cooperation? What is it?" As in this case, Kohlberg consistently urged us to think more deeply about authors' statements.

CONCLUSION

In his own way, Kohlberg underscored two points I had learned from Goethals. The first point concerns words. Through his own classroom presentations, Kohlberg illustrated that verbal facility isn't everything, that a person's thinking may be much deeper than one would guess from his or her way with words. This doesn't mean that I took a lack of verbal clarity as a good model for teaching. But Kohlberg made me respect the possibility that a person is saying more than one might assume from his or her words alone. Moreover, Kohlberg helped me see how verbal sophistication can cloud issues. He pointed to the need to get to the crux of an issue by trying to express it in simple, ordinary language.

The second general point Kohlberg drove home to me was the value of the Socratic method. Kohlberg acknowledged that he wasn't particularly adept at this method, but he tried to ask questions that stimulated us to think. For Kohlberg, Socratic questioning was central to his Piagetian view of how the mind develops. Piaget argued that teachers cannot promote intellectual development through the transmission of information and ready-made ideas. Instead, teachers must stimulate students to engage in active thinking. Teachers must prompt students to question statements and assumptions and to figure things out for themselves. This is what Kohlberg, like Goethals, tried to get us to do.

SUGGESTIONS FOR FURTHER READING

Kohlberg, L., Kaufman, K., Scharf, P., & Hickey, J. (1975). The just community approach to correction: A theory. *Journal of Moral Education, 4*, 243–260. Kohlberg describes his view on how active thinking is stimulated.

Piaget, J. (1971). *Science of Education of Education and the Psychology* of the Child. D. Coltman, trans. New York: Viking Compass Book. Kohlberg was strongly influenced by Piaget's educational thoughts, as expressed in this work. See especially pages 150–180.

Crain, W. (2005). *Theories of Development: Concepts and Applications.* Englewood Cliffs, NJ: Prentice Hall. See especially pages 136–141 on the Piaget's theory of how thinking develops, and pages 159–160 and 169–172 on Kohlberg's similar views.

Azrin, N. H., & Lindsley, O.R. (1956). The reinforcement of cooperation between children. *Journal of Abnormal Psychology, 52* (12), 100–102. This is one of the studies Kohlberg asked students to more critically read, focusing on whether the investigators actually studied cooperation.

CHAPTER 21

STRANGERS, MENTORS, AND FREUD

Daniel K. Lapsley
University of Notre Dame

The teacher who makes a difference sometimes shows up in one's life in decisive but unexpected ways and at a time that could not be anticipated. Moreover, such a person may not even be a teacher in the professional sense of the term, and the influence that makes a difference may not be understood fully until years later.

This is a story about fortuitous influence. It is a story about the decisive role that individuals have played in altering the trajectory of my life, although I am hard-pressed to call some of them teachers, nor can I even remember the names of some of them. So much for making them eternal. This story also is contrarian to the main thematic intentions of this volume. In truth, I am hard-pressed to nominate a single teacher, not one that "made a difference" during my formative adolescence in the sense required of this volume.

I did, of course, have good teachers growing up in the Steel Valley of Pittsburgh. Mrs. Sexton, my sixth-grade teacher, spent a long day teaching us how to take notes in outline form to better prepare us for when we went to college and had to sit through the impenetrable lectures of fast-talking

The Ones We Remember: Scholars Reflect on Teachers Who Made a Difference, pages 189–194

professors—a skill that paid dividends, indeed, when I went off to college. My tenth-grade civics teacher, Tom Tyskiewicz, adroitly combined high expectations with easy familiarity. Earning his respect was important to me, and over the years we became close friends (although he has since left the teaching profession). I look back fondly and with gratitude to my undergraduate years at the Indiana University of Pennsylvania (IUP), where I received by B.A. degree in Psychology.

But my narrative locates the decisive influences elsewhere. Here's one example. Just before I made the transition to junior high school, my friends and I often played basketball at the outdoor courts of our elementary school. Afterwards, we would walk up to the nearby gas station to find water and to hang-out, sometimes for hours. One day there was a young man there waiting for his car to be serviced, and we struck up a conversation that soon turned to the events of the Vietnam War. We got into an argument. In retrospect, I was unusually knowledgeable about world events for my age. I read voraciously. I studied the newsmagazines. And I was a hawk on the war. I wonder if there is something about young adolescent boys that finds the trappings of military and presidential power irresistible. I supported President Johnson but cried when he decided not to seek re-election. I read Richard Nixon's *Six Crises* and judged him heroic.

And I defended the Vietnam War. I believed strongly in the "domino theory" of Communist conquest, stood up for our treaty obligations under SEATO, railed against the naked aggression of North Vietnam against a sovereign state. My interlocutor took the other side. He was a college student (but he seemed much older), and I wondered if he was a draft dodger. When his car was ready he said something to this effect: You are an extraordinarily bright lad. Have you thought about going to college? I should definitely go to college. He then asked me (for reasons unexplained) if I had read Dante's *The Divine Comedy* and how much I would enjoy it—but implying, too, that I was up to it. I was in sixth-grade.

I walked home as if striding mountains. Imagine this stranger urging me to go to college, wondering if I've read Dante's *The Divine Comedy*. I met my father when I got home and told him, somewhat joyously, what this man had said about me. He was nonplussed, but I don't remember being particularly disappointed by his flat reaction to my story. My father, after all, had stocked the house with subscriptions to newsmagazines and, at one point, to poetry and writer's periodicals. If my father sensed that I was college-bound it was all news to me. When I reflect on the course of events that have led to my present station in life, the encounter with the stranger at the gas station looms larger than any teacher, larger than anything that happened in any school. The stranger at the gas station planted an idea, raised a possibility that had not occurred to me. He gave me information about myself that was opaque to me. It made me feel special, talented. It was grist for the identity work that was now before my rising adolescence.

This clear, vivid memory I have never shaken. And I credit this encounter, this stranger, with setting me on the path that was unusual for kids in the steel town of my birth, the path "less traveled by" that led towards academic life, and (in the words of Robert Frost) *"that has made all the difference."*

I sometimes tell this story to undergraduate students in my classes on adolescent development to caution them in what they say to youngsters. Here was a random fortuitous encounter with a stranger that proved to have enormous consequences, in a way that could not have been anticipated, and from which I took strange gain away. But imagine the consequence if the stranger's reactions to my muscular defense of American foreign policy was not one of bemused admiration and encouragement but one of ridicule, sarcasm and belittlement; if my reaction to serious discussion was not exultant satisfaction but anger and humiliation. There are enough occasions for humiliation and discouragement in adolescence without adults piling on; and one can never really know the far-reaching consequence of simple encouragement; or of simply mirroring to the child his or her own sense of possibilities, even if fantastic. The dreams of adolescence should not have to bear too much realism.

One person, then, who made a difference in my life, was not a teacher at all but a stranger who passed the time in conversation with me while his car was being repaired. A second person was Sigmund Freud. This must sound peculiar, yet I don't know what would have become of me had I not encountered Freud's remarkable, terrifying theory. I was in the habit of checking books out of the school library that were quite advanced now that I fashioned myself quite the little intellectual. I did the best I could with these works on politics, poetry and philosophy, but the real effect was simply to show-off to my friends as I lugged them around.

But one day in junior high school I checked out from the library a short biography of Sigmund Freud. And my eyes could not believe the words I was reading. Infantile sexuality, penis envy, castration complex, defense mechanisms, libido, erotogenic zones, unconscious motivations, dream interpretation, incestuous desires, Oedipus complexes—oh my! So shocked was I that I wanted to validate what I was reading by pulling an encyclopedia off the shelf to read the entry on Freud. Sure enough, it was all there. I suppose it was like throwing a match into a gas can for a pubertal adolescent boy to read Freud's account of psychosexual development, but it was not just the shocking sexuality revealed in these pages that captured my interest: it was the fact that Freud, by means of psychoanalysis, appeared to have occult knowledge of the secret inner lives of individuals. And I wanted some of that!

After putting down Freud's biography there was nothing else that I wanted to do except study whatever it was Freud was doing. Of course, at that age, I knew nothing about the difference between psychoanalysis, psychiatry, and psychology. But the die was cast. For the remainder of my high school years I fashioned myself the resident expert on all things psychological. This amused my friends but it became a predominant pose that preoccupied my identity exploration, and when I went off to IUP there was no doubt that I would be studying psychology as a major. But I knew this back in eighth-grade.

The trajectory of my life, then, took two decisive turns, and both before I entered high school. The encounter with the college student at the gas station oriented me towards something other than entering the steel mills upon graduation from high school; the encounter with Freud gave sense and direction to a possible future self.

The third decisive turn does indeed involve a teacher (in a conventional sense) whose influence made a difference. I first met Robert Enright when he was a new visiting assistant professor at the University of New Orleans (UNO), and I was a new graduate student entering a terminal masters degree program in its Department of Psychology. How I ended up in New Orleans and what happened next is crucial to the lesson I want to draw.

I managed to graduate from IUP *cum laude*, and with my interests still rooted strongly in clinical psychology. Like most undergraduate psychology majors (to this day) I wanted to be a working clinician, and gave no thought at all about the professorate. In retrospect, my naiveté about postgraduate careers in psychology was boundless. My attempt to gain admission to graduate programs in clinical psychology was not going well (given a rather mediocre quantitative GRE score), and my advisor told me to apply to southern schools where the competition might not be as keen as the "prestigious northeastern schools." I took down the big APA book of graduate programs and found an entry for UNO that listed a degree program in *applied behavior analysis*. I did not know what this meant, but I saw the word "applied" and that seemed as close to clinical as I was going to get. So off I went to the Crescent City.

The program turned out to be a rigorous study of basic experimental and behavioral science (for which I was grateful). Some of my professors wore lab coats and ran rats through mazes. It occurred to me that I was being trained to impose reinforcement schedules on mentally disabled or mentally-ill patients in residential settings that manage patient behavior by means of "token economies"—and probably in some far off bayou community. The meaning of "applied behavior analysis" was now clear to me, and it was not quite the heroic career that I imagined for myself.

Bob Enright joined the faculty just as I entered the program. He seemed unimaginably young for a professor. He had just received his Ph.D. in human development from the University of Minnesota, and he signed on at UNO on a one-year visiting basis (this was not entirely clear to me at the time). Bob was personable and ambitious. I heard he was looking for graduate students to help him with his research, so I stopped by his small windowless office. It was a mess, papers everywhere, and mostly on the floor. As I waited for him to get off the phone, my attention drifted towards some reprints on the floor—and they had his name on them. This astonished me. Here I am sitting in the office of a published author! Seeing Bob's name in print on published papers galvanized a radical reappraisal of my aspirations and career. Whatever Bob was doing to get his name in print—I wanted some of that!

I did work with Bob on a number of his projects, publishing some of them with him. My very first publication was a small idea that I brought to him which paid off with good data and favorable reviews. One project required me to write an extensive literature review, which Bob highly praised. The first summer I took a night job in a private mental hospital so my days could be free to work on research with Bob, a commitment that endeared myself to him. Bob left UNO to take a position at the University of Wisconsin-Madison, and I followed him there after receiving my master's degree. The UW-Madison was never on my radar screen, and I would never have had the courage to apply there to such a prestigious research university were Bob not there. He became my mentor and friend. We collaborated on many papers. He is my "professional father" and nothing in my present academic life would have been possible had I not met Bob Enright.

There is a difference between being an advisor and a mentor; and, on the other side, between an advisee and a protégé. I think the main characteristic that makes for a mentor-protégé relationship is the shared sense of common purpose. We were working to advance each other's careers, certainly, but there was a personal element, too. I knew always that Bob would hear out my ideas, no matter how ill-formed, and he would yield when it was warranted (which was not often!). Add to common purpose, then, a sense of mutual respect when only my unilateral respect for him was required.

What lessons, then, do I draw from this narrative? I often think about the odds of meeting Bob in New Orleans. Here I was a new graduate student coming down from Pittsburgh meeting Bob at UNO as he took his first academic job after graduating with his doctorate from the University of Minnesota—two paths crossing in a place far from our homes. What are the chances that I meet a guy at a gas station whose good opinion of me opens up possibilities not envisioned? Or that I read a biography that sustains an avocation across adolescence? There is something fortuitous about each of these examples, but the lesson is not that random chance is the most important influences in one's life. Rather, the lesson is that one cannot see very far into the future. The trajectory of one's life is open to altered courses in ways that cannot be anticipated. And what seems like fortuitous interventions are possible only if one is in a position to capitalize on the seemingly lucky things that happen. It is often said that "Luck is the residue of design," which can only mean that cultivating one's talents in continuous learning is the only sure way to catch a break. Meeting Bob in New Orleans would not have paid off like it did unless I brought something to the table— an ability to write well and to work hard.

A second lesson is that at least some important elements of education during adolescence do not place in schools, are part of no formal curriculum and are not the object of instruction. The fabric of adolescence is richly appointed with occasions for teaching-and-learning, and researchers are paying increasing attention to those that take place in contexts other than the formalities of classrooms. We should be careful what we say to adolescents because we are all potential teachers of life-altering lessons.

My final thought concerns what is owed to mentorship. Shared purpose, personal investment, mutual respect, these were some of the qualities that described my relationship with Bob Enright, my mentor. I owe Bob simply everything, but this is the sort of debt that cannot be repaid easily. It is rather like what Origen said of the debt of love: "The debt of love abides for us and never ceases; for it is good for us both to pay it everyday and yet always to owe it." The debt that I owe my mentor is best paid in those occasions when I can be a mentor for others.

And what of the debt owed to the other two decisive influences on my life? My debt to Sigmund Freud was paid (I like to think) when I wrote an entry on Freud for the Encyclopedia of Human Behavior. As for my interlocutor at the gas station many years ago—one of these days I will get around to reading *The Divine Comedy*.

SUGGESTED READING

Bandura, A. (1982). The psychology of chance encounters and life paths. *American Psychologist, 37,* 747–755.

CHAPTER 22

A CULTURE AND ITS REPRESENTATIVES

David C. Berliner
Arizona State University

Vygotsky got it right. Everything intra-psychic is some transformation and representation of what was learned from participation in the social systems of which we are a part. I started at the Stanford University School of Education in Summer of 1964 and, unaware and unprepared, I found myself in an environment that exerted a powerful socializing effect on me. It didn't affect everyone the same way, but at Stanford I entered a culture I had not encountered before, nor had I even imagined its existence, and it changed me. The mentoring and friendship I received from natives of that culture, particularly by two of its most distinguished faculty, taught me what it meant to be an academic. Though they were nothing but encouraging throughout my surprisingly successful career, I continually feel I cannot live up to the standards set by them and the culture that they represented.

One learns to pass as a native quickly in a foreign culture, or perish. I arrived at Stanford with a wife and two children, and enough funds for about 4 weeks. I was nervous about my ability to compete as an educational psychologist, barely knowing what that field was and what it is that one did as an educational psychologist. At that time Stanford was arguably number

The Ones We Remember: Scholars Reflect on Teachers Who Made a Difference, pages 195–203
Copyright © 2008 by Information Age Publishing

one in psychology and in education, and that contributed to my feelings of inadequacy. The money problems subsided when I quickly landed a research assistants' job with the National Longitudinal Study of Mathematics Ability (NLSMA). That was part of the "New Math" curriculum reform led by Edward Beagle, and it employed such notable future scholars of mathematics education as Jeremy Kilpatrick, Thomas Romberg, and James Wilson. They were talented enough to scare me even more during those first weeks at Stanford. My boss on the project eventually became my closest friend, the remarkable Leonard Cahen, who seemed to intuitively grasp research and evaluation in ways I have never be able to match. He too initially added to my anxiety. But my first Stanford course moved me from merely anxious to completely terrified! That was a course on Social Foundations of Education with then dean I. James Quillan. We had a paper due early in the course, about the third week, and another due at the end of the course, the twelfth week. The teaching assistant for the course was the now distinguished policy analyst James Guthrie, who served most of his career at UC Berkeley and is now a professor at Vanderbilt University. I was called to the deans' office after my first paper because the assistant and the dean needed to inform me that my writing was unacceptable. In their judgment my paper was awful. They informed me that my work was not up to the standards they expected of a Stanford Ph. D. My worst fears were realized when the dean informed me I was in danger of flunking out of Stanford.

Nine weeks later I was again called to the deans' office, sure that my nascent career had ended. Instead the dean told me that my second paper was excellent, both well-written and creative, and if I'd like to get it published he could help me do that. Moreover, if I wanted to work with him on that topic he thought we might be able to co-author work in that area. Terror certainly motivates student learning, though it probably is not to be recommended for every student. But terror did help me go from a potential failure to a successful student in 9 weeks.

I learned quickly that I was in a culture that depended on the written word and thus I had to get used to communicating my thoughts in ways that the culture valued. I never became a terrific writer, but I have won some writing awards of which I am proud. I thank Stanford's culture in general, and Dean Quillan in particular, for scaring me into learning how to write passably. What Stanford taught me is not at all mysterious. Revise everything you write a few times, and then, when you think it ready, have an editor go over it (your spouse if you have a strong marriage!) in order to point out all the additional places where you were a long way from perfect in your thinking and mechanics.

Once I thought I could survive, and had this belief validated by the faculty, Stanford became an intellectual feast. Lee J. Cronbach and N. L. Gage were the newest educational psychologists in the program, but we studied psychology also with Richard Atkinson, Albert Bandura, William Estes, Jack Hilgard, Quinn McNemar, and Patrick Suppes, to name a few of the better known of the psychology faculty. Individually and collectively the Stanford psychologists and educators had an impact not just on the knowledge acquired from their teaching, but much more importantly, I think, they communicated the habits of mind to help me understand my discipline in ways that were both subtle and powerful. In abundance at that time, and in that place, were first-rate thinkers in psychology and education. From such distinguished faculty students learn many things that never make it into the textbooks. It's the stuff not easily written about; the tacit knowledge that makes one a professional within a discipline. The amount of this tacit knowledge distinguishes experts from novices, and the most articulate of these experts can help make the tacit explicit. In the Stanford environment I had experiences with experts like that.

The best teachers help you to learn their habits of mind. You learn how to frame problems, such as the problems inherent in studying teaching. You learn their views on the nature of science in the social sciences. Through them you discover the weakness of science and the power of politics to affect evaluation. Or you might learn the reasons that criticism is so important in the sciences. You learn to do research, of course, as in most educational psychology doctoral programs, but at Stanford I learned also the etiquette and ethics for the conduct of research, and its reporting. I was asked to craft research reports in my first year; I designed experiments, ran subjects, and wrote reports on micro-teaching in my second year, resulting in an AERA paper that year; I wrote ancillary materials for Fredrick McDonalds' well respected educational psychology text; and I worked as an assistant on one of the first reports of the National Academy of Education. Each of these apprenticeships was a setting for learning about a scholars' life. Each job provided the chance to acquire the tacit knowledge and normative behavior that must necessarily guide research. Stanford provided a powerful culture that I wanted to identify with, and so I allowed it to exert a good deal of influence on my life. But two of that culture's representatives, Lee J. Cronbach and Nathaniel L. Gage, were particularly influential in shaping my professional life.

An incident with Cronbach exemplifies the man and his dedication to teaching and his students. In a course on human abilities he was explaining the variance-covariance matrix and that prompted me to ask a question. I said " Dr. Cronbach, I see correlation, I have a scatterplot in mind when I think about that concept. And I can see variance. I can visualize how the deviations from the mean form and grow. Is there a way you can show covariance visually?"

Cronbach stared at me in silence before the class. He stared and stared, and as time went on I broke into a sweat. He continued to stare and stay silent still longer, and by this time the whole class was in a sweat! Many of us thought, I learned later, that he had a seizure. None of us knew what was going on or quite what to do as we all sat, distressed and silent. Finally, after what seemed an eternity to us all, he said. "No" and continued on just as if nothing had happened. We all let out a collective sigh of relief. But that is not the end of the story.

A few months after this incident I was passing his office in Cubberly Hall, at Stanford, and said "hi." He said "David, come in here. Sit down." He then went to his black board and began sketching things out on the board and uttering what I first believed to be incantations and chants. I never did understand fully what he was saying to me. But when he was done, he looked at me like a little kid, all pleased with himself, and I realized that he had just informed me that what he had drawn was a picture of covariance. I had trouble remembering that I had even asked that question, but he had spent the ensuing three months worrying about it.

I cannot draw it for anyone, as I didn't take notes. I am afraid that like Fermat's theorem, this visual representation will remain lost because I was too startled and too unprepared to remember it. But what I do remember is that this incident defined, in part, what it means to be a great teacher. You must take your students seriously. And if you don't know the answers to their questions you have to go get them. Although not all of my cohort felt as I did, I found that this respect for students permeated the Stanford culture. Another example that makes this point clear comes from an encounter with Quinn McNemar. McNemar was a great statistician of an earlier era, a former president of the APA. On a day I remember well I had just completed my final examination in his statistics course. I was satisfied enough with my performance that I turned it in, even though I knew I had some problems with certain items. I went out to the hall to wait for my friends to finish. Many of them were sweating over the test, competing for the highest grade, but I had done the best I could and so I simply relaxed. As I sat waiting and watching the stressed students still in the class, Professor McNemar came over to me and asked me what I thought of the test. I told him that I thought the test was fair, and that I thought I did alright on it, but "I simply could not answer the Chi-Square problem at all." I told him that I had tried and tried, but I just couldn't come up with any way for solving it so I finally left it blank. He chuckled and said yes, that was a tough one all right, he had been working on it for a few years and he couldn't solve it either!

As I thought of my own struggle a few minutes earlier, and looked at my sweating colleagues, I thought Quinn McNemar the cruelest person in the world. But when I questioned him he explained himself. He said he put that item on the test because he thought that under the pressure of the test some smart student might crack the paradox that the problem presented. It turned out that it was not cruelty that motivated him at all. Instead, he put this apparently intractable problem on the test out of his genuine respect for the intellects of his students. I do not recommend this technique to anyone reading these memories of my graduate school experience. But, it is illustrative of what I found. With few exceptions, I found that Stanford professors, certainly among the busiest psychologists and educators in the world, genuinely respected their students' intellects, questions, and contributions to research.

LEE J. CRONBACH AND N. L. GAGE: EXTRAORDINARY ROLE MODELS

Cronbach and Gage had worked together at the University of Illinois, and came to Stanford at about the same time. They eventually logged over 50 years of work on the same faculties, and early in their careers they did some joint research. As Cronbach's biography notes, he and Gage eventually decided to split the world—he would do psychometrics and Gage would do research on teaching. I had the honor (and difficulty) of working as Cronbach's research assistant for one year of my graduate training. My job was officially 20 hours a week but I had to work 40 hours to keep up with what I was given to do, and also so as not to look too ignorant in Cronbach's eyes. Every time we did something and I thought it was great, Lee tore it up and revised it again. He respected my opinions which made me feel wonderful. But it was he who had the high standards and creativity to always say about both my work and his own, "lets try this instead." Revision was a constant, and so his writing was always remarkably lucid. He sent me to libraries, to do interviews, to follow him around at meetings, all while he and Patrick Suppes worked on the book *Research for Tomorrow's Schools.* This was the first book put out by the National Academy of Education, on whose board of directors I now proudly serve. Cronbach had me do meticulous referencing and quote checking, modeling perfectly the scientists obligations to be clear in thought, parsimonious in writing, and meticulous in referencing. Standards few of our colleagues and I reach as frequently as did Cronbach.

Cronbach was one of the Terman gifted, with a childhood IQ that was off-the-charts. It was clear to me in working with him that there was absolutely no diminution of that IQ in his adult days. Every one who knew him appreciated that his mind was both quick and quirky. Being around him was being in a room charged with intellectual energy focused on solving educational problems and communicating well-warranted ideas.

Although he was perceived by many to be "cold," and occasionally was rude to faculty and students, there was a human side to Cronbach, as well. He found time to visit me when I had a hospital emergency—the only faculty member to do so—and always treated me in an avuncular way. He also treated warmly a young colleague whom he admired greatly, Richard E. Snow, who became my dear friend during this time period. Snow was a master at "psychologizing," that is, thinking through the *psychological* meaning of aptitude and instructional environments as we all tried to design aptitude-treatment-interaction (ATI) studies. Dick Snow was also a part of this powerful environment, a *learning community* in today's parlance, and he was also one of the warmest and wisest psychologists I ever met. The modeling by Cronbach and Snow in particular, shaped the kinds of educational psychologists that came through Stanford's program at that time. I feel lucky to have been there at that time.

I knew N. L. Gage slightly while at Stanford. I had a course with him and worked on projects related to those he worked on in the Stanford Center for the Study of Teaching. But I was not close to him. On graduation I left Stanford to work for Dwight Allen, a Stanford professor that had just become dean of education at the University of Massachusetts. Dwight was a prolific generator of ideas and an exciting person to be around, still exercising a fertile mind as a distinguished professor at Old Dominion University in Virginia. But the match of my family with New England, in the tumultuous years of the late 60s, didn't work out well. I began to negotiate for a job back in the San Francisco Bay area, and as I was doing so Nate Gage, on Dick Snow's recommendation, asked me to co-author an educational psychology text. The Stanford culture of which I was a part provided me this wonderful opportunity to work with one of the finest scholars in the social sciences. His is a lasting influence on me, for as I write this review of individuals that shaped my life, N. L. Gage is just over 90 years of age and still working on his magnum opus, a book on a theory of teaching. On most mornings he is in his office at 10am, and he leaves at four. The scholar in winter, for sure, but a scholar still in fine form.

Gage influenced me more than any other scholar since we were writing together frequently for 25 years. An example of the man and his values are found in the following story. In the early 1990s I had been a respondent at an APA convention where all the other panelists criticized the schools. I had been doing a great deal of research in schools and classrooms around that time and shared my observations with the panelists and the audience. I said that America's students were actually doing fine, that our teachers were remarkably able and humane, and that the book "A nation at risk," published a few years earlier, was bull! Nate Gage was in the audience that day and immediately after the session came up to me and asked if I had the data to back up what I said. I replied that the data were all around if any one wanted to look for it, but it seemed that people would rather just spout off and blame the schools, instead. Gage looked me squarely in the eye and said, with a touch of sadness about my errant behavior, "David, you need data if you are going to say things like that." N. L. Gage did not want to hear arguments ex cathedra, or anecdotes from a frequent visitor to the schools. Gage is a data man!

I thought a lot about his comment over the next few days, and decided to do what he wanted. So I went out to look for the data. This resulted in a speech I gave a few months later that changed my life. I challenged the lies and distortions that had been told by Reagan era media darlings such as William Bennett, and I tore into the distortions about the productivity of the schools put out by the business community, all dutifully reported by an ignorant media. My wife, on whom I inflicted the paper the day before I was to give it, predicted that this speech would result in a change in my career. I delivered the talk and received a wild, standing ovation from a group of educators, and as predicted by my wife, my career changed. I drifted away from traditional educational psychology into policy work, particularly after writing the best selling book "the manufactured crisis" with the morally outraged, indefatigable and impeccable scholar Bruce Biddle as my coauthor. But it was N. L. Gage, as my friend and colleague, and as a representative of that Stanford culture, who pushed me to "get the data."

I had started working with Gage some 20 years before the incident I just recounted. During the first 5 years of that relationship, from 1970–1975, we met virtually every Friday and Saturday. They were great years as we crafted our educational psychology text and talked of many things personal and private, as well as those of a professional nature. A hundred little things Gage things did as a scholar shaped me. For example, early in our writing relationship Nate bet me a nickel that a long quote I had for our book was wrong. I took that bet, sure that I would win. But, after checking the quote I paid up my nickel. Most long quotes are copied wrong, although it may only be a comma left out or a comma inserted where it didn't belong, or it might be a phrase or sentence garbled just a bit. But the chances for getting quotes wrong were high! Gage never got them wrong and he taught me to watch out for this common error.

He has a remarkable memory for dates and events, and could tell me in exquisite detail the day he met his beloved Maggie, as well as every detail about the people and the events at the meeting that launched the first *Handbook of Research on Teaching*. That was no mere publication, but an intellectual event that launched that very active field of research on teaching within educational psychology. His handbook was not just beautifully edited mechanically because Gage is one of the clearest and parsimonious writers in our field, but it is also brilliantly edited social science reviews. Nate's ability to conceptualize the structure of our field, and to articulate what it needed in order to be both scientifically credible and useful were on display in that first handbook, and always on display for me, as we worked together. His social science knowledge, methodological sophistication, and his encyclopedic knowledge of all the details of all the important studies in research on teaching pushed the idea that it was possible to obtain warranted assertability in the area of research on teaching. His faith that we could create a scientific basis for the art of teaching drove a whole generation of scholars, including me, to attempt that in a field that barely existed until the Gage *Handbook* came out. N. L. Gage's influence is on an entire field of study and along the way, on a host of educational psychologists who trained at Stanford and began their distinguished careers under his influence.

CONCLUSION

I was blessed by the chance discovery of a great institutional home for learning how to be a member of a profession I have loved. My experience at Stanford taught me a lesson that relates to training teachers, or to physicians and those in the hospitality industry, as well. What I learned was that individual teachers matter, but so does the culture of the institute doing the training. Powerful learning environments, now so often studied by our European colleagues, are cultural, not individual, creations. In powerful learning environments there is consistency in the messages sent by the instructors who are representatives of the culture. The subtle messages communicated about what is acceptable behavior, what constitutes excellence, how criticism is framed, how to do a review, and so forth, constitute the hidden curriculum of the training institute, and it is as powerful as the more formal curricula to which students are exposed. Though I am not sure how one goes about it, I believe that each of us in a school of education or department of psychology should attend as much to culture building across divisions and departments, as we do to our own courses and syllabus design.

Two of the most famous representatives of the Stanford culture gave me encouragement and shaped my values. Not a day goes by but that I am grateful to N. L. Gage for his unwavering belief that reliable knowledge can be obtained through research on teaching, and that such hard won knowledge can be communicated in such a way as to be useful to teachers. His faith influenced my career. Somewhere along way, however, Cronbach lost that faith. Cronbach argued that social science findings are quite limited. He asserted that the real world is one with myriad interactions, thus limiting the ecological and population generalizability of all but the simplest psychological and educational knowledge.

From both of them I received well-reasoned arguments about why I should have faith in psychological and educational research, and also why I should not. I honor them both by alternating between doing research of the type that Gage would admire (I hope), and doing policy and political work, which Cronbach saw as the more likely way to change the educational system. Gage sits on one shoulder, Cronbach on the other, but both admonish me to be the clearest thinker and most lucid writer I can be.

CHAPTER 23

HOW TO BECOME THE TEACHER WHO MAKES THE DIFFERENCE

An Anti-Romantic Theory of Pedagogy— Principles, Not Personalities

Marshall Gregory
Butler University

MUST A TEACHER BE CHARISMATIC AND SEXY IN ORDER TO BE THE ONE WHO MAKES A DIFFERENCE?

Like Duke Orsino in Shakespeare's *Twelfth Night*, American culture is in love with love. That is, Americans are generally in love with feelings, and frequently give feelings an automatic credibility, especially if they are intense, merely because they exist. Like the feel of sex and the taste of food, intense emotions are compelling to experience or observe, and many Americans respond as if emotions possess a default legitimacy on the grounds of intensity alone. Our culture endlessly extols the virtues of "listening to your heart," "letting go," "not living in your head," "being swept away by love,"

The Ones We Remember: Scholars Reflect on Teachers Who Made a Difference, pages 205–226
Copyright © 2008 by Information Age Publishing

"being lifted up by passion," and so on. In thousands of narratives from soap operas to romance novels to the persistent message in Star Wars that warriors and lovers should connect with "The Force" using instinct rather than reason, our culture reinforces the notion that the heart, not the head, is not only the real authority in human affairs, but also the ultimate justification for our actions. One of our culture's most common clichés about romance is, "you can't choose who you love." Translation: love is all about feelings. Thought, judgment, and reason play no role in love. We don't choose. Love chooses, and sweeps us up in rhapsodic flight (until, not uncommonly, rhapsodic love loses its lift and drops us from 300 feet above the cement).

Moreover, our culture combines its prejudice in favor of rhapsodic emotions with its endless appetite for celebrity worship in a way that turns celebrity watching into a kind of pop art form for the ceaseless expression of our passion for passion. *Entertainment Weekly* is available in a print format once a week, in a TV format nightly, and on the web constantly, not to mention an endless stream of stories about celebrity high jinks that come from the mainstream media. It is a disquieting thought but an obvious truth that there are millions of people in America who really *care* about whether or not Angelina Jolie and Brad Pitt, Tom Cruise and Katie Holmes, Jennifer Aniston and Vince Vaughn, and hundreds of other well-known celebrity couples are having affairs, getting married, getting divorced, getting fat, getting thin, getting drunk, getting sober, getting religion, looking bad, looking good, having liposuction, having babies, getting rich, getting bored, getting it on, or just getting along.

What does this cultural wallowing in passion for passion's sake combined with celebrity worship have to do with teaching? Unfortunately, it has a lot to do with teaching, not because these cultural obsessions form an explicit ideology about teaching, but because they form a kind of cultural atmosphere that makes teachers feel as if charismatic performance is obligatory. This atmosphere soaks itself like a dye into every expectation that students have about their teachers and classes. It would be better, actually, if the American love of passion for its own sake and its love of celebrity worship for the sake of titillation *did* yield an explicit ideology of teaching, because an ideology would be easier to resist than a general cultural atmosphere that carries immense force because it seems to exist everywhere in general, yet is profoundly difficult to corner or attack because it also seems to exist nowhere in particular.

One pernicious effect of this general cultural atmosphere is that, in America, both teachers and students enter their classrooms mostly unaware of how intensely the atmosphere of contemporary culture leads them to expect that good teaching and effective learning will depend on teacherly charisma and pedagogical sexiness—by which I mean the teacher's ability to make class seem as exciting as a TV game show, and to give it a slight smattering of glamour to boot—or at the very least that success will depend on the teacher and the student feeling that they have compatible personalities. Often, a teacher and a student who grate on each other will readily and easily accept a diagnosis of "personality incompatibility" as a terminal judgment about why they do not need to listen seriously to each other. Students and teachers alike hope to wind up *loving* each other, not often sexually, of course, but in the passionately emotive way so frequently represented in such movies as *Children of a Lesser God, Dead Poets Society, Renaissance Man, Dangerous Minds*, and *Freedom Writers*. In consequence, expectations about intimacy of emotional compatibility, teacherly charisma, and pedagogical sexiness *matter* both to students and teachers more than it needs to and much more than it should. The conflation of good teaching and teacherly charisma is so deeply entrenched in the psychology of American schooling that neither students nor teachers (who may have fleeting intuitions about the poverty of such expectations) will find few cultural resources to help them think their way around them. Thus they are often trapped by bogus expectations, and both groups wind up feeling disappointed and frustrated with their classroom experience on the grounds of personal incompatibilities that, in fact, are not of central importance to either good teaching *or* effective learning.

In what follows, I intend to argue that not only do teachers *not* have to rely on teacherly charisma and pedagogical sexiness to be good teachers, but that they also do not have to rely for their teaching—as they are so often left to do by graduate schools that mostly gloss over teaching—on trial-and-error, good will, and intuitions alone. Trial-and-error, good will, and intuitions are neither valueless nor irrelevant to good teaching, but in this country the typical system of graduate education and the typical modes of professional socialization for new college teachers leave teachers who want to be good teachers thinking that trial-and-error, good will, and intuitions are the *only* tools available to them. In the pedagogy seminars for college teachers that I began conducting as long ago as the mid-eighties, I have seen over and over again how surprised—and relieved—college teachers are to discover that this is not the case. The idea that teaching can be thought about systematically *apart* from personalities and charisma is a notion that many college teachers, already committed to the value of systematic thinking within their disciplines but who did not know that it was a possibility in their teaching, heartily welcome.

There are more than personalities in the classroom. There is also more in the classroom than content information, explanations, tests, and discussions. There are *principles* of teaching that those who hope someday to become the teachers who make the difference can appeal to both for general orientation and even, sometimes, for specific guidance. In this essay I will be laying out a taxonomy of what I take to be the most salient and useful pedagogical principles, in the hope that what I say may help both experienced and inexperienced teachers alike liberate themselves from the bogus expectations forced on them and their students by a society in love with passion, charisma, and teacherly sexiness. My aims here do not qualify me as the heroic specialist who flies in from the coast and saves you from a pedagogical heart attack with dramatic surgery worthy of a TV drama— "Just think, Louise: he's the only pedagogical doctor in the *world* who knows how to perform the over-and-under-in-and-out-behind-the-back-glandular-splenetic-visceral-stint-and-general-all-purpose-*brain*-transplant"—but I have learned to think about teaching issues the hard way and in the company of many thoughtful colleagues and friends who have helped me shape and condition my own views. Writing essays such as this is one way of paying my debt to all of those persons whose thinking has enriched my own. Just as all medicines these days are accompanied by caveats and warnings, the principles I discuss below demand a few caveats of their own.

CAVEATS

Caveat #1: Results Not Guaranteed

There are no sure-fire nostrums, boluses, or homeopathic pills that guarantee teaching success. "Teaching," as Bartlett Giamatti has said, "is an instinctual art, mindful of potential, craving of realizations." The principles that I offer here are not about guaranteed results, but about nuanced ways of thinking. They are particularly about ways that teachers might learn to navigate themselves through and around their own prejudices and blind spots, most of which they do not fall into out of carelessness or indifference, but which they inherit from an educational system in America that nearly always leaves students in the dark about its underlying educational aims—other than strict, instrumental aims such as "getting a job"—and from short-sighted programs of graduate education. When bright students are left mostly in the dark about the underlying aims behind their own education, it is easy for them to turn into bright teachers who love their disciplines but who don't know any more about explaining to students what's *educational* about those disciplines than their own teachers did. The wall of opacity between students and teachers about meta-educational aims—the reasons that teachers *might* be able to offer but mostly *don't* offer for why studying the poems of John Donne or the biology of cell division might be *educational*, not just useful for passing tests—is one of the great reasons behind "results not guaranteed."

Caveat #2: "Readiness is all"

Right before Hamlet leaves his apartment to face the duel with Laertes that leads to the climactic events at the end of Shakespeare's great tragedy, he compresses a vast deal of human wisdom into four short sentences—"If it be now, 'tis not to come. If it be not to come, it will be now. If it be not now, yet it will come. The readiness is all." (*Hamlet* 5.2). In these sentences, Hamlet is resisting Horatio's urgent advice to play things safely by reminding Horatio that one can never play safely enough to guarantee results, that one can never count on winning, and, by implication, that sometimes even the best people do not get what they want or deserve. In the face of ineradicable existential chanciness, Hamlet concludes that human beings should approach life not looking for success but preparing themselves to deal with whatever comes, whether it is success or setbacks. "The readiness is all," says Hamlet.

I have never heard Hamlet extolled as an educational philosopher (although there could well be a dusty doctoral dissertation lying inert in some research university's library on just this topic; if there is, neither your nor I should disturb its repose), but, truth be told, the perspective that Hamlet articulates to Horatio articulates a good pedagogical caveat for teachers to be aware of: be prepared, but don't count on steady success. On any given classroom day or in relation to any individual student, teacherly success can be forestalled and undercut by a hundred variables beyond the teacher's control. Life happens to both teachers and students, and what happens in life—everything from roommate troubles to abortions to family deaths to hangovers to the flu to sleepless nights to general grumpiness, and a zillion other ailments to which flesh is heir—cannot always be kept out of the classroom. Moreover, any given student in any given semester may not be ready for what the teacher has to offer, no matter how much the student may need it and no matter how much the teacher may want to give it. Sometimes what happens in the classroom is the tiniest speck on a particular student's radar screen of life, and, when this is the case, hardly any degree of teacherly enthusiasm and good will be sufficient to bring the classroom content into focus for the distracted or distraught student. All that good teachers can do is be *ready*: ready to see, quick to notice, swift to respond. Sometimes they get the chance, sometimes not.

Caveat #3: No Instant Results

Students are developing organisms, not computers that can be programmed or machines that can be predicted. What students "get" one day they may seem to "lose" the very next day. More often than not, the acquisition of developmental skills presents itself as a herky-jerky, three-steps-forward-and-two-steps-back kind of movement. The teacher who expects a steady forty-five degree angle of student ascent toward intellectual and ethical maturity is not remembering his or her own period of stumbling, bumbling, and confusion. *Patience* will generally lead to less wear and skidding on both teachers' and students' mental tires than urgent speeding and desperate braking. A growing organism tends to grow according to an internal clock that the teacher needs to respect, and teachers need to remember that they are more like gardeners than clock makers.

WHY IS BEING A GOOD TEACHER SO HARD?

Caveats aside, it may seem unfair that in light of the low pay and long hours, being a good teacher is at least as difficult as being a rocket scientist or a brain surgeon. Unfair or not, however, "it is," to quote my students, "what it is." (This zippy nugget of wisdom is a recent addition to undergraduate small-talk that I find persistently amusing, especially since it is usually uttered in the tone of one who has just untangled a major conundrum of life.) Anyone who wishes to become the teacher who makes the difference must begin by recognizing that good teaching is much harder than good scholarship (because it requires good scholarship, and much more). This is another front on which the default legitimacy that our culture bestows on charisma and passion is misleading. Many people tend automatically to assume that personally charismatic, pedagogically sexy, and emotively passionate teachers must be good teachers, but the truth is that charisma, sexiness, and passion in teaching, just as in politics, can blind the audience—or a room full of students—to a multitude of sins. Teachers who know how to turn on the charm are not thereby bad teachers, but neither are they thereby good teachers. Every teacher who has charm should use it, but only as a tool that s/he has under full control, not as a substitute for hard thinking about pedagogical principles. The teacher who wishes to make the difference soon learns by experience that good teaching is often rewarding and joyful, but seldom easy. Why is this so?

Resistance from Popular Culture

Teaching is hard, in the first place, because the skills that most teachers work hard to help their students learn generally cut across the grain of popular culture that has swaddled our students in its embrace since their birth. On the intellectual front, teachers help students develop skills of critical thinking, historical and political analysis, close observation and close reading, computation and calculation, effective use of evidence, logical argumentation, and skepticism about common sense versions of complicated issues. On the personal front, teachers help students develop the ethical skills of empathy, honesty, fairness, kindness, self-control, and compassion. The trouble that teachers constantly run into is that what they do on both of these fronts almost always positions them as challengers of the commonplace truths that students have heard all of their lives. In the Western world generally, and especially in America, market values, spin politics, and the mindset of advertising manipulations now saturate society so deeply that when teachers help students develop the kinds of intellectual and ethical skills I have just described, one common consequence is that teachers and their strange skills of analysis and skepticism get put on the defensive, while students scramble to retain their grip on the familiar notions that they never before knew were vulnerable to challenge. Skepticism about common sense? "*Why*, for pete's sake? Common sense is my best friend." Kindness and compassion as everyday principles of conduct? "Only in Christmas movies and Thanksgiving Day turkey dinner lines at homeless shelters. Everyday life is too hard and too harsh." To many students, a binding, *practical* commitment to ethical virtues will seem too demanding, except, of course, as a distant ideal possessing neither authority nor bite. How can teaching *not* be hard when it challenges students to reconsider every verity that they thought was founded on bedrock?

Teachers Point, Students Squint

Teaching is hard, in the second place, because the teacher is always in the position of trying to describe the compelling excitement of objects and ideas that students, try as they might, simply cannot at first bring into focus. They squint, they cock their heads, they peer into the mist, and they often wonder half-angrily if their teacher just isn't crazy at worst or eccentric at best. Much teaching has the frustrating character of the color-sighted person or the hearing person trying to explain the beauty of sunsets or symphonies to persons who are color-blind or deaf. The only way this dynamic can work is for the student to have sufficient trust in the teacher to believe that, in time and under the teacher's direction, s/he will also come to see the colors and sounds that so animate the teacher's voice, countenance, and manner.

Fear of Failure

Teaching is hard, in the third place, because failure on the part of the students is always a real possibility, and because students always know this.

A huge part of every teacher's job is not the importation into the student's mind of disciplinary content, which is comparatively easy, but the much more difficult job of supporting learning by also supporting the real risks that students must take in the face of failure. As snails shrink from sun and salt, students shrink from failure. This is a pedagogical problem because students set their thermostat for failure dysfunctionally low—"B"s are the new "C"s; "A"s are the new norm—but a truth that everyone already knows about human beings in general is that their *perceptions* generally drive their behavior more directly than do facts. The fact that there is no growth without risking failure is not a fact that, by itself, powerfully motivates students to override their perception that failure—looking bad or scoring low—is a catastrophe. The X-factor, the agent in whose absence students can seldom be persuaded to risk sun and salt, is the teacher. The teacher is often the single most crucial influence in the student's willingness to take the risks that real learning requires. The teacher must model the complex truth that *when real learning occurs, failure is inevitable for everyone at some points,* but that this sort of failure is never terminal, and in the long run doesn't really detract from eventual success. The great home run hitters always have more strikeouts than ordinary players, but no one remembers or cares about their strikeouts.

Specialist Education vs Liberal Education

Teaching is hard, in the fourth place, because teachers are specialists in disciplinary information and methodology but are often confused by a tension that they feel between their strong commitment to cover as much disciplinary territory as possible and their deep intuition that some of their most important work is not disciplinary at all. It is natural for students to be confused about this tension, but it can be pedagogically terrible when *teachers* are also confused about this tension. Teachers' confusion is clearly visible, however, when they list liberal arts learning objectives on their syllabi—critical thinking, concern for justice, imaginative resourcefulness, and so on—but then do not know how to make these objectives show up as accountable learning aims in their courses' tests or paper assignments. Students mostly do not have an educational agenda; they are too used to supposing that education is "giving the teacher what s/he wants." The task of articulating the relationship between disciplinary content and liberal arts aims is the teacher's job, and a great many teachers are not sure how to perform this difficult task.

Can-Opener Education

Teaching is hard, in the fifth place, because some teachers and almost all students—not to mention students' parents—tend to define and value education in instrumental terms, while many teachers try to persuade students to value their education in terms of self-development and human excellence. Thus teachers and students often talk past each other, sometimes without realizing it, and, in any event, often employ two incommensurate sets of value that tend to fracture educational discourse. What makes teaching even harder, however, is when teachers share students' confusion, and when teachers also advocate education in mostly instrumental terms, as if education were a kind of can opener for getting at the world's goodies, and as if the difference between a good education and a poor education were to be measured by the number of bells and whistles on the can opener, or as if the value of the can opener were synonymous with the academic status of the manufacturer's brand name. "So your can opener is made by Harvard! It must be a really *good* can opener!" When teachers are not clear about the difference between instrumental and liberal education, then glib teaching becomes very easy and good teaching becomes very hard.

The Difficulty of Teaching Yourself

Teaching is hard, in the sixth place, because the teacher can never escape the reality that s/he is not only teaching a discipline and not only teaching general intellectual and ethical skills, but is also teaching himself or herself. Teaching is a highly complicated balancing act that requires great attentiveness, great self-awareness, a deep sense of nuanced rhetoric and self-presentation, and a vast amount of energy to pull off with conviction, liveliness, and effectiveness. When I say that teachers can never evade teaching themselves, I am being neither hyperbolic nor metaphoric. Every teacher models his or her distinctive way of dealing with information, his or her distinctive way of dealing with ideas, and most of all his or her distinctive way of dealing with students. It is not possible for a teacher *not* to model himself or herself, and, given that students years after graduation seldom report being able to recall anything from distant class content but often report surprisingly vivid recollections of their teachers' self-presentation—manner of speech, body language, passions, interests, style of dress, jokes, and so on—it follows that teachers' lessons of themselves *stick*. There are at least two plain but serious ethical and intellectual implications that follow. First, when the memory of class content disappears but the memory of the teacher remains vivid, then whatever the teacher has modeled in the way of ethical virtues such as charity, civility, respect, and fairness; or what the teacher has modeled in the way of intellectual virtues such as lucidity of argument or skillful use of evidence may be the deepest and most formative lessons of the student's experience, even though the teacher concentrating almost exclusively on disciplinary content may not only have not been concerned about what he or she was modeling, but may not even have recognized that s/he *should* have been concerned about modeling. Second, just as students shrink from the sun and salt of perceived failure, many teachers shrink from thinking about teaching-as-modeling because it makes them feel too vulnerable, and, perhaps, inadequate, but this issue cannot be dodged. Teachers teach *at least* as much by modeling as by explaining. The teacher who squirms away from thinking how to handle this complex feature of teaching is like a surgeon who wants to perform great operations but refuses to face up to the fact that the sight of blood makes him faint.

PRINCIPLES TO HELP TEACHERS AVOID PEDAGOGICAL MUDDLES

So if teaching must be approached with all kinds of caveats, and if good teaching is so difficult, what are some of the most important and useful principles that the ambitious and conscientious teacher should think about and appeal to? I'm not talking about principles as some kind of inoculation guaranteed to produce success and certainly not guaranteed to forestall failure. Thinking about principles, however, can prevent a teacher's pedagogy from becoming intellectually thin and personally anemic because of a starved imagination and an excessive reliance on routines, clichés, and trodden paths. Most weak teaching does not derive from indifference, stupidity, and certainly not from malice, but from the failure on the part of teachers to engage in certain kinds of thinking before entering the classroom—primarily, thinking about principles—and it is this failure of prior thinking that trips teachers into all kinds of miry teaching pits and renders them vulnerable to all kinds of teaching sneezes and rasping coughs. What cognitive and intellectual principles can help prevent these mishaps and ailments?

In what follows I discuss the following issues in the following order: seeing things from the students' point of view, learning how to gain students' trust, figuring out how to help students get past the dead-end question about "what am I going to *do* with my education," and approaching pedagogy on the foundation of a developed *philosophy of education* rather than simply relying on intuition, good will, and trial-and-error. Although I consider all of these issues extremely important, I have ordered them in what I take to be, roughly, ascending order of importance, and will spend more space and time discussing the last issue than I spend on the other three issues together.

Seeing Things from the Students' Point of View

A teacher unable to see things from the students' point of view is as crippled in the quest for good teaching just as a conductor or choral director is crippled in the quest for beautiful music if he or she is unable to hear the right pitch. If a conductor or choral director can't tell when the instrumentalist or the singer is *on* or *off* pitch, s/he can beat out the right time till the cows come home, but her music is still going to sound terrible.

Seeing things in a classroom from the students' point of view is at least as hard as conducting an orchestra or directing a choral group—some days it seems as hard as breaking rocks—but many teachers seem blind to this fact and are quite complacent in their confidence that they know everything from students' incomes to students' motives to students' feelings and thoughts. I am always struck by the strangeness of this glib confidence coming from people who within their disciplines know that easy assumptions not backed up by investigation or evidence are shaky at best and bogus at worst. Worse, many teachers indulge in stereotypes instead of searching for evidence. In my pedagogy seminars I am often shocked to hear teachers employing precisely the kinds of stereotypes about students that teachers hate when students employ the counterpart stereotypes about them. Students sometimes use stereotypes such as "dry as dust," "head in the clouds," "using yellow notes from the sixties," and so on, while teachers rely on stereotypes such as "frat boy," sorority bubblehead," "snot nosed rich kid" (there's a rich sociological tale to be told here, but that's for another day), "brown nose," "nerd," and "slacker."

Teachers don't really know what students are thinking unless they ask. Furthermore, unless they ask students in ways that invite authentic responses and that are transparently non-directive, they won't find out even if they do ask. I use short, warm-up exercises at the beginning of my first-year and sophomore classes,[1] in which students are invited to tell briefly something about themselves: sometimes a funny memory, a favorite Christmas present, a favorite vacation, a favorite band or vocalist, or whatever. The point is that students gradually become acquainted with each other, and instead of sitting all semester long amongst a group of strangers before whom the last thing they want to do is expose their ignorance or lack of skill about *anything*, the class gradually turns into a community of citizens who become supportive of each other, friendly to each other, and pursue class aims as a group rather than a random collection of contiguous but personally indifferent agents. As this transformation occurs, students will tell you what they think, and it becomes easier to see their education from their point of view.

I encountered an extreme correction to any complacency that *I* may have fallen into about seeing things from students' point of view when I took an undergraduate course in Shakespeare acting three years ago. I took the complete course: attended class every day, did all of the exercises, accepted my roles and performance responsibilities, and was hands down the worst student in the entire class. Suddenly, the students' point of view was not one that I had to imagine or speculate about. I was experiencing it directly. It was not always pleasant. Being in a class where I was not only not in charge but wasn't even any good was a marvelous reintroduction to the world of being a student. It was also a potent education in the gut as well as the head about the kinds of anxiety, disconnection, and temptations to blame the messenger that all frustrated students must feel. I'm sure that at least some students come into my classes feeling as awkward, stymied, and embarrassed by their difficulties reading and interpreting a John Donne poem or a Charles Dickens novel as I did by the demands of playing Malvolio in cross-tied yellow garters. Being a student again reminded me vividly of the huge difference between teachers' *claims* on their side of the educational fence that they see things from the students' point of view, and the students' actual *experience* on their side of the fence. Not all teachers may be able to duplicate the opportunity I had to place myself in my students' shoes, literally, by becoming an undergraduate again, but all teachers *can avoid* making hasty, superficial inferences about students based on their dress, hair style, mode of speech, zip code, model of car, and other unreliable indicators of student ethos.

How to Gain Students' Trust

There are hierarchies of trust, ranging from your comparatively light trust that the person ringing up a small sale is going to give you the correct change, to the profoundly deeper trust that some person holding your happiness hostage in his hand—a parent, lover, spouse, or child, for example—is not going to betray you. The trust that teachers should reach for lies somewhere mid-point between these two extremes. There are times (often without preface or preparation) when students trust a teacher with some deepest secret, fear, or confession, but teachers should seldom solicit this kind of trust and should *never* solicit it as a matter of habit. Such exchanges are more likely to undermine a good teaching/learning relationship than support it.

What are students' generic secrets, anxieties, and desires that (a) typically block their effective learning, and that (b) could be diminished by an appropriate trust in the teacher? These are not likely to be secrets or anxieties about students' sexual orientation, marital problems, or resentments about their parents' childrearing failures. They *are* likely to be secret anxieties about not being smart enough, about not being accomplished enough, about not being liked or admired by the teacher, about looking stupid in front of other students (most of whom are strangers), and most of all about failing. The fact that most students are not at all clear about what they mean by "enough" or by "failure" not only does not diminish their anxieties, but, in fact, increases the nightmare aura of these threats. Not being good enough and fear of failing are more scary to students *because* they aren't sure what either of these means than if they faced these specters directly, diminished them by defining them, and ultimately stared them out of countenance. Teachers would be better able to offer students effective modes of overcoming their fears if they would cease seeing those fears as rooted in students' excessive feelings of pride or entitlement, and, instead, come to understand student fears as rooted in feelings of shame. Many teachers get angry at what they misdiagnose as students' excessive pride when they really should be more sympathetic to students' excessive sense of shame for not being good enough.[2]

This is where trust in the teacher enters in, but what is the paradigmatic nature of trust? Teachers should not mistake students' civility, niceness, and pleasant head nods for trust. Nor should they mistake students' appreciation for trust, although appreciation is closer to trust than mere civility. Trust is a highly complicated interpersonal dynamic saturated with ethical considerations. There are many kinds of superficial social projections that look more or less like trust, but down deep in the region of the heart where lie the roots of need and love, genuine trust is slow to develop and wary of putting itself at risk because doing so places the trusting person, potentially, in harm's way. Having one's trust trivialized, unappreciated, or betrayed is one of the most painful of human experiences. The gate in the fence that trust dwells on the other side of swings on the hinges of ethical evaluation. A positive ethical evaluation swings the gate open; a negative evaluation keeps the gate closed. Person A trusts Person B because Person A believes in Person B's integrity, honesty, fairness, and good will. Ultimately, there is nothing that merits the name of *deep* trust other than a kind of existential faith in the goodness of the person that one decides, finally, is trustworthy.

In other words, the kind of trust in teachers that helps students fight their fears of not being good enough and of failing is based on students' ethical evaluation of their teachers' integrity, honesty, fairness, and good will. They come into class already prepared to trust your disciplinary expertise (why would students not believe from the get-go in your competence about American history or calculus?), which means that all of those teachers, and they are legion, who are mostly insecure about precisely this issue—their authority as disciplinary masters—are failing to focus on the issue of teacherly *ethos* that ultimately has much more to do with the success of their students' learning than disciplinary expertise. What students need to know is not how many "A"s their teachers got in graduate school or how many articles and books their teachers have published since then, but whether the teacher understands their own anxieties and fears with sufficient sensitivity that if they take the risk of (fearfully) letting go of those anxieties long enough to walk out on the tightrope of new experience, the teacher will be there to catch them with encouragement, assistance, understanding, and support should they fall.

How to Deal with, "But What Can I Do with Courses or a Major in X?"

Students and their parents ask this "What can I *do*" question *only* about courses or majors in the humanities and basic sciences, and the incidence is not just occasional. They almost *always* ask this question about courses or majors in the humanities and sciences. They do *not* ask this question about courses or majors in business, nursing, pharmacy, teacher education, dance, or arts administration. Saying this highlights at once the nearly universal presumption that the right paradigm for defining the aims of *all* courses and majors is the instrumental paradigm that advances the can opener view of educational utility I discussed earlier. This is an inadequate paradigm, but, sadly, it is a paradigm that has been repeatedly been sold to students by their parents and that vast network of high school counselors who sometimes seem to have no other goal in life than to prime all freshmen to come to college with the "what can I *do* with" question literally *leaping* from their lips in the first English, history, chemistry, math, or philosophy class they encounter.

I do not think that students who ask the "what can I *do* with *X*" question do so in a captious, casuistical, or insincere manner. In my experience, they have not the faintest notion that this question applied to courses and majors in the humanities and sciences forces them to look in the wrong direction for a meaningful answer. Even more sadly, however, *many* teachers in the liberal arts and sciences also fail to realize that this question turns their heads in the wrong direction. For these teachers, therefore, the "what *do* I do with *X*" question becomes a trick question with a dead-end no-answer, a termination that they desperately wriggle to avoid by sweating hard to construct instrumental defenses of liberal arts education: "Well, here's what you can *do* with the liberal arts: they're a very prestigious kind of can opener for getting at the world' goodies! You can learn to *communicate* better, by god, and that's always a good thing, right? Or, whew, you can learn to *write* better.

Employers always like that, *trust me.* Just the other day I was talking to this recruiter from Comcast (or Viacom or CitiCard or General Motors) who was complaining to me about some terribly misspelled memo he got from an underling, and I'll bet *you* even know how to spell "Foucault's episteme." See how *useful* we liberal arts teachers are to your material prosperity and professional success? What else are we here for?"

When liberal arts teachers start constructing this desperate, sweaty palmed discourse of instrumental defenses for liberal education, they may as well toss in the towel and become taxi drivers or corporate moguls because they have already lost the game and don't even know it. Instrumental arguments in favor of instrumental training to serve instrumental aims will always be more logical and sound more convincing. *The appropriate question to ask about liberal arts courses and majors is not what you do with them, but (a) who you become because of them, and (b) what kind of life you lead because of them that you would not otherwise have had available to you.* The great value of courses in philosophy, history, physics, literature, languages, and other liberal arts courses is not that one *does* anything particularly instrumental with them. The great value of these courses is what they do to the student. They change the very architecture and quality of one's intellect and sensibility.

Liberal arts courses are designed to change the fundamental operations of the student's powers of reasoning, introspection, imagination, sociability, aesthetic responsiveness, linguistic sensitivity and expression, and ethical and moral deliberation. Instrumental courses and majors generally employ mechanistic metaphors of education, and tell the student how to get the most power out of the intellectual engine s/he already possesses. Liberal arts courses generally employ organic metaphors, and lead the student into forms of mental and imaginative exercise that constantly invite the growing organism to achieve a more robust and fully developed version of its own capabilities. Instrumental activities are indeed supported and improved by liberal arts skills such as critical thinking and linguistic sophistication, but arguing that these skills are foundational to the value of instrumental courses is as silly as arguing that one pursues good health because good health also supports and improves instrumental activities. Of course it does, but even if it didn't, no one would accept being sick over being healthy on the grounds that, in the absence of instrumental projects, the difference between being sick and being healthy is a wash.

No one wants good health only for instrumental purposes. One wants good health because it is a superior form of existence to stunted development, sickness, paralysis, and pain. The student who *absorbs* the benefits of working with, say, languages, scientific hypotheses, or literary texts—as opposed to merely storing recallable facts *about* these domains—has his or her intellect and sensibility reconfigured in ways that make one's overall life more vital, more varied, more thoughtful, more curious, and more aware of the interplay of tragedy and luck, good and evil, hopes and failure, and the paradoxical nature of the drive to live that is always played out within the context of death's inevitability. An intellect and sensibility shaped by a liberal arts education may not be a happier existence than the life of someone who never learns to think about these things, but the happiness of those who do not learn how to think is the kind of happiness that those who do learn how to think would never trade away, because the sometimes sadder, more thoughtful life that thinkers live seems—not despite its complexity but *because* of its complexity—to provide deeper and more accurate insights into reality, as well as giving a sense of connection with the primal forces in our nature that the final lines of Wordsworth's "Intimations of Immortality" capture so richly:

> The clouds that gather round the setting sun
> Do take a sober coloring from an eye
> That hath kept watch o'er man's mortality;
> Another race hath been, and other palms are won.
> Thanks to the human heart by which we live,
> Thanks to its tenderness, its joys, and fears,
> To me the meanest flower that blows can give
> Thoughts that do often lie too deep for tears.

It is not a denigration of instrumental education to say that it does not and cannot configure the intellect and sensibility to feel the force of such insights, to appreciate the language in with it is uttered, or to support the introspective and social deliberations prompted by such intellectual reflectiveness. One should not fault instrumental education for failing to do what it never was designed to do and never promised to do. But one should not fault liberal education courses and majors for doing something profoundly different from instrumental courses and majors. The difference most emphatically does not stem from any cheap claims about superior intelligence or moral goodness on the part of the liberal arts major. Such claims are indefensible. The point is that *instrumental studies and liberal arts studies are two different kinds of studies producing two different kinds of intellect and sensibility.* This does not mean that students must choose either one or the other. Most students can pursue both sets of aims if they choose to, but they will have little incentive to do so if their teachers always and forever allow themselves to be trapped into offering instrumental arguments in favor of liberal education, arguments which often begin the moment any student—entirely unaware of the panicked response that s/he is about to provoke—parrots the tired query from his parents or her high-school counselor, "what can I *do* with a major in *X*?"

Don't Go Into the Classroom Without a Developed Philosophy of Education

Far too many teachers substitute the structure of content in their disciplines for the philosophy of education that *should*—but that all too often *doesn't*—provide the foundation of the teacher's pedagogy. Many teachers are not even *aware* of making this substitution. Doing so is the standard form of socialization for almost all academics. However, the fact that we are socialized into our profession *not* to see the difference between the content of our disciplines and a philosophy of education is only one reason that that practice is so insidious. It is certainly not the last reason that this practice is so pernicious.

A teacher who walks into a classroom without the foundation of an educational philosophy is like a chef in the kitchen with no idea of what kind of meal he wants to cook, or like a gardener at the nursery with no idea of what kind of garden he wants to create. Until both of these agents get clear about what kind of overall project they intend to embark on, the chef and the gardener either stand in dismay among the foods and the plants, or, if they face a hard and fast deadline for the finished meal or the garden—just as the teacher whose class meets at 9:00 a.m. faces a hard and fast deadline for walking into class and saying *something*—they can begin cooking and planting by grabbing whatever foods and plants are closest at hand rather than making a plan or having a philosophy. For teachers, the material always closest at hand is the content of their disciplines, but mistaking this content for a philosophy of education is like mistaking the ability to nap for a scientific understanding of the physiology of sleep.

In what follows I will share with my readers my own working philosophy of education. This philosophy provides me with both a beginning point and an end point for my pedagogy. It is, as Shelley says of poetry, "the center and circumference" of what I do in the classroom. It is not eternally fixed. It has developed over many years, and as I think more and more persistently about matters, I keep changing it by adding a part or reformulating a part, but these constant revisions are unimportant to the role of this philosophy in my teaching. The point is that *it helps me see where to begin and where I want to go.* Since my philosophy of education is several paragraphs long, I will demarcate it from my commentary about it by placing it in italics and using bold face type for emphasis. When I share this philosophy as a document with my students, I do not call it a "philosophy of education." I call it…

The Primary Markers of an Educated Mind

*First, the person with an educated mind possesses the **cognitive** maturity to pay **prolonged analytical attention** to the interlocking sub-components of complex structures,* *whether material or conceptual (buildings, machines, works of art, scientific hypotheses, philosophical arguments, mathematical proofs, political theories, historical analyses, literary and dramatic texts, foreign languages, natural phenomena, social phenomena, and so on);*

*Second, the person with an educated mind possesses the **intellectual** maturity to apply concepts, ideas, and methods of argument acquired from the intellectual, artistic, scientific, and academic traditions of the world's great civilizations to the thoughtful and judicious solution of problems of all kinds (existential, moral, political, medical, social, legal, material, environmental, procedural, and so on; this also includes, of course, problems within traditional academic disciplines);*

*Third, the person with an educated mind possesses the **ethical** maturity to apply the benefits of knowledge, learning, and trained intelligence to social problems of injustice, dishonesty, poverty, sexism, racism, and political oppression. Well-educated men and women acknowledge that other people's pursuit of happiness, prosperity, and autonomy is as legitimate as their own.*

*Fourth, the person with an educated mind possesses the **emotional** maturity to accept hard work, delayed gratification, and persistent criticism as the price that anyone must pay for the inestimable advantages of infrastructure forms of self development such as self-discipline and moral courage.*

*Fifth, the person with an educated mind possesses a **personal** commitment to the comprehensive cultivation of a cluster of intellectual, emotional, and ethical capacities such as curiosity, open-mindedness, intellectual playfulness, and critical reflection.*

*The first of these markers of an educated mind—the ability to pay prolonged analytical attention to the interlocking components of complex structures—is perhaps the most difficult skill to teach, yet it is the most important skill to teach as early and as effectively as possible. It's difficult because paying prolonged analytical attention to **anything**— especially to complex structures—is a highly **unnatural** kind of cognition for human beings. (The exceptions to this claim are humans' ability to pay close attention to a few things that we come into the world apparently hard-wired for, such as, for example, other people's facial expressions and body language, which begins to explain the universal fascination that human beings have for movies and television, but that's another story.) Apart from these kinds of exceptions, however, we do not come into the world hard-wired to pay prolonged analytical attention to the component parts of complex structures such as sonnets, bridges, tax forms, historical artifacts, or scientific data. We can **learn** to develop analytical attentiveness—and when anyone acquires a level of expertise at doing it within any given area of accomplishment, such as writing well, playing the piano well, doing mathematical proofs well, and so on, then we all wind up loving to do this kind of thinking—but the truth is that it's difficult and unnatural, especially in the early stages of learning it.*

Because narratives, spectacle, and sensory pleasure are natural dispositions, most human beings are much better at telling and remembering stories or describing and remembering social events than remembering the periodic table, mathematical formulas, or logical proofs. The mind as shaped by evolutionary forces seems to be a perceptual and cognitive system that developed to help our species to survive, but not to achieve *deep understanding of things in any philosophical or scientific sense. Survival depends on many cognitive skills and operations of luck, but not on deep understanding of the sort represented by literary analysis, scientific hypothesizing, historical interrogation, or philosophical argumentation. Although the human species is vast, those who have **deep** understanding of anything are few.*

In general, human minds do not insist on precision and do not favor complex explanations. Our minds like to make quick, "close-enough" determinations about events, usually in terms of causal agents, and then move on. Partly we do this to save energy, partly to prevent boredom, partly because moving on was a safer adaptation in early stages of evolution than sticking around for a prolonged look, especially if the flicker of movement that excited our curiosity turned out to be a predator, and partly because in the ordinary course of things "close-enough" is, well, close enough. In everyday life, most people's understanding of political events, history, science, technology, mathematics, and so on tends to range from "close-enough" to profoundly ignorant—Jay Leno's "jay walking" episodes on The Tonight Show *reveal the shocking range of many people's ignorance within the kinds of domains I just listed—but this ignorance (and this is a fact that teachers should reflect on daily, daily) seems **not** to be a serious impediment to anyone's ability to be socially acceptable to others, nor a serious impediment to anyone's ability to find a mate, hold a job, travel abroad, vote in elections, win an election, get rich, get famous, and so on. In everyday life, "close-enough" often **is** close enough.*

But in the pursuit of excellence or truth, "close-enough" is not close enough, and prolonged analytical attentiveness is the most powerful educational counterbalance to the allure of stereotypes, quick guesses, clichés, and social bromides.

*It seems to me that **education "takes" in the only sense that matters when it transforms the structure of human desires,** when it alters what we do by changing what we want. Changing what we want also changes who we are. Education accomplishes such transformation by complicating, enriching, and diversifying one's desires, not to mention giving one standards for evaluating some desires as better than others on any number of fronts ranging from sheer functionality to moral profundity. If students leave college with the same structure of desires they had when they entered college, then they leave not having been educated but merely entertained. If college is only about skills and never about transformation, then it's nothing but an expensive shopping experience— "I picked up a few nifty items in the English, History, and Psychology departments," students can say: "items that will wear well at either the beach or the office"—but faculty members should not be confused, even when their students are, about the profound difference between academic shopping and getting a real education.*

*The teachers in American society who already possess highly developed skills for changing people's structure of desires are commercial marketers. They actually know how to make consumers shape their identity and their conduct around the perceived (created) desire for certain products and a certain style of life. **Marketers know how to shape and alter what people want and who they desire to be.** The problem is, the aim of such transformation is company profits, not the consumers' self-development as civic participants or moral agents. But if teachers in college stick to the transmission of skills without thinking about transformation, then transformation is left by uncontested default to the commercial marketers.*

Education is less about improving the knowledge one owns than about improving the choices one makes. I say this not to depreciate knowledge, but merely to reflect the reality that in every discipline, knowledge is always changing. The "truths" of any discipline fifty years ago are not the "truths" of the discipline today. Knowledge is provisional, constructed, and, generally, temporary. Most truths wind up being scrapped and replaced by "better" truths as research moves forward and as new theories get articulated. In any event, knowledge, however important, is not the central ingredient in one's ability to lead a life that is intellectually perspicuous, socially responsible, personally enriched, and morally defensible. Persons who thought that the earth was flat, for example, were surely able to live thoughtful, morally defensible lives, and when they failed to live thoughtful lives it is absurd to think that their failure could be traced back to their ignorance that the earth is round. The relationship between having knowledge and living a thoughtful life, in other words, is not a simple matter than can be expressed in the formula "greater knowledge equals greater thoughtfulness or guaranteed happiness." The choices one makes, however, are always at the center of whether one's life is thoughtful and considered rather than impulsive and selfish.

Many important consequences for my teaching follow from this philosophy, but I shall discuss here only the single most important recommendation that I base on it, in the hopes that what I say may help other teachers clarify their teaching aims. What do I do with my educational philosophy? How do I put it in motion in my teaching? As journalists say of stories that stick around, how do I "give it legs?"

Share Your Philosophy of Education With Your Students. Over my years of teaching I have taught myself to do what no one in college or graduate school ever breathed to me might be possible. I chart two paths of discourse in my classes. One is the path of disciplinary content. The other is the path of meta-educational discussion, in which I share with my students—*only in stages*, not all at once—my philosophy of education, and I try to make clear for students how the disciplinary content that I ask them to work on is connected to the educational aims described in my philosophy of education.

This transparency about meta-educational aims has had a wonderfully salutary effect on my teaching. In the first place, my students understand my philosophy, and it gives them a reason to understand that the goals of the course are *theirs*, not mine or the university's or the discipline's. In the second place, my philosophy of education relieves students of the necessity (or the temptation) of pretending to like the course content as a way of winning my favor. I could not care less if all my students learn to love Shakespeare sonnets, Jane Austen novels, or literary theory the way I do. Insofar as they might, fine, but I am clear in my own mind that the material I teach is a means to an end, not an end in itself. I tell my students that their education actually occurs not when they attempt to store content information for later recall—this is a futile enterprise since most of us forget most of what we learn unless we continue to use it over and over—but education occurs when they *work* with the material not for the sake of the material or for me, but for the sake of how the *labor* itself changes, develops, and strengthens the very architecture of the capacities they must deploy in order to do the labor in the first place: the capacities of imagination, reason, introspection, moral and ethical deliberation, aesthetic responsiveness, linguistic sensitivity, and so on.

We say that we are educators, and that our purpose in being teachers is helping students become educated agents in the world, yet we seldom talk to our students in any systematic way about what being educated means—as opposed to talking to them a *lot* about what it means to learn our disciplinary content—and how an educated mind operates differently in the world from an uneducated mind. This is a curious disjunction for people who call themselves educators, and the only way I can explain it is to refer to the overwhelming tendency of disciplinary content to move like thick syrup into all the crevasses, cracks, and corners of the classroom experience, and to substitute itself for any kind of discourse about the ways in which that content might be educational rather than merely interesting or useful. I might also refer to the inertia of habit and tradition. The approach to teaching that allows the structure of knowledge in the discipline to substitute itself for a philosophy of education has been going on for so long that few teachers have any idea that alternative approaches on this front even exist. Teachers can do better, and the teacher who wishes to become the teacher who makes the difference *must* do better. Otherwise we slip perilously close to becoming mere entertainers, and if we are really good at entertaining, then we become the stars who collect a gaggle of groupies around us, and we *appear* to be the teachers who make the difference when, in reality, we are merely giving our students the thrill of being backstage with the man or woman who knows how to bang the bejeesus out of the guitar and sell a song with charisma.

Charisma is always impressive, but performance artistry is not the same thing as being a musician, and being the kind of teacher whose charisma charms your students into little puddles of affection for you personally is not the same thing as educating them to think for themselves. Students with stars in their eyes and stars behind the teacher's podium are not learning autonomy, nor are they learning how to think critically and deeply about the difference between learning content information and dealing with that information in ways characteristic of educated minds. They are not learning to deal with it, that is, with intellectual perspicacity, with some sense of social responsibility, with a deep sense of personal enrichment, and with the ambition of putting that information to work in the world in morally defensible ways. This is what educated minds do, and if we are not helping our students acquire this orientation toward life and learning, then we are not doing nearly as much for our students as we could. We can do better, and I am convinced that appealing to thoughtful principles of pedagogy, and thus negotiating our way around the pressure to be charismatic, is a good way to start doing better.

NOTE

1. At my home institution, the English majors who share junior- and senior-level courses have usually had enough classes together such that they know each other pretty well, allowing me to dispense with the warm-up exercise that I use in 100- and 200-level courses.